W9-CXC-219

The Modern
Olympic Games

The Modern Olympic Games

John Lucas

South Brunswick and New York: A. S. Barnes and Company
London: Thomas Yoseloff Ltd

A. S. Barnes and Co., Inc.
Cranbury, New Jersey 08512

Thomas Yoseloff Ltd
Magdalen House
136-148 Tooley Street
London SE1 2TT, England

Library of Congress Cataloging in Publication Data

Lucas, John Apostal, 1927-
  The modern Olympic Games.

  1. Olympic games.   I. Title.
GV721.5.L8   796.4′8   79-52025
ISBN 0-498-02447-4

Printed in the United States of America

Contents

Introduction

Language is that marvelous instrument that separates and elevates man from all other living things. Language accentuates the uniqueness of man, but it is also abundantly clear that language too often serves as a barrier between people. More than ever before, the human animal needs an increasing number of effective alternative means of communication besides the written and spoken word. Music, art, the dance, international cultural exchanges, and sport can serve as these alternatives to language. They must do so at an accelerated rate during the last decades of the twentieth century so that they might act as potentially effective means of international communication. Few collective human behaviors seem more important. Sentimentality and grandiose schemes must be put aside in this continuing search for a universal language. The modern Olympic Games were, unfortunately, conceived amidst an air of sentimentality and excessive grandiosity. And yet, the idea at its core was and is sound. The Olympic Games are distinctly different from the championships of World Cup soccer, Super Bowl football, and World Series baseball. The Olympic Games, at their best, can function as one singular instrument among many toward initiating real communication among and between all men and women. We are still far from a stable, rational, and loving world. Yet, as never before, the potential for progress toward such a state exists. Under no circumstances can the Olympic Games wipe out war, violence, brutality, repression. These quadrennial games can only underscore and therefore possibly accelerate a perpetual human hunger for communication, a natural curiosity about one's fellow creature. To say that a hundred years of Olympian communication might aid in the collective plight of mankind is presumptuous, but what do we have that is distinctly better?

A half century ago the German Minister of the Interior, Dr. H. E. Wirth, in paraphrasing the mystic genius, Goethe, pointed out that "bodily culture is a primordial element of general human culture." Modern scholars might phrase it differently, noting the universality of the play instinct as well as mankind's passion for competitive games. The modern Olympic Games are a genuine attempt to channel these two forms of human energy into what sport philosopher Francis Keenan called "competitive cooperation"—which is not only the Olympic rationale, but, more importantly, might well be the proper goal of mankind. *Washington Post* columnist George F. Will was incorrect when he stated that the Olympic Movement is incapable of healthy growth and that only political and commercial motives are "strong enough to sustain this quadrennial farce." On the contrary, way back in 1913, Sir Arthur Conan Doyle felt strongly that the termination of the Olympic Games would have "an enervating effect" on the few cultural ties that try to join people together. Such was the case at the beginning of the century. The statement continues to ring true near the century's end. There are hundreds of thousands of young men and women in every land whose athletic thrust toward excellence is a vital force that needs nurturing in both spiritual and temporal terms. Harvard philosopher George Santayana saw the unselfish athlete as the last of the knights, and his physical prowess as a natural prelude to mature aspirations and self-liberation. This doesn't work everytime, but nothing ever does. Jim McKay, of Olympic television fame, once concluded that the games are both a symbol of hope and a representation of disappointment. They are, he said, "the largest regularly scheduled gathering of mankind." Konrad Lorenz once visualized the Olympics as an opportunity for men and women to "give scope to a number of truly valuable patterns of social behavior," and, at the same time, reduce rather than aggravate excessive nationalism. Just the opposite can happen, too. Olympic athletes are not gods. We can only hope that, while in attendance at the Games, most of their behavior is god-like. Ideally, for these non-professional athletes, the Olympic experience is an intense, brief, meaningful encounter, engaged in jointly with preparation for a larger and longer career. I believe that, amidst all the Olympic venality, there exists a strong comradery, something 1956 Olympic champion Chris Brasher called, "a sort of freemasonry among the competitors—a common interest and enthusiasm, producing the kind of mutual understanding that seems often to exist between scientists of different races."

I believe in the Olympic Idea and the Olympic Games. I believe in them so strongly that, after two decades of Olympic Games attendance and an equal time in library research, I must echo, once again, the need for carefully accelerated Olympic reform. Each of the Olympic presidents—Baron Pierre de Coubertin, Count Henri de Baillet-Latour, J. Sigfrid Edstrom, Avery Brundage, and Michael Morris, Lord Killanin—has pronounced the need for changes in the Olympic Movement structure and in the format of the game themselves. Responsible journalists and other editorialists have, since 1896, leveled thoughtful and legitimate accusations at the Olympic Idea and the Olympic Games. Usually, in these criticisms, meaningful suggestions for change and improvement are included. And then there is that veritable army of nincompoops who, over the decades have served up an undirected and inflammatory mishmash against the whole Olympic concept. Most of this criticism is based on "incidents" and sometimes tragedies that have occurred at every single one of the eighteen regular games. Throw in the triple jump dispute and bitterness against American domination of the unofficial 1906 Games in Athens, and one has a complete critical chronology of Olympic malevolence. And yet, to me, this kind of mindless Olympic tattletale is unproductive, proves little, and fails to address the possibility of larger, more fundamental issues of international sport. The Olympic Movement, like all institutions and governments, must have rules and regulations, because, as Alexander Hamilton said, the passions of men will not conform to the dictates of reason and justice without constraint. There must always be constraint, and, along with it, hope. From Reverend Robert S. DeCourcy Laffin's 1913 conviction that "the Olympic Movement answers to the deepest needs of our time," and Ken Doherty's 1960 insightful analysis that "youth throughout the world yearns to be challenged to its utmost energies in enterprises whose rules are related to their needs and seem reasonably fair to all," there emerges a kind of Olympic preamble. Doherty, the athlete, scientist, coach, and philosopher, concluded by declaring that "no area of human action is so fertile for providing such a challenge as sports, especially Olympic sports."

Few human institutions have been as durable, widespread, and imaginative as the modern Olympic Games. All too infrequently, humanity has been robbed of displays of peaceful heroics, or, as the ancient Greeks called it, noble *aristeia*. The Olympic Games afford this opportunity to the youth of the world more generously than any other human invention. That this dream of inner excitement and equilibrium is just that—a dream yet unfulfilled—is not condemnation of the Olympic Movement or the human race. Rather, it is a never-ending challenge for mankind to seek and gain some kind of balance, never allowing human passions to gain ascendancy over spiritual qualities. The Olympic Games need to be preserved. No other social institution in the world has, as its sole reason for existence, the brotherhood of man, the physical health of mankind, and the joy of international athletic competition. Monumental problems connected with these games may not allow them to last out the twentieth century. This book is an effort at scientific sport history; it is based on the optimistic hope that factual information is the basis for rational decision-making. The author's bias is laid bare and is contained in the text's dedication to the eventual fulfillment of that persistent human yearning—universal peace.

The Modern
Olympic Games

1 • The French Baron Pierre de Coubertin

Baron Pierre de Coubertin, the founder of the modern Olympic Games, was an aristocratic Frenchman who took great pride in the fact that his mother's family was descended from companions of William the Conqueror, while his father's ancestor was Pierre de Fredy, Lord de la Motte, chamberlain to the fifteenth century King of France, Louis XI. Coubertin was born in Paris on 1 January 1863, and lived seventy-four years, passing away on 2 September 1937 in Geneva, Switzerland. Through the centuries, his people had been prominent civil servants, churchmen, soldiers, artists, merchants, jurists—all monarchists and Catholics. In 1577, Jean Fredy purchased the Estates of Coubertin near Paris, thus introducing the familiar French name into the family. Much later, in the nineteenth century, Pierre's father, Charles Louis de Fredy, married Agathe Gabrielle de Grisenoy de Mirville, whose wealthy family came from the region of Havre in Normandy. It was at the manor house of Mirville that their son, Pierre, spent his holidays for thirty years. The future Olympic Games revivalist was the fourth and last child of Baron and Baronesse de Coubertin. Pierre's father, Charles Louis (1822-1908), belonged to what might be called the middle aristocracy and was a gifted painter of religious and historical pictures. One of his works depicted the discovery of the famous Laocoon by his own ancestor, Felicia de Fredy. Another of his compositions, "Pontifical Procession," is in the Vatican. His murals, sketches, and church paintings won him knighthood in the Legion of Honor in 1865. It was in this atmosphere of culture and affluence that Pierre de Coubertin was born in 1863, eight years before France's humiliation by Prussian armies.

The Franco-Prussian War was a disaster for the Coubertin family and for all of France. France's struggle to once again attain status as a nation was the initial incentive in Coubertin's efforts at educational and sport reform during the early years of the Third Republic. He was among the Jesuit students in their exclusive and reactionary day high school in the Paris Ecole Saint Ignace. Coubertin's long-time friend, Professor William

Pierre de Coubertin (1863 –1937), founder of the modern Olympic Games. Credit IOC Archives.

Milligan Sloane of Princeton University, called Pierre's life at the parochial school "so narrow, so gloomy, so deadening, so repellent, that, like others of his birth, he entered on a course of thorough self-examination". No matter. The boy had a good mind and was a brilliant student of letters, history, and pedagogy, not to mention skill in fencing, horsemanship, and gymnastics. Like many of his school friends, a military education at St. Cyr followed by an attractive career in the army tempted the young Coubertin. "I resolved to change careers," he said, "and attach my name to a great pedagogical reform". He entered the University of Paris, where he obtained successively the degrees of bachelor of arts, bachelor of sciences, and bachelor of laws. He continued postgraduate studies at the Free School of Political Science in Paris where he became familiar with French philosophy, English educational history, and a range of subjects challenging to a keen and eclectic mind. "His memory was prodigious," remarked Geoffrey de Navacelle, great nephew of the Baron.

During these formative years of the 1870s and early 1880s, the young man continued a deep appreciation of his roots, which included Italian aristocrats, Norman ancestors, distant French relatives like Cyrano de Bergerac, and the immediate heritage left him by his father and grandfather. The most influential Jesuit in Coubertin's life was Father Caron, professor of humanities and rhetoric, who taught him Greek and Roman history and the glory of ancient games at Olympia. At age seventeen, Coubertin read Hippolyte Taine's *Notes on England,* where, among other things, the philosopher-historian noted the vigorous, athletic life of English adolescents and contrasted it with the dreary existence of French schoolboys. Even earlier, in 1875, he had read a French translation of Thomas Hughes's English classic *Tom Brown's School Days.* The impressionable Coubertin was euphoric about the vigor and physicality depicted in English life at Rugby School. So taken was Coubertin by this overdrawn picture of English life that for all his life he continued to refer to it as the epitome of moral, physical, intellectual education—and in that order of importance. Coubertin's writings are replete with liberal and democratic declarations—much of them influenced by the French sociologist Frederic Le Play, who upheld Christian morality, supported existing institutional forms including the family, but also urged that powerful social reforms needed implementation in order to effectively aid working people. Coubertin's eventual creation—modern international Olympic Games—was his own kind of radical reform.

As a boy, Coubertin accompanied his parents to Italy, Germany, Austria, and Switzerland. But it was the half dozen trips to Great Britain in the early 1880's that had a profound and lasting effect on the young man. The figure of Dr. Thomas Arnold, headmaster of England's Rugby School from 1828 to 1842, was the single most important influence on the life and thought of Pierre de Coubertin. The Baron's philosophical approach combined the "wholeness" of Greek antiquity with the extreme nineteenth-century moralism taught by Thomas Arnold. Coubertin's concept of Athenian philosophy, exemplified in the trinity of character, intellect, and body, was inexorably fused with the image of disciplined austerity and sportsmanship of the English Rugby School. Coubertin's already low opinion of French education was intensified by the contrasting picture at Oxford and Cambridge Universities, and at the elite Public Schools of England. He was especially taken by the graduates of these schools, most having had ten years of organized and competitive athletics in their youthful backgrounds. Coubertin's modern version of the Greek scholar-athlete was the English sporting gentleman. The Baron perceived the Aristotelian virtue of *eutrapelia* as the consummate trait in his idealized athletic Englishman—a romantic meld of vitality, courage, versatility, and, above all, a sense of proportion. It was a concept that was to dominate his life and writings. It was a code of life that, when transposed to the amateur and Olympic code of athletics, profoundly affected tens of thousands of athletes through most of the twentieth century.

Baron Pierre de Coubertin was a man possessed. The turmoil and reform that so agonized France after the war of 1870–71, accentuated, among other things, the nation's fragile tradition of organized sport and physical education. In an old Catholic country like France, a sporting point comparable with the neighbor across the English Channel had never been reached. The young baron was moved by patriotism, a sensitivity to the educational needs of his people, and most of all, by the extraordinary things he had learned during his two trips to North America and many pilgrimages to England. His romanticized version of Anglo-American organized, competitive athletics was rivaled by his youthful conviction that these nations were the greatest powers in the world, due, in large measure, to a tradition of honorable and exhilarating games-playing. Coupled with his knowledge of ancient Greek athletics and the medieval chivalric code, Coubertin began to formulate a larger international and Olympian festival.

In his study of the Rugby School during its nineteenth-century history, Coubertin concluded that its school life was an adult world in miniature. Nowhere in France could he find a counterpart. It was with the catalyst of athletic competition that Arnold and especially public school teachers trained future leaders. Coubertin praised the moral, social, and physical values derived by the students at Rugby. Even though the Frenchman vastly overstated the influence of Arnold, he was convinced that the sports-centered English Public School system was the rock upon which the vast and majestic British Empire rested. He felt the same way about the emerging international giant, the United States. The Anglo-mania of Pierre de Coubertin pervades much of his writing. In a chapter from his *Pages D'Histoire Contemporaire* titled "Britannic Power," the genesis of this power is said to be a peculiar "Muscular Christianity" which originated in Thomas Arnold's Rugby School. At least, so Coubertin believed. Actually, Arnold's passionate attempt to make boys freely functioning individuals never led him to overemphasize athletics. This was left to succeeding generations of schoolmasters. The impression of sports predominance at Rugby during Arnold's administration was created by Thomas Hughes and his immense best seller, *Tom Brown's School Days*. All of Dr. Arnold's efforts were directed toward obedience to God, to school, and to himself. He was able, through instruction in the classics, in history, and through weekly theological sermons to mold his students to an astonishing degree. Pierre de Coubertin seized upon the uniqueness of the English public school and vowed to introduce it into French education. He saw in these English schools what he wanted to see—the phenomenon of total athletic participation and the resultant strengthening of boyhood moral and physical fiber. The Frenchman, unencumbered by modern research, passionately believed that the English Public Schools, like the ancient schools of Hellas, produced athletes, men of character, and Empire builders.

Through a literary career that spanned fifty years and over 55,000 pages of written material, Baron Pierre de Coubertin's philosophy of "Olympism" emerged as a strongly "Muscular Christian" attitude—a sporting philosophy that was firmly established before the first Athens Olympic Games of 1896. Back in Paris, Coubertin addressed the "Societe d'economie sociale," emphasizing that English "Muscular Christianity" had profoundly affected and uplifted every military and political area of influence in that country. It was just the kind of exaggeration that highlighted the man's weakness as a historian but underscored his evangelic fervor. Just before Coubertin's first trip to America in 1889, France had taken positive steps to introduce sport and physical education into its schools. The fast-rising aristocrat had been helpful in the implementation. Just before his departure, he spoke at the French Open-Air Tennis Society on Britain's greatness as a commonwealth of nations and her unrivaled love affair with sport. He arrived in Boston, Massachusetts, firm in his conviction that the Rugby School and English society had spawned a unique world force—interscholastic and intercollegiate athletics. Monsieur de Coubertin was secretary of the French Educational Reform Association at the Boston Conference on Physical Training. American physical educators, completely divided on what European system to adopt as their own, may have been helped by Coubertin's unrestrained outburst in support of the English athletic system "as understood and explained by the greatest of modern teachers, Thomas Arnold of Rugby." With characteristic zeal, Coubertin tried to spread the English gospel of Muscular Christianity. Don't be surprised, he said, if forced to choose between academic subjects and competitive sport, both the Public Schools of England and America's West Point would embrace the latter. There is hardly a large piece of Coubertin literature that does not dwell on what he conceived as a precious English gift to the world. To insure its transport, the young baron created a bold plan of reconstituted Olympic Games, not just for Frenchmen, but for all mankind.

Coubertin's mind dwelt in the distant and recent past. To him, the two greatest forces for good were "Hellenic Completeness" and the ideals embodied in English sport. From the beginning and through the first ten Olympic Games, these two concepts served as motive and philosophy for the perpetuation of this world sport festival. After ten years of backbreaking work, Coubertin was rewarded with the first modern Olympic Games in Athens, Greece. A dream had been fulfilled for him and in a 26 March 1896 letter, he was overly optimistic, noting that the Greeks had overnight become conscious once again of their great heritage: "the skeptics have been eliminated; the Olympic Games have not a single enemy." Thirteen nations participated in a highly successful first venture, and plans began immediately for Paris Games in 1900. "It is clear that sport is gradually spreading over the whole world," he said on the eve of the games of the Second Olympiad. Coubertin admitted the inadequacy of the Paris Olympics and promised to do better four years later. For the second consecutive time, Coubertin was mistaken that his Olympic Games might gain strength and stature by being associated with a world's fair. The third Olympics were held in conjunction with the 1904 Louisiana Exposition in St. Louis. Coubertin was not present to witness the ineffective games that lacked international representation and were nearly devoid of that precious Coubertin ingredient—"beauty and reverence". The emergency Olympics in 1906, held in the safety of the Athens stadium, may have saved the Olympic Games. Massive Greek support and enthusiasm resulted in a genuine international sport festival, prompting local authorities to insist that Athens be designated the logical, permanent site for the new Olympic Games. Coubertin fought hard, insisting that peoples in every geographic area of the world be privileged to host an Olympic Games. Despite mounting administrative problems and disturbing nationalistic fervor by some nations, especially the United States and Britain, the 1908 London and 1912 Stockholm Olympic Games were significant forward steps in Coubertin's unflinching dream of the brotherhood of man through the medium of sane, international, athletic competition.

The Olympic Games scheduled for 1916 were cancelled due to war. The fifty-one-year-old Coubertin was rejected for military service, serving through the bitter years as an interpreter. He never faltered in his unfulfilled dream of peace through Olympic sport participation. On 24 February 1918, before the Hellenic Society of Lausanne, Switzerland, he repeated his belief that international sport, rightly conducted, might contribute to world health and world pacifism. The 1916 games in Berlin had been cancelled, although the chronological passage of time, 1916–1919, was unassailable and labeled, "The Sixth Olympiad of the Modern Era." Brave and foolhardy efforts culminated the Seventh Olympiad in the Antwerp, Belgium, 1920 Games. The war-ravaged city worked things out, although imperfectly. Coubertin was getting repetitious as he pleaded with diplomats and the media to view the Olympic Games with pride, but with nationalistic restraint, and with a sense of and hope for universal progress.

The aging warrior, Coubertin, attended the Paris Olympics of 1924, but, due to illness, was unable to participate in the 1928 Games at Amsterdam. Nothing stands still, especially in sport. Paavo Nurmi of Finland startled Parisians and the world with his relentless distance running. Paris was broiling in daily temperatures of over 100 degrees Fahrenheit. Tempers flared, and the *Times* of London cried, "No more Olympic Games." Coubertin replied that it is precisely at times of international tension that world physical education and well-organized sport can play an essential role in the cause of peace. He stepped down as president of the International Olympic Committee in 1925, only to renew his beliefs in the social and physical restorative powers of sport. On 17 April 1927, speaking from Olympia, Greece, he looked forward to the entire youth of the world taking part in sport, "with honor and disinterestedness." The ancient Greek custom of combining art, music, and cultural events in harmony with intense athletic competitions was an idea conceived by Baron Coubertin in 1906 and continued in 1928. Larger numbers of women competed in the Amsterdam Games, much to the disgust of the retired Olympic president. Pierre de Coubertin was, after all, a Victorian-Edwardian child of his times. The old man did not attend the 1932 Olympic Games nor those held in Berlin four years later. Coubertin had long since spent his entire fortune on Olympic business, over the objections of long-suffering Madame Coubertin. From his headquarters in Lausanne, Switzerland, the Baron reminded the young of the world, once again, that "the main issue in life is not the victory but the fight; the essential thing is not have won but to have fought well." The International Olympic Committee (IOC) fought a bitter, partially successful, and hidden struggle with Adolf Hitler for ideological control of the 1936 Games.

Pierre de Coubertin was a small man, always well-dressed, with a strong mustache and "piercing, lively eyes." In 1895, he married Marie Rothan, of Alsatian origin. Her father, Gustav Rothan, was a historian, minister in the French embassy, and good friend of Pierre's father, Charles de Coubertin. Marie and Pierre met in 1892 and were married on March 12, 1895 in the Paris Reformed Protestant Church. She had two children, a son Jacques (1896-1940), and a daughter, Renee, born in 1902, who was talented, intelligent, "but of fragile mental health." Both children were a constant source of concern to the Coubertins. The long-suffering Baroness de Coubertin could never get her husband to stop spending his money on Olympic ventures. Biographer Marie-Thérèse Eyquem commented that Madame Coubertin was "of a difficult character," yet supportive and loving of her single-minded husband. Coubertin loved his wife, said Eyquem, "and could not do without her, but suffered from her behavior and her unstable disposition." The literature is nearly void on this relationship. We do know that Marie de Coubertin passed away in Lausanne, Switzerland on 6 May 1963, in her 102nd year.

Baron de Coubertin retired in 1925 and was haunted by mounting problems for the rest of his life. Not the least of these troubles was a lack of money. He did not attend the 1928, 1932, or 1936 Olympic Games partly because he could not afford it. For nearly half a century he had devoted all his time and monies to the Olympic movement. He had tried in vain to find a job. He refused to touch the small treasury of the International Olympic Committee. Some evidence exists that Coubertin's long-time admirer, the great German educator and Berlin Olympic Games organizer Dr. Carl Diem, interceded on the Baron's behalf, and an honorarium of 10,000 DM from the German government supported the French baron during the last years of his life. He was further sustained during these difficult years of the 1930s by Fr. M. Messerli, Paul Martin, IOC Secretary, Mme. Zanchi, and others. Coubertin was never a good athlete, and yet, from childhood, had experimented in competitive sport and fitness activities. In his last year, he was seen frequently rowing his boat on Lake Geneva. He had never fully reconciled himself to the fact that Adolf Hitler and his gang had attempted, with considerable success, to turn the recent Berlin Olympics into an aggressive instrument of German propaganda. The Baron was old, destitute, and deeply melancholy. And yet his unceasing rhapsodical tune continued to call the Olympic Games "not simply championships of the world, but a dedication to noble youth—a universal and viable religion." Hard times had apparently been unable to dent an essentially idealistic attitude toward the role of his brand of international sport.

The baron appeared in good health, and yet the end of his life came abruptly on 2 September 1937 as he was strolling through Geneva's Lagrange Park. The diminutive Coubertin, white-haired and seventy-four years of age, suddenly stopped, dropped his cane, lost his balance, and fell dead on the gravel path. An era had come to an end. Apoplexy or a heart attack were listed as the cause of his passing. The *New York Times* obituary noted that "Baron de Coubertin looked upon sports with the eyes of an artist, a dreamer and an educator." It was an accurate assessment of an eventful life. His name had been forwarded as a candidate for the 1928 Nobel Peace Prize. "The Baron was a descendent of Rubens and Cyrano de Bergerac," said the *Times* of London, "and there are those who attribute many of his remarkable qualities to his famous forebearers." Coubertin's many admirers were convinced that a good and noble man had been in their midst. According to his wishes, Coubertin's body was buried in the Lausanne cemetery of Bois-de-Vaux, while his heart, placed in a green stone urn, was transported to Olympia, Greece. On 26 March 1938, the heart of Pierre de Coubertin was buried with solemn ceremony at a site close to the ancient Olympic stadium. A white marble stele adorned with a head of Zeus marked the spot. Prince Paul represented the King of Greece at the ceremony, carried out on the 110th anniversary of Greek independence. The Greek and International Olympic committees gathered there, as did scores of dignitaries and thousands of spectators. The Greek Minister of Education praised the Olympic founder in lavish language so dear to Coubertin himself: "You achieved the great aim of your life; may you sleep in peace! Your great soul will be satisfied to have set a high goal before humanity." Coubertin's friend, Dr. Messerli, eulogized more simply: "May his works, his ideas survive." Honor and praise was heaped on this high-minded Frenchman, and yet, in the penultimate year of his life, Coubertin was filled with sorrow, concerned about his own sanity, and decidedly sure that he had made mistakes and had left much undone. It may be that Coubertin's frank admission to having left "unfinished" the Olympic "symphony," is the strongest testimony to the strength and uniqueness of the man.

Coubertin never promised that watching and participating in the games would guarantee that we would all love one another. He was convinced, however, that these quadrennial sport festivals lifted the level of physical fitness for hundreds of thousands, and breathed out an atmosphere of chivalry, courage, beauty, and a mutual respect for and between young men and women from all over the world. "Games for all nations" was his creed. "I believe in the future of mankind," he said in the year of his death. The pageantry of the Olympic Games, its symbolisms, even mystical meanings, so often the target of some journalists, were all Coubertin's efforts to build into these games a Greek dignity and intensity, a medieval chivalric idealism, and a modern sense of pride and passion. He succeeded in this to an astonishing degree, despite powerful intrusions from ultranationalists and the money crises of Olympic sites construction.

Coubertin was old-fashioned enough to believe that a sense of personal destiny, individual toughness combined with dignity, might remain with young people who trained for and participated in the Olympic Games.

The great experiment began on Easter Sunday, 1896, appropriately in Athens, Greece—site of the ancient games and spiritual origin of sport as it is understood in the western world. Speaking at the Athenian Parnasse Society, Coubertin paid tribute both to the ancient Greeks as creators of the ideal formula for sport, and to nineteenth-century Englishmen for having spread the doctrine of honorable and competitive sport throughout the western world. Coubertin was a life-long "Muscular Christian"—with less emphasis on the "Christian" than the "Muscular." He was born a Roman Catholic but remained unconvinced as to its dogma. Rather (and he said so many times), his was the religion of amateur sport. The sports field is a holy temple, he said, "a laboratory for manliness . . . an incomparable pedagogical tool . . ."—and it was all the invention of the Reverend Thomas Arnold. The Rugby School experiment, he said, gave birth to Muscular Christianity—"a Greek formula perfected by Anglo-Saxon Civilization."

Coubertin frequently wrote in an unclear and pedestrian manner. He was (and is) poorly understood because of this literary disorder, and because his ideas were innovative to many. The amateur spirit—the concept of absolutely no material gain was to him "a religion, with church, dogma and cult." Coubertin's conception of sport was the most obvious aspect of a grand attempt to fuse academic training with moral and physical education. The catalyst would be sport. His habitual "Pollyanna" view of sport was a fortress as well as a continuing puzzle and weakness. This grandiosity and philanthropic overkill is emphasized by the Olympic headquarters wall poster: "Olympism tends to bring together in a radiant gathering all the principles contributing to the perfection of man." In the mind of the founder, the definition of Olympic philosophy was well established by the war's end, 1920, and the Antwerp Games of the Seventh Olympiad. For Pierre de Coubertin, Olympism embraced the best of ancient Greece, the proven power of English Muscular Christianity, rhythm, art, beauty, and balance. Olympism encompasses an understanding that the body and the mind and the soul of man have an integrated glory. It is this symbiosis that can lead man to understand, as Socrates said, "his chief and proper concern—knowledge of himself and of the right way to live." All of us who love beauty, peace, athletics, who have done no impiety or sacrilege, who believe in fair play, are advocates of Olympism, and are Greeks in the highest sense. This was the language of Coubertin; he rarely deviated from this tone in more than fifty years of continuous writing. And yet, in all that time, he never failed to realize the tenuous nature of his Olympic Games experiment, the thin line between pride and fanaticism, the specter of nationalism gone mad.

Coubertin was a man of monumental ambivalence. He was never able to untrack himself emotionally, to distinguish between his basic world leadership role as either (1) philosophical leader of a new, twentieth-century pedagogical, humanistic "sport-for-all" thrust, or (2) promoter of the world's most important, competitive, and, therefore, exclusive sporting event—the Olympic Games. He wanted, simultaneously, to write about and work toward a world revival of physical education, and he labored to accomplish this through enlarging the scope and influence of the Olympic Games. In other words, his hope was that every Olympic Games competitor might exert a powerful influence on the masses for health and fitness. Throughout his writings, Coubertin fluctuated between egalitarian concern for the physical well-being of all peoples and also for that tiny fraction—the world's greatest athletes. His writings are frequently a tortuous laybrinth of inconsistencies—and I believe the main reason for such obtuseness was his life-long inability to deal with each phenomenon separately.

I believe that Coubertin denied himself an even larger measure of greatness by failing to recognize the quadrennial festival as an extraordinary gathering of champions—men and women who deserved and demanded very special treatment. Had he devoted himself fully to the other great task of expanding the sport-for-all, lifetime sport philosophy, Coubertin might today be recognized as one of the most important physical educators of the twentieth century. After reading Coubertin for nearly twenty years, I am convinced that his all-too-frequent habit of ascribing the same criteria, rules of conduct, and philosophy to Olympic athletes and to recreational sportsmen was the single greatest weakness of his Olympian philosophy. There are very few of us that are too idealistic. The French baron was very idealistic; he missed the mark in failing to recognize in the Olympic athlete a specially privileged person, an elitist, who for a brief few years, is deserving of a patron. He and she deserve some minimal, basic financial assistance, thus allowing them to develop into something approaching their full potential without even remotely running the risk of categorization as high-salaried professional sport entertainers.

Coubertin was a consummate romantic and a very good man. He fervently believed that his international experiment—the Olympic games—might contribute "to the general welfare and the betterment of humanity." As an old man with more than the usual share of triumphs and disappointments, he urged youth to never give up, to experience the joy of sport, to devote themselves to a life of "complete and unremitting altruism." In 1898, he wrote Harvard University president Charles Eliot inviting him to send several representatives to the next Olympic games, provided, of course, they be first-class athletes, good sportsmen, and pure amateurs. He was always sensitive to the need for the multidimensional athlete—a kind of Greek reincarnation, a modern-day medieval knight, a slightly modified aristocratic English gentleman-athlete. He dreamt on, never losing hope; his dream, while impossible of full fruition, bears remarkable testimony to the man. In a new biography, Yves-Pierre Boulongne unashamedly calls Coubertin one of the great modern teachers, educational theorists, humanists, and a "puritan in ethics." The Baron's dream of speaking a common language through the medium of cosmopolitan and honorable sport was a grandiose and unique idea. The fact that it has fulfilled some of his visionary plans, yet fallen short of full potential, can only act as a catalyst for today's sports leaders. By several standards, Pierre de Coubertin was a great man. This French citizen but spiritual "child of Albion" was emotionally and intellectually dominated by the impossible dream—the apostolic mission of introducing untrammeled Muscular Christianity to the whole world. No one, especially the revisionist historians, however, should judge him too harshly; Coubertin did, in the last analysis, believe in the intrinsic goodness of the human race, and, along with Charles Beard, Jacob Bronowski, and others, saw in mankind's gradual ascent and progress some kind of universal "mundane republic." Pierre de Coubertin rendered an enormous service to the community of nations. The many flaws in his Olympic jewel only highlight the fact that it is a precious commodity constantly in need of care, polishing, and, possibly, a sharp blow now and then to cut it into manageable parts.

A Glance at Coubertin's Written Works

The massive published works of Pierre de Coubertin, enough to fill twenty-five normal-sized volumes, are both mundane ramblings and an excellent example of a creative, unique mind. He wrote voluminously on sport history, sport psychology, sport sociology, and sport philosophy, long, long before they became contemporary and fashionable areas of scholarship. He also wrote on politics, geography, archaeology, theology, pedagogy, social, cultural, and military history, as well as education, physical education, physiology, medicine, and literature. The trouble is that almost all his commentaries in these areas of specialization are unscientific, and, in almost every case, incomplete. How could it be otherwise? He wrote compulsively for more than fifty years. The truths that his works contain, and there are many, are largely the results of a powerful, life-long habit of eclectic reading, intuition, empiricism, and a kind of metaphysical revelation. He was too busy all his life to ever become a recognized expert in any area. He is listed nowhere in the encyclopedia of world scholars. The long list of distinguished French scholars of the nineteenth century, in that nation's listing of its own first-rate thinkers, contains no mention of Pierre de Coubertin. But this may not be a good example, for Coubertin's native land, France, consistently ignored him in almost every one of his endeavors. Coubertin's most lucid writings occurred when he was a young man. The only book, I believe, that gave him some degree of recognition and praise from area specialists was his 1896 *L'Evolution Francaise Sous la Troisieme Republique*. The work was translated into English in 1898 and published by Thomas Crowell Publishers. Albert Shaw, editor of the *American Review of Reviews*, called it a "remarkable volume," and heaped praise on the young Frenchman whose "international and comparative cast of mind has come to be second nature with M. de Coubertin." Hedley Peck in *The Bookman* commented that Coubertin's book was written "with unusual fairness and philosophic insight," a lucid account of French history from 1871 to the end of the century. Political corruption, the hazards of a democracy, French literature, the position of the Catholic Church, Malthusian economics, and public education were all handled by Coubertin with thoroughness and controlled passion.

Unfortunately, Pierre de Coubertin was frequently obtuse, rambling, and, on occasion, incoherent in his vast writings. His fifteen years of impressions between 1885 and 1899, before the heavy burdens as Games organizer, are his most lucid work. A blizzard of articles—several score of them—appeared during this pre-twentieth century period. The phenomenon of sport, French politics, and life in England and the United States, make up the essence of this material. *Souvenirs d'Oxford et de Cambridge* (1887) was followed quickly the next year by *L'Education en Angleterre*. His passion for anything English or American continued in his *L'Education Anglaise en France* (1889). His rhapsodical impressions of the United States permeates *Universites Transatlantique* (1890), while second impressions of the USA appear in Coubertin's *Souvenirs d'Amerique et de Grece* (1897). In England, he watched Harrow School cricket in fascination and cried that English life and politics thrived in a free environment, one unencumbered by "suffocating interference from the state." He saw "the essential individualism of these Englishmen." Cambridge University, with its student self-government and rugged sport, was a revelation to him. Drifting over to Ireland, ever-alert to new images, the sport-starved Coubertin was fascinated both with the game of hurling and the warm, melancholy, yet peculiarly happy people. Only weeks earlier, he had seen football, lawn tennis, gymnastics, and rowing in the city of London. All of this is replete with a kind of moral and athletic education taught certain English youngsters—students "laying the ground work for citizenship." The tidy Baron de Coubertin worshiped the name of Thomas Arnold and in his own way credited the English headmaster with initiating the revolution of Muscular Christianity. Musing in the Rugby Chapel, the young French romantic stared at Arnold's tomb and "meditated on this cornerstone of the British Empire." Coubertin's two trips to the United States in 1889 and 1893 are well documented in these early impressions, and underscore his growing conviction that no system of education stands higher than the Anglo-American university training, a unique enterprise in leadership, he said, with the yeast of manly intercollegiate athletic competition leading the way.

From 1900 through World War I, Pierre de Coubertin reached his zenity of literary productivity. He seemed never to stop writing, and it is estimated that he published (a great deal of it at his own expense) something like 8,000 pages of material during the period. Almost no subject escaped his curiosity and perpetual commentary. His periodical articles touched on "The Future of Europe," fairly objective analyses of the five Olympic Games between 1900 and 1912, "The Psychology of Sport," "A New Form of Physical Education," French education, "Shakespeare and Victor Hugo," "Nudity and Sport," "A Model University," Franco-German politics, commentaries on Ancient Greece, "Why I Revived the Olympic Games," "Roosevelt and Tolstoi," "The Negro Question," "Reminiscences of Olympic Diplomats, Count Zeppelin, Colonel Balck, Jean Charcot." This is only an arbitrary selection of a much larger bibliography. His textbooks during this period include *France Since 1814* (1900), *Notes Sur L'Education Publique* (1901), *The Education of Twentieth Century Adolescents* (1905), his informative 1909 autobiography, *A Twenty-one Year Campaign*. That same year he published *Pages D'Histoire Contemporaine*. His *Essays on Sport Psychology* in 1913 was followed by *Pedagogie Sportive* in 1919.

From 1920 to the end of his life in 1937, Pierre de Coubertin's written bequests to those that were interested (and there were few) were frequent, hugely theoretical and idealistic, and frequently repetitious. It almost seemed that he was at his best during the years of struggle for recognition. Once he became world famous, his literary and didactic skill weakened. It may also have been that financial, family, and physical problems robbed him of some of his powers. In 1921, he wrote *Leçons de Pedagogie Sportive* and a more expanded *Pedagogie Sportive* the next year. The year after his retirement, 1926, Coubertin published four volumes called *L'Histoire Universelle*; they were subtitled, *The Asian Empires; The Mediterranean Drama; Celts, Germans, and Slavs*; and *The Formation and Development of Modern Democracies*. In the third volume, the Baron eulogized British education, especially that of Thomas Arnold, and pointed out for the hundredth time that athletics, when "exalted and coordinated," can act as a catalyst to bring together high intellect and moral courage. He had absolutely nothing new to say, but then Coubertin must have recognized that, after forty years, his ideas were hardly universal precepts. Coubertin faltered but did not stop writing. In 1930, he wrote *Notre France*, and, in 1931, a second autobiography, *Memoires Olympiques*, his most quoted work. Only recently, in 1977, the International Olympic Committee's official periodical, *Olympic Review*, translated and published in monthly installments this entire 248-page personal history. Lastly, Coubertin's *Anthologie* (1933) was largely fragmentary history woven with personal impressions.

His essays, newspaper editorials, and published periodicals were formidable during this period, 1920–1937. And yet it was his speeches that stirred the imagination, for Pierre de Coubertin was always at his very best when he was on his feet. On the hundredth anniversary of Greek Independence (1930), Coubertin addressed the Swiss Society of the Friends of Greece, reminding them that the original spirit of Hellenism taught us how to grow socially and morally. "Let us not lose this heritage, exchanging it for something of lesser value," concluded Coubertin. Ten years earlier, on 17 August 1920, in the presence of the IOC, the King of Belgium, and hundreds of guests from all over the world gathered for the Games of the Seventh Olympiad, the Baron de Coubertin was in his usual speaking form. The personal qualities that make for athletic success, he said, are the same qualities that each of us need for individual fulfillment. They are three in number: "hard work, boldness, tempered with sanity; controlled passion, a kind of idealized disinterestedness; and daily good deeds and life-long altruism." This Coubertin was indeed old-fashioned . . . in a timeless sort of way.

2 • Genesis of the Olympic Games Movement 1890 –1896

Baron Pierre de Coubertin's attempts to introduce compulsory school physical education in France met with little success. Efforts to make competitive athletics at the club level a national pastime never received a national mandate. The thought among most Frenchmen during the 1880s and 1890s was that playing games was not pedagogically sound or socially desirable for the development of future citizens. Coubertin never lost hope for a revitalization of sport and physical culture among his own people, but, in one of his infrequent practical moments, he decided that an international renaissance of sport, difficult as it would be, might be more easily accomplished than large-scale reform in his own country. After all, Britain, North America, Germany, and Scandinavia were in the midst of significant athletic progress during the century's last decade. Coubertin was well aware of these rumblings. The twenty-six-year-old baron organized the first international congress for the promotion of physical education, held in Paris 8–15 June 1889 in conjunction with that city's Universal Exposition. During the fall of that same year, he traveled to Boston, Massachusetts, as the French advisory expert to the Director of Secondary Education in the Ministry of Public Instruction. Addressing 2,000 delegates to the Physical Training Conference—most of whom were unsure which European system of sport and exercise should dominate the American scene—Coubertin made it clear that the English system of competitive interscholastic and intercollegiate athletics was supreme. His five months of continuous travel throughout North America convinced him that Canadians and Americans had already made their decision about sport. Coubertin fully agreed with his friend Albert Shaw, editor of the *American Review of Reviews,* that honest rather than deceitful athletics must be continually fought for, that Greek and calculus may be optional courses in our schools, "but proper care, discipline and development of the physical man . . . should be uniformly required of every student."

During the years 1890 to 1892, Coubertin and his small group of reformers were successful in the creation of playing fields at several hundred schools, and in widening the influence of the newly formed French Union of Athletic Clubs. International rowing, rugby, and athletic matches now attracted small bands of French athletes. But progress was slow. After painful negotiations, Coubertin and his club associates received permission to lay down a cinder running track in Paris's palace grounds, the beautiful gardens of Tuileries—only to be told that from time to time it would be necessary to roll up the track and carry it away. "Such were the bureaucrats of the day," moaned a slightly cynical Coubertin. On 4 July 1891, the powerful track team from New York City's Manhattan Athletic Club visited Paris, met the neophyte French athletes from the Racing Club, and administered "valuable lessons" to the host athletes. It was all a heady mix for the young Coubertin; a master plan for a truly cosmopolitan gathering of athletes was gaining momentum and clarity in his thinking, as well as the publication of a niagara of bulletins, essays, and periodical articles. He knew exactly what he wanted. For a decade, the young aristocrat had been preoccupied with idealized concepts of English education, the Age of Chivalry, and the very best of ancient Greece. As he said, "Long before I thought of drawing from Olympia's roots a new principle, I had the idea of rebuilding it in spirit." The idea seemed ripe for translation to a more tangible form.

By the fall of 1892, Pierre de Coubertin was convinced that significant progress in popularizing sport among the French masses was several generations away. He couldn't wait that long. Besides, a more grandiose idea continued to ferment in his active mind. He recognized that an entire conference could not be devoted to the idea of an Olympic Games revival. Quite coincidentally, Coubertin's club, the Union des Sports Athletiques (USFSA) was five years old that year. Club secretary Coubertin quickly called a meeting of members, guests, and friends of sport for 25 November 1892 in the main auditorium of the great Sorbonne University. The Baron remembered it well from his own undergraduate days only a decade earlier—that old amphitheatre "where so many candidates used to turn pale in their frantic endeavor to decipher Greek or Latin texts." Coubertin had masterminded the whole thing, and the great hall glittered with famous sportsmen, influential politicians, and well-known figures from the literary world. It was to be a trademark of Coubertin, who, time after time, gathered about him men of influence whenever he felt the need to achieve some personal Olympian goal. Several provocative issues faced the large Sorbonne audience. The proliferation of French sport, the new tempo of international athletic competitions, and the omnipresent amateurism problem were all legitimate items on the agenda. But Pierre de Coubertin had a singular and private wish to share with the students and with his friends. The all-important preliminaries must take place first, he thought.

The week's activities included a fifty-kilometer cycling race, all-day fencing matches, a cross-country race for boys, foot races, a grand picnic, and a special-invitation banquet on Sunday, 27 November. Nothing was overlooked; Coubertin had requested and received 1500 francs from French athletic clubs and from James Gordon Bennett, the remarkable editor of the *New York Herald,* who had established a Paris division in 1887 with the hope of cementing relations between the United States and France. Planning for the all-importance Sorbonne conference on the twenty-fifth had begun back in March of 1892, when Coubertin had convinced the President of France, Sadi Carnot, to act as patron of the festival. Paris resident Russian Grand Duke Wladimir agreed to preside over the meeting. The Russian and French national anthems were played, followed by Ernest Callot's "Ode de Circonstance" sung by Segond de l'Odeon, from Sophoclean verse translated into French. The evening of the conference was cold and gray, but, inside the Sorbonne, the stage was sparkling with personalities. The president of the USFSA, Janze, was there, as were university President Octave Greard and Russia's Prince Obelensky. French and Russian flags filled the room. The remainder of the evening was devoted to lectures on the world history of sport and physical education. Noted historian Georges Bourdon, in typical flowery tones so typical of the age, spoke of the ancient Greek glory during the Age of Pericles, and of the close association of "purified athletics" with this Athenian greatness. J. J. Jusserand gave the next speech on "Sport in the Middle Ages," quoting passages from Deschamps, Villon, and Rabelais's *Gargantua*. Jusserand, future French ambassador to the United States, was to write the authoritative history, *Sports and Games in Ancient France* (1901). This part of the program ended with a comedy presentation by Coubertin's brother, Paul Fredy, called "Dante and Virgil at the Union of Sports."

Coubertin was now ready for what he hoped would be a dramatic and effective finale. In Coubertin's autobiography, *Memoires Olympique,* he admits that his plan called for a sensational finish to his speech—the revival of the Olympic Games. "The time had come to take the plunge," he said. He started modestly, tracing the modern history of physical education and sport, especially in France. He warmed to the task, and then, at first imperceptibly, shifted the focus of his talk. The spirit of ancient Greece, a king of universal Hellenism, continues to be a powerful intellectual, social, and spiritual force, he noted. Significant manifestations of this most important period of our European heritage need greater emphasis, and, in some cases, a modern revival, he continued. He paused for emphasis and concluded with a timely analogy dealing with tariffs and free-trade—two of the most keenly discussed matters of the 1890's:

> Let us export our oarsmen, our runners, our fencers into other lands. This is the true Free Trade of the future; and the day it is introduced into Europe the cause of Peace will have received a new and strong ally. It inspires me to touch upon a further step I now propose, and in it I shall ask that the help you have given me hitherto you will extend again, so that together we may attempt to realize, upon a basis suitable to the conditions of our modern life, the splendid and beneficent task of reviving the Olympic Games.

It was Coubertin's best shot. He had left nothing undone. The arrow had been shot into the air, said one writer. It was an idea "audacious, eloquent, and cunning," said another. The audience applauded, many smiled inanely, most seemed genuinely impressed with his skill and sincerity. But not a single person in that large and diverse audience took his proposal seriously. Somehow, that gathering of university students, faculty, sportsmen, intellectuals, and members of Parisian society had completely missed the point, thinking Coubertin's speech a mere clever piece of oratory. The young French baron was crushed. He had prepared himself for any audience reaction—"opposition, irony, protest, but not complete indifference and a complete lack of understanding." Following his brilliant failure, he mingled with the audience, trying to convince them that he was seriously proposing an Olympic Games revival. But they continued to think he was talking in parables, equating the Olympic Games "in their mental museums along with the mysteries of Eleusis or the Delphic Oracle—dead things that could be revived only in the theater." Somehow, Coubertin's proposal was seen as purely symbolic. Four years later, at the first Athens Olympic Games, a woman approached Coubertin and told him that she had been present during his Sorbonne speech, confessing that she misunderstood him, thinking he was referring to a theatrical production called "The Olympics" that she had enjoyed at the San Francisco Opera house. In fact, a good many of Coubertin's listeners thought he was proposing an animated theatrical reproduction of the ancient Olympic Games. Coubertin must have weakened when one woman asked if the Olympian actors would perform in the nude. No, he replied; these games would be real and worldwide. "Oh, then," she replied, "will we see Indian, Negro, and Chinese performers?" Coubertin weakened on the spot and "smiled rather than fight them." The contemporary French newspaper *L'Auto* commented that the time was not ripe for Olympic Games. Both the French and Germans failed to understand the scheme, while the British, concluded the newspaper editorial, saw the Olympic

Games proposal as most exciting, but much too vast, even unattainable. Coubertin retreated from all this as gracefully as possible. He admitted that he had been hasty; much more work needed to be done. A sober Coubertin was prepared to pitch his tune in a lower key.

After the Sorbonne conference of 1892, the Baron more fully understood that not only had he blundered, but that domestic political life, the dominant ethos of the French Third Republic at that time, prevented easy acceptance of a cosmopolitan athletic gathering. During these last years of the twentieth century, most educated Frenchmen were looking and thinking inwardly rather than on a global scale. A modern historian, Allan Mitchell, noted that the German empire was fashioned in a victorious war, the French republic by a humiliating defeat. The French people "underwent a period of introspection and self-recrimination." Both the military and clergy joined French politicians in proclaiming a kind of "mystique of national regeneration." Anything un-French was suspect. Professor William Milligan Sloane called it a "perverted and chauvinistic concept of nationality." Any new form of athletics smacking of a foreign element was suspect. "Let us be French," cried the militant nationalists. Charles Maurras, ultra-nationalist, felt that the Olympic Games revival would profane a beautiful idea and result in serious national and world disorder. If the truth be known, he said, international sport would reveal weaknesses among Latin nations while highlighting "Anglo-Saxon predominance." France, unprepared to embrace neighboring countries, could not accept Coubertin's Olympic internationalism. The Baron was in a bind; his Olympic dream lay dormant, much work needed to be done, he had already spent far too much of his own money, and only a few volunteered to help. French sporting clubs were divided, suspicious of one another, and operating under widely differing amateur rules.

Coubertin was persistent, and, fortunately, there seemed to be a starting point for a return to his Olympic Games proposal. The delegates at the 1892 Sorbonne meeting had received in their packets a proposal for a future meeting on the problem of amateurism. Adolphe de Pallissaux had framed the document. The two friends approached the French Sports Union, requesting a high level meeting in Paris. On 1 August 1893, the USFSA Committee met at its usual place, 27 Boulevard des Italiens. Baron Pierre de Coubertin, secretary-general, presided. Around the table were Monsieurs Agnel, Fenwick, Depont, Saint-Chaffray, Reichel, Harvey, Pallissaux, Mercier, Jung, Grisel, Sloane, Marcadet, and Louis-Philippe Reichel. "Not one of these men is unknown in the history of French Sport revival; a historic date for prideful Frenchmen," recalled the secretary. The committee drafted seven questions on the problems of amateurism; Coubertin added an eighth proposal, which read: "Regarding the possibility of the revival of the Olympic Games. Under what conditions could they be re-established?" Coubertin's friends quickly approved all eight discussion topics. But Coubertin was unconvinced that ready approval by the committee, especially his Olympic Games revival proposal, was any guarantee of their larger acceptance. He could not forget the previous year's Sorbonne conference. Determined to gain international support, Coubertin decided to return to North America and England. International sport competition was growing, but slowly. The baron had been instrumental in starting rugby and track competitions between the French Racing Club and foreign teams. He had worked hard for French rowers to gain admission to the 1893 Henley Regatta. Just before his departure to seek the support of "high-minded sportsmen," Coubertin spoke at the Lycée de Chartres. He reminded the students that patriotism was not a hatred of other peoples; it was, rather, a love of one's own country, a deep respect of peoples other than themselves, and a determination to uplift one's personal moral and physical health.

The baron had his own reasons for making this trip, but he was also on official business. In the autumn of 1893, he left for the States as official representative on French Higher Education to the Chicago World's Fair. Talks with former Prime Minister Jules Ferry and President Carnot had prepared him for the official part of his mission. He also desperately needed to talk to friends and, hopefully, supporters of his Olympic Games dream. The thirty-year-old Frenchman enjoyed Chicago, its athletic club, the World's Fair, and the Congress on Higher Education. He took the train to California, looking with fascination at the Plains states and Rockies along the way. He stayed at San Francisco's Palace Hotel, made frequent use of the Olympic Club, visited Stanford University, and awarded a medal at the University of California, Berkeley, to the best student speaker on French history or politics. On his return trip, he stopped at Tulane University in New Orleans, looked closely at student life at Michigan University. Of course, he made the trip to Harvard University, and then the University of Virginia, Georgetown University, the city of Washington, D.C., and finally on to Princeton University, spending three weeks with his good friend and professor of European history, William Milligan Sloane. The historian Hippolyte Taine was of the opinion that "Sloane knows France better than any other foreigner." Sloane made every effort to help his younger collegaue, and, on the eve of Coubertin's departure from Princeton, a dinner party was arranged for 27 November 1893 at New York City's University Club. Although Sloane had hand-picked the Harvard, Yale, Princeton, and Columbia sportsmen present at the dinner meeting, the affair was not considered a success by Coubertin. Even at this early date in American sport history, the eastern universities were engaged in a bitter, prolonged struggle for power with the Amateur Athletic Union (AAU), and had no time to give Coubertin's Olympic

Games proposal any more than polite disinterest. Coubertin, ever-eager for straws, hoped at least that there would be no American opposition at a June 1894 meeting that was already churning in his mind. Thanksgiving Day 1893 was on the thirtieth of November, and the young Baron joined 50,000 others at Manhattan Field for a "Yankee football match between Yale [0] and Princeton [6]." His American adventure, a qualified success, had gained some friends. He had learned a great deal, and was hugely impressed with his version of the multidimensional American athlete—a kind of Greek reincarnation, an idealized modern-day medieval knight. Coubertin always had a way of seeing what he wanted to see. He returned immediately to Paris, and, as was his habit, wrote a travelogue called *Souvenirs d'Amerique et de Grece*.

The unifying leadership of Pierre de Coubertin had been sorely missed among French sporting circles during his four months absence. He found things "difficult and uncertain" in the early weeks of the new year, and with characteristic zeal, wrote an open letter, dated 15 January 1894, addressed to all sporting societies and clubs the world over. With some knowledge of Olympic Games history and of human nature, Coubertin warned that any revival of these games must be accompanied by eternal vigilance in order to preserve their essential honesty. As fragile as sport amateurism is, he said, the international experiment needs to be tested; only then would an Olympic Games revival

. . . bring together every four years the representatives of the nations of the world, and we can well believe that these courteous and peaceful contests would constitute the highest of international activities.

In his near frantic efforts to drum up Olympic Games support, Coubertin attended a dinner in February of 1894 at London's University Sports Club. Sir John Astley welcomed "the prophet of the new era;" the Prince of Wales and the Right Honorable Arthur Balfour also agreed to support the cause of sport. Coubertin's way was to ingratiate himself with men of influence. He worked hard and was rewarded with support from the duke of Sparta, the king of Belgium, the crown of princes of Sweden and Norway, the Duc d'Aumale, and other prominent Frenchmen. There were rumblings of discontent, of course. American support was nearly non-existent; British support had been less than robust, for, as Coubertin correctly guessed, they regarded sport as their own "exclusive property." A month before the June 1894 Congress, Coubertin visited the German embassy in Paris, vainly trying for support from their powerful gymnastic socities. The French gymnastic group immediately threatened withdrawal from the Sorbonne meeting if the hated Germans were invited. The shadow of the Franco-Prussian War lingered; the thin line of athletic communication between the two countries was irreparably shaken. "Touchy patriotism" was a pervasive European phenomenon during these last years of the nineteenth century and too many European sporting clubs agreed with the Belgium gymnastic leader that Coubertin's version of sport represented "Anglomaniacs importing into France the school games of the United Kingdom just as hunting dogs and race horses are imported." Coubertin's January circular, sent around the world, received "a very irregular and scattered response." His pet project was in poor shape, and he reacted in characteristic fashion. He asked his friend and famed Greek archaeologist Charles Waldstein to write the King of Greece urging him to accept an invitation as honorary member of the June meeting. King George accepted. When France's Minister of Foreign Affairs, M. Casimir Perier, was unable to accept Coubertin's request to chair the Paris International Athletic Congress in June, the Baron immediately asked and received a positive reply from another baron, the distinguished Senator de Courcel, former ambassador to Berlin, and, in December of that same year, ambassador to England. All seemed to be ready. The eight-day meeting was under the over-all organization of three distinguished sports leaders representing major geographic areas. Coubertin had quite arbitrarily, but, for him, logically, divided the world into three parts, appointing a leader for each. There would be the British Empire's representative, C. Herbert, secretary of the AAA; Continental Europe's, M. de Coubertin; and the North American world's, William Milligan Sloane.

On Saturday 16 June 1894, in the Palace of the Sorbonne, over two thousand guests were present to discuss the continuing problem of amateurism, to be exposed once again to Coubertin's Olympic Games proposal, and, just as importantly, to enjoy the extraordinarilly well-planned musical and artistic celebration. The great amphitheater had only recently been the scene of the Louis Pasteur Jubilee. This time, the impossible task of defining amateurism and regulating the conduct of all non-professional athletes was to be discussed. Proposals eight, nine, and ten belonged to Coubertin. Even at this early date, Coubertin was pessimistic about solutions to the amateur problem. He frankly admitted that once again, at least for him, the matter of creeping athletic professionalism would be used as a convenient camouflage to somewhat mute the real reason for the Congress. Seventy-nine delegates from forty-nine sporting societies, representing twelve countries, were on hand, ready to listen, and to vote. Coubertin and his associates had outdone themselves, and the great hall of the Sorbonne was filled with art works and sumptuous decorations; an atmosphere calculated "to please and impress" the delegates had taken months of planning. Baron de Courcel's inaugural address was a plea for all Frenchmen to recognize sport and physical culture, not as incidental pastimes, but as a national necessity. Excessive French intellectualism is dangerous, he said; the timeless wisdom and balance of an ancient Athenian education needs immediate introduction into public schools. The heady atmosphere inside the Sorbonne was heightened by the poet, Jean Aicard, president of the French Association of Men and Letters, whose speech, "enflamed in idealism," spoke of the universal power of righteousness combined with robust physical health.

The walls of the Sorbonne had only recently been decorated by Puvis de Chavannes, one of France's greatest muralists. His commissioned works decorated hotels, museums, and galleries, while his most famous work inside the Boston Public Library brought him 200,000 francs. Coubertin was delighted at the way things were unfolding. The year before, 1893, the French School of Archaeology in Athens had uncovered at Delphi some rare poems and musical scores carved on marble tablets. It was an extraordinary find, for almost no music had survived from ancient times. This Greek musical fragment had been translated by Theodore Reinach and adapted for music by the famous composer-conductor Gabriel Fauré. Coubertin worked hard and got both of them to perform at the June Congress. Reinach first read the music; then this haunting, ancient "Hymn to Apollo" was sung by Madame Jeanne Remaclé; a choral group accompanied by harps and directed by Gabriel Fauré was so impressive that a London newspaperman present at the Sorbonne wisely observed that the audience was vastly more impressed with the poetry, music, and scenery, than by any talk of revived Olympic Games. He was convinced, as was Coubertin, that the educated audience would respond positively in the presence of "fine and large ideas," that almost any proposals on sport reform and Olympic renaissance would receive full support. Coubertin readily accepted credit (or blame) for the eminently church-like atmosphere of the whole opening day.

The International Athletic Congress tackled the entire amateur-professional problem on Sunday 17 June. Of course, the thorny issues spilled over into the next several days, but not without delicious interruptions for footraces, torchlight parades by the military, athletic exhibitions on the Bois de Boulogne, horse races, mock battles on horseback, trumpet voluntaries, receptions, banquets, lantern parades, and fireworks displays. By Friday, 22 June, some unanimity regarding amateurism had been agreed upon. All was most pacific, and Coubertin reflected that "behind this peaceful facade I had been able without hindrance to get my conception of the modern Olympic revival unanimously endorsed." On the following day, Coubertin put before the delegates the proposal that, in order to promote physical education and international friendship, world Olympic Games should be held every four years.

Coubertin had been instrumental in creating an *"ambiance esperée,"* or accepting atmosphere, at the week-long conference. Long before its conclusion, Coubertin said, "I knew instinctively that nobody would ever consciously or otherwise vote against the revival of the Olympic Games." The motion carried unanimously. That evening, Baron de Courcel hosted a triumphant dinner. Coubertin was jubilant and spoke of "Olympism"—the spirit and philosophy that would cement the new games into something unique among world sporting events—a triumph of the integrated mind, body, and spirit. "I lift my glass to the Olympic Idea," he said; it is an antique concept which has "returned to illuminate the threshold of the twentieth century with a gleam of joyous hope." An encouraging telegram from the King of Greece focused on Athens as the first Olympic Games site. The newly-formed International Olympic Committee had already agreed on Athens and Paris Olympics in 1896 and 1900. The new IOC president was the Athenian delegate and historian, Demitrios Bikelas. The brilliant French philologist, Michael Breal, offered a silver cup as trophy for an Olympic Marathon race, and predicted great financial and spiritual benefits for the host city. "Palmes academique" were presented to William Milligan Sloane, to Pallissaux, and Jules Morcadet. Bill Henry, American journalist, director of the 1932 Los Angeles Olympics, and an admirer of Coubertin, noted that a "mystic spell" had been cast over all the Sorbonne delegates, and under "the inspired stage management of its great protagonist, the Olympic dream of Baron Pierre de Coubertin took definite shape for the first time." The baron put it more simply, declaring, "As for myself, I hereby assert my claims for being sole author of the whole project."

Although Bikelas was its president, the IOC was under the direct control of Pierre de Coubertin. He alone selected for membership, in addition to himself: Ernest Callot of France, General Alexander Butowsky of Russia, General Viktor Balck of Sweden, William Milligan Sloane of the United States, Jiri Guth-Jarkovsky of Bohemia, Fr. Ferenc Kemeny of Hungary, Herbert and Lord Ampthill of England, Dr. J. B. Zubiaur of Argentina, Leonard Cuff of New Zealand, Count Lucchesi Palli and Duke Andrea Carafa of Italy, and Count Maxime de Bousies of Belgium. Coubertin could expect knowledgeable hard work from only a few of them. His would be a lonely, difficult task. As it turned out, the passionate Greeks, animated at the thought of an Olympic Games on their soil and fired with patriotic zeal, tried to ignore the Frenchman in Paris and never included him in their organizational plans. However, not all the Greeks believed that the games should be returned to their "rightful place." The combination of Anglo-American indifference, lackluster enthusiasm in Paris, no knowledge of the movement on most continents of the world, fiscal bankruptcy and near political anarchy in Athens, made for no guarantee of an Olympic revival. The eighteen-month period from July of 1894 to early spring of 1896 was painful for everyone concerned. In London, the *Spectator* editorialist wrote an article calling the Olympic Games revival efforts, "The Latest Athletic Whim," and bitterly criticized "the absurd importance" attached to the improbable plan. But the Greeks had pride and were stung by the European press that had heaped abuse on them because of the Greek treasury's inability to make foreign loan payments. The government was determined to save face and remind the world of the nation's immense heritage.

IOC President Bikelas was in Athens, sending hopeful letters to Coubertin. A less cheerful note was received in October of 1894. Greek Prime Minister Tricoupis was disenchanted with the whole Olympic effort; Bikelas strongly urged that Coubertin come to Athens. Despite his marriage plans fixed for 12 March 1895, the Baron took the train to Marseille, and boarded the steamer *Ortegal* bound for Piraeus, the port of Athens. In the Greek city, Coubertin was met by Bikelas, who handed him a copy of a letter from Stephanos Dragoumis addressed to the baron in Paris, dated 1 November. The influential politician and member of the Zappeion Athletic Club repeated that Greece was broke, and the excellent Olympic Games idea might better be postponed until 1900, as part of the Paris Universal Exposition. This was the last straw, for Coubertin had exchanged letters with Ferenc Kemeny, IOC member from Hungary, regarding the possibility of holding the 1896 Olympic Games in that country to celebrate its thousandth anniversary. Initial enthusiasm by Kemeny turned to gloom when his government insisted that there was absolutely no money available for such a venture. It had to be Greece or nothing. It was Coubertin's first trip to Greece. The day after landing, he and his host, Bikelas, toured the city, including the recently excavated ancient Olympic stadium. After several days of frantic talks with minor politicians, interspersed with careful attempts to gauge the mood of the average Athenian citizen regarding new expenditures on modern Olympic Games, Baron de Coubertin leveled his best weapon—the art of oratory—at the Parnassus Literary Society on 16 November 1894. He started well, reminding the audience that western culture, including sport and physical education, had its beginnings in Athens. "Your ancestors," he cried, "created the truest integration of muscles and ideas." The demise of Greek culture left a centuries-long void, he went on, only to be rescued by a new nineteenth-century moral and physical imperative— English Muscular Christianity. The educational principles taught by Thomas Arnold, Charles Kingsley, and others represent a movement that is "world-wide and gathering speed," said the animated Baron. He was always good on his feet, and instructed an attentive audience that the proposed new Olympic Games are not only very Greek in nature, but represent a modern "need for peace and brotherhood." He finished with a reminder that the Athenian celebration

> . . . would entail only a minimal expenditure of 150,000 francs, which would soon be more than recovered. Do not allow your enthusiasm to be dampened by the prospect of athletic defeat at the hand of strangers. Dishonor would not lie in defeat, but in failure to take part. You may be sure that in working for the cause of sport, you are working for your country.

President Bikelas and Coubertin now sought financial help from the Athenian family of Zappas, sponsors of the Zappeion Athletic Club. The brothers Zappas had left to the state a rich legacy for the erection of a sports training institute, the Zappeion. Director Dragoumis said "no" to any request for monies, but softened after Coubertin's calculated editorial in the newspaper *Asty* in which the Frenchman admitted that the Athenian Olympics would be difficult, but, he said, "the French have a proverb that says the word 'impossible' is not in the language. I have been told the word is Greek. I do not believe it." However effective Coubertin may have been, the key to successful games was the royal family. King George was in Russia for the funeral of Emperor Alexander III. George's three sons, Constantine, George, and Nicholas took charge of the organizing committee, and, especially, of raising public monies. Coubertin had been in Athens three weeks and, just before his departure, the public treasury announced that donations had reached exactly 332,756 drachmas. It was not nearly enough, but the baron had to return to Paris for, among other reasons, his marriage. A quick trip to Olympia to see "the sacred landscape," a speech on 7 December 1894 at the Naples Philological Society, described as "a waste of my breath," and his return to Paris followed rapidly. The fate of the New Olympics was now completely in the hands of the Greeks, and they were seriously divided on the worth of the whole affair.

His Royal Highness, Prince Constantine, President of the Olympic Games Organizing Committee, called for a meeting on 13 January 1895 in the Zappeion Building. By encouraging these new international Olympic Games, he said, world friendships will be enhanced, and, at the same time, "we pay homage to our ancestors who established the Pan-Hellenic Games in Olympia." He reminded all that despite serious problems and individual opposition, "all the Hellenes show their eagerness to promote this great enterprise, . . ." He then asked that key patriots, a Council of Twelve, be assigned the task of raising public monies. He was sure of success, despite the shortness of time. After all, he concluded:

. . . I draw from the patriotic pride which animates our nation, and the pure and sincere veneration, with which every Greek remembers the glorious traditions of ancient Hellas. Gentlemen, I reckon not less on your intelligent activity to bring to a prosperous end the work which has begun under such happy auspices . . . We must at once set to work vigorously if we want to gain the desired goal.

Thus, almost by royal decree, arguments against the Olympic plan were frowned upon, and a massive campaign to raise more monies for a new stadium now reached international dimensions. Greek royalty became patrons of the scheme. Wealthy Greek merchants all over the world contributed $100,000.

It was still not enough. Timoleon J. Philemon, former Athens mayor and now general-secretary of the Olympic organizing committee, immediately set sail for Alexandria, Egypt, to plead with George Averoff. The rich merchant and well-known Athenian benefactor needed little convincing, and promised to cover all the expenses for a complete restoration of the Olympic stadium. The sum would eventually approach one million Greek drachmas. The savior had been found, and, when the prince was informed, he immediately commissioned George Vroutos to create an Averoff statue, to be placed in front of the stadium as a token of national gratitude.

IOC president Bikelas, who had returned to Athens, worked around the clock for the cause. He kept in constant touch with Paris-bound Coubertin. After all, it was Bikelas who had suggested to Coubertin that the first restored games be held in Athens. A February 1895 meeting at the Zappeion created nine subcommittees, each charged with specific tasks to be completed a year from that date. It was tough sledding, for, as secretary Philemon said at the time, "There were still a number of people left who continued to throw ridicule on the whole enterprise." Back in Paris, unfortunately, Coubertin couldn't collect a French franc from the government to support his Olympic idea. For over half a year, the strongly nationalistic German gymnastic societies eyed with suspicion this French-sponsored, international sporting festival, heavily infiltrated with Anglo-American competitions. Richard Mandell, in his excellent little book *The First Modern Olympics* paraphrased the Germanic point of view. "If the Germans were to participate in modern Olympic Games, they would have to be *national* Olympic Games for Germans alone." The Swedish crown prince was interested, but no more than that. General Butowsky wrote that the Russian press was manifestly uninterested in the Olympic movement. "Our press," he wrote on 2 February 1895, "finds the question of physical training unworthy of mention in a distinguished newspaper." Small but hardly overwhelming interest was shown in

England, and, most shocking of all, the United States was far too absorbed in American football and baseball to be any more than casually interested in a far-away Greek festival.

The German question deserves elaboration for, as usual, it was complex. Dr. Willibald Gebhardt, a chemist from Berlin, differed from his countrymen in that he understood and sympathized with Pierre de Coubertin's grandiose plans for sport cosmopolitanism. Gebhardt felt he could better serve his country and the Olympic Idea if he were a member of the IOC. Coubertin unfolded the whole story from memory in his autobiography, *Memoires Olympique*. His version and several others seem to agree that out-of-context remarks by Coubertin (possibly unconsciously biased against France's traditional enemy) had slandered Germany, thus alienating whatever little sympathy existed there for Olympic Games. In a 12 June 1895 interview, Coubertin had said Germany was not present at the previous year's great Sorbonne Congress, and that the late invitation sent to that country to attend the Paris meeting might not have been accidental. Coubertin also pointed out, insensitively, that German and Greek political relations were bad; furthermore, he said, as far as the members of the Greek royal family were concerned, "their sympathies were French." Mandell's research further points out that Coubertin's remarks were published in gymnastic periodicals, and on 24 December 1895 in the influential *National-Zeitung*. Coubertin's immediate denial to the Greek minister in Berlin was answered with a promise that the widest possible publicity would be given the denial—including a copy to sports-loving German Chancellor Hohenlohe. Coubertin's spiritual friend, Gebhardt, assured him by telegram of his wholehearted support in the joint Olympic enterprise. "He was kind enough," said the harassed Frenchman, "to send a copy of this message to the French ambassador, Mr. Jules Herbette." It seems that politics and the Olympic Games, even at this germinal stage, became inescapably coupled. It may have been that Coubertin was still miffed at his two unanswered invitations addressed to Prussian Minister von Podbieiski to send athletes to Athens. But the usual Coubertin persistence and single-mindedness won the day, and despite German gymnasts refusal to participate, a representative team from that country did compete in Greece. In the end, not only Gebhardt but also Baron von Reiffenstein forgave the baron for any alleged discriminatory remarks.

Another kind of discrimination was occurring, and it didn't sit very well with Coubertin. The zealous Greeks, in perpetual motion during the pre-Olympic year of 1895, almost never mentioned the name of the foreigner from Paris who had revived the entire movement. Coubertin's name was absent from official Olympic bulletins, tentative programs, royal edicts, organizing committee instructions, and the Greek press. One

Athens paper did answer the absent Coubertin's claim as Olympic Games renovator, calling him "a thief, seeking to rob Greece of her inheritance." The Baron replied vigorously to critical remarks in the *Times* of London and the *Messenger of Athens*. In Bill Henry's *Approved History of the Olympic Games*, the author states that a new Greek national passion at the time made it nearly impossible for the Greeks to recognize the organizer of these new Games. "The Greeks," said Henry, "were not as interested in ignoring Coubertin as they were in claiming what they felt was theirs—and theirs alone." Even the hard-working Olympic enthusiast, Philemon, may have believed some of the anti-Coubertin rumors and reports. At least, Coubertin believed he did, compounding matters by accusing the Greek statesman of "evil designs" in attempting to do away with the newly-formed International Olympic Committee. The whole affair smacked of the unbelievable, but comparable anecdotes are told of every Olympic Games preparations from that pre-Athens period to the present day.

The physical restoration of ancient Athens, including the construction of an athletic stadium, is associated with heroic names—Pericles, Lycurgus, Demosthenes, Heracleitos, and finally, in the second century after Christ, the Athenian sophist, Herodes Atticus. In the space of four years during the reign of Roman Emperor Hadrian (117-138 A.D.), the stadium was transformed and covered with beautiful marble. Pausanias noted that the work nearly exhausted the Pentelic marble quarries, but that the sight of the new stadium "was splendid beyond description." The passage of more than seventeen and one-half centuries eliminated almost all traces of the once-great sports arena. Excavations from 1869 to 1878, and again in 1895, stimulated interest in its reconstruction. The awarding of the new Olympic Games to Athens and the generosity of Averoff generated frantic efforts to completely rebuild the stadium as a reflection of a new modern Greek age and glory. Time was short, not much more than a year, and architect Anastas Metaxas and nearly five hundred workers began the impossible task of a complete, classical restoration of the Panathenaic Stadion, all in pure white marble. They didn't quite make it, but, at the opening ceremonies in April of 1896, it was the largest and handsomest stadium in the world. James E. Sullivan, long-time American Olympic Chief, was enormously impressed with the "tiers of marble seats that go to the clouds." It was a grand place for the Olympic Games, he said, and "In size and dimensions, it is unsurpassed; in form and construction, it is unequalled." The cigar-shaped cinder track, built along classic lines, with long straightaways and incredibly sharp turns at both ends of the stadium, was groomed by groundskeeper Charles Perry, brought to Athens from the London Athletic Club.

Open communication between the IOC and sports organizations around the world did not exist on the eve of the Games of the First Olympiad.

Coubertin's frantically persistent efforts to invite all amateur athletes to compete in Athens were barely successful. The world press had cooperated in only the most marginal way. Coubertin was right in his self-praise that he had acted as a catalyst for international sport, that without his Games it might have been years more before the fruition of his idea, a world confederation of sportsmen. In the United States, only William Milligan Sloane was directly connected with the IOC; a few Amateur Athletic Union (AAU) organizers and an even smaller number of college people were aware of Olympic Games plans. Professor Sloane did his part, arranging for six weeks off for four Princeton undergraduate students: Robert Garrett, Francis Lane, Albert Tyler, and Herbert Jameson. They paid their own way, of course. The Boston Athletic Association team to Athens consisted of Thomas Burke, Ellery Clark, Thomas Curtis, Arthur Blake, W. W. Hoyt, and Manager John Graham. It seems that during the January 1896 indoor games, Blake's spectacular win in the thousand-yard run prompted him to say, in jest, "Oh, I'm too good for Boston. I ought to go over and run the Marathon, at Athens, in the Olympic Games." A month later, it was all arranged. Harvard University's Dean Briggs gave senior Clark special permission to miss classes and go to Greece. But Harvard freshman Jim Connolly was not so fortunate. He was refused a leave of absence from Harvard. On his eighty-seventh birthday in 1956, Connolly remembered that the school administration "said if I left I'd have to resign and might not get back to school when I returned. So I quit." He joined the others and set sail for Greece on 20 March 1896, aboard the German steamer *Fulda*. The seventeen-day trip was tiresome, and it was frightening when they arrived in Athens on 5 April, to find that the next day marked the opening of the games. No one had informed the Americans that their own Roman calender and the official Olympic Games Greek calender differed by twelve days. It didn't seem to matter, and the entire American team stayed up all night, enjoying the rare spectacle of an entire city population gone crazy with anticipation of their very own Olympic Games.

Athens was ablaze with lights and festivities. Myriads of lanterns lined and spanned the streets, bearing the letters *A* and *O (Olympiako Agones*—"Olympic Games"). Coubertin was back in the city for the games and a week-long meeting of the IOC. Most members were present (Sloane was unable to attend due to the press of university responsibilities). At a meeting in the magnificent Hotel Grande-Bretagne on 6 April 1896, three cities, New York, Berlin, and Stockholm were discussed as possible sites for the 1904 games. It was all highly theoretical talk, and the committee knew it, for in that very city the Greek Olympic Organizing Committee would listen to no plan other than the one marking Athens as the permanent home of the modern games. On 7 and 9 April, seven members of the Committee met at President Bikelas's home. At the second of these meetings, Dr. Gebhardt discussed the creation of national Olympic Committees. Most of the Greeks were involved in far more exciting things than such mundane talk. On Sunday, 5 April 1896, the Orthodox Easter and also the seventy-fifth anniversary of the Greek War of Independence, a large crowd collected in the early morning outside the new stadium to participate in the unveiling of the Averoff statue. A company of infantry in their very best dress, special police, a marching band, ministers, guests, deputies, foreign representatives, IOC members, athletes, and priests all participated. Also, the streets and surrounding hills "presented a living mass of densely packed spectators." At 11 A.M., after the arrival of the Royal Family, Philemon's speech on the significance of Averoff's great gift was interrupted by a heavy rain shower, but, as he finished his hymn of praise to a man "deserving the gratitude of the whole nation," the crown prince drew a string, the Greek flag covering the statue dropped, "and all bystanders could behold the imposing figure of the noble son of Epiros." We do not know if Pierre de Coubertin, thirty-three-year-old French nobleman, was present. We do know that he was caught up in his own dreams, as well as in the electric Athenian atmosphere. He spoke rhapsodically, convinced that no one present in Athens that spring could fail to understand "the new reunion of body and mind, the return of a harmonious Hellenic athleticism." It is not that there were no critics; their voices were muted during the brief time of the festival. Coubertin was understandably overjoyed, optimistic. The advantage of hindsight proves he was overly optimistic in noting that:

> The sun shines, and the Olympic games are here. The Greeks have overnight become conscious of the native strength and suppleness of their race . . . The fears and ironies of the year just passed have disappeared. The skeptics have been eliminated; the Olympic games have not a single enemy.

3 • Olympic Trial and Tribulation 1896 –1911

Much as a child must experiment during its formative years, and, as a child, endure trial, tribulation, and youthful joys, so did the actors in the new Olympic drama experience these feelings. The great undertaking could not have begun under more dramatic circumstances. It seemed that all of Athens followed the Royal Family to the marvelous new Olympic stadium. The Greeks, despite their legendary heritage as the inventors of western sport, were wildly naive about most forms of organized athletics. A tenth of a million spectators gathered inside the area and also clung like locusts on the nearby hills. The Royal Family formally opened the games of the first modern Olympiad, the chorus and orchestra presented an original Olympic cantata, and the immortal spirit of antiquity was asked to "give life and animation to these noble games." It was all very exciting for a predominantly Greek crowd, despite the doubly unkind remark of an American visitor who said that the modern Greek knows nothing of organized sport; "All are unknown to him," he said, "as they are to a Chinaman." And yet a special cosmopolitanism was evident even at this first Olympic Games. *Harper's Weekly* of 18 April 1896 noted that Greek street merchants in the city of Chicago left their pushcarts at home, attended a high mass, and marched in an Olympic inaugural parade through the city's main streets.

Three hundred and eleven athletes from thirteen countries participated in nine sports during the Greek celebration, 5 April through 15 April 1896. Austria, Sweden, Switzerland, Australia, Bulgaria, Chile, Denmark, Germany, France, Great Britain, Hungary, the United States, and Greece were represented. Unfortunately, Italy was not. Their only entry, who walked from Milan to Athens in order, as he supposed, to get himself into proper training, was disqualified on his arrival. The modern Olympic Games precedent was established as track and field athletics occupied center stage, with uneven notoriety given to gymnastics, weight lifting, shooting, lawn tennis, cycling, wrestling, swimming, and fencing.

Yachting, rowing, rugby, and equestrian sports received varying degrees of consideration, but were not contested. As in all Olympic cities, there was an inflationary spiral in Athens during the month of April 1896. But there has always been a way to beat this game, and Sir George Stuart Robertson, looking back sixty years, recalled that he and his Australian friend, E. H. Flack, winner at 800 and 1500 meters, "hired a small, furnished flat and fed at Greek restaurants, thus having the advantage of paying drachmae and not in sterling." A New England lady, Miss Maynard Butler, watching the street festivities from her balcony at the Hotel Angleterre, had pointed out to her Queen Olga "walking incognito and in the very closest crush of the untidy but quietly devout throng." One reason for the relative success of these games was the enthusiasm and full cooperation of the entire Royal Family.

Britain's parsimonious attitude about entering these games made American victories in track-and-field a foregone conclusion. Athletes from other countries knew no more than the barest rudiments of the sport. The very first victory in Athens was Jim Connolly's easy win in the hop, step, and jump. A 200-piece band played his national anthem, two Greek sailors hoisted an American flag, sailors from the USS San Francisco stood at strict attention. The more than 60,000 polite and curious Greek spectators set the tenor for the entire eleven-day festival. As for Connolly, he was to say many years later, "Why, it was a moment to inspire." Tom Burke won the 100 and 400 meters in 12.0 and 54.0 seconds; Tom Curtis hurdled to victory; Ellery Clark won his silver first-place medals in the long and high jump; W. W. Hoyt only had to vault 10'9¾" to capture the pole vault. Bob Garrett won the shot put, and stunned everyone, including himself, by beating the Greek champion, Georgios Paraskevopoulos, in the discus throw. The impressive Australian, Flack, won at 800 and 1,500 meters. An absolutely unbridled enthusiasm took control of the Greeks as Spyridon Louis won the marathon, his countrymen taking four of the next five places. The *Times* correspondent called it "a scene of indescribable excitement" as the young Greek entered the stadium and headed for the King of Greece, with tall Prince Constantine and even taller Prince George jogging at his side. Coubertin called the wild scene "extraordinary," and was "convinced that psychic forces play a much more active role in sport than is generally believed." Nothing like it had been seen in nineteenth-century European history.

Marksmanship honors with the rifle, pistol, and revolver belonged to the Greeks and to the two military officers from Boston, Captains John and Sumner Paine. France and Greece won all the prizes in fencing, while British, Greek, and German athletes won the strictly informal single and double lawn-tennis tournament. Gymnastics took place in the main stadium and was popular with the crowd. German, Greek, and Swiss performers dominated the parallel and horizontal bars, the side horse, flying rings, rope climb, and long-horse vault. Karl Schuhmann, the German turner, was only five feet four inches, but "crafty and quick." He was immediately a crowd favorite, winning the vault, and then, astonishingly, the Greco-Roman heavyweight wrestling championship, defeating Georgios Tsitas of Greece and the English giant, Launceston Elliot. The swimming competition was no more than a bizarre series of shivering plunges in the Aegean Sea. Alfred Hajos of Hungary won at 100 and 1,500 meters, an Austrian and several Greeks winning the remaining freestyle races. Hajos must have been a brave and clever young man. Just prior to his long-distance victory, he smeared himself with a half-inch of grease, plunged into the icy, thirteen-degree-centigrade water, and cut through the water ahead of his eight opponents, hoping to avoid cramps. "I won ahead of the others with a big lead," he recalled, "but my greatest struggle was against the towering twelve-foot-high waves, and the terribly cold water." Elliot of Britain won first place in the one-hand lift, far ahead of Denmark's Viggo Jensen and Alexandros Nikolopoulos. Jensen and Elliot tied at 111.5 kilograms in the two-hand lift, with local hero Sotirios Versis in third place. France and Greece split honors in fencing. The presence of the royal family and the impressive central hall of the Zappeion sports club gave an added dimension to what was, after all, limited competitions in épée, foil, and saber. Cycling was very prominent at these Athens games, a reflection of its intense popularity in Europe and North America. An extraordinary road race of 87 kilometers from the velodrome to Marathon and back saw the brave and battered A. Konstantinidis finish first in 3:22:31. The Frenchman, Paul Masson, won the 1,000-meter time-trial, the 2,000-meter sprint, and the 10-kilometer track race. Leon Flemeng of France took a little over three hours to win the 100-kilometer track race. German, British, and Greek athletes raced well in all cycling competitions. The last of the cycling races was the twelve-hour endurance race on the track. Of the six entries, only three exhausted riders finished the ordeal, Adolf Schmal of Austria (314 kilometers, 997 meters), F. Keeping of Britain, and Paraskevopoulos.

The young men representing the United States at Athens were easily the most popular of the foreigners. United States consul George Horton commented that many Greeks wished "first to win ourselves, but after us let it be the Americans." One eyewitness calculated that the lionized Americans "were the heroes of the hour," while an elderly Greek classics professor volunteered that the Americans are like the ancient Greeks, having "proved their intellectual preeminence by their splendid victories in athletics." At the impressive awards ceremony on 15 April, King George leaned closer to double-medal winner Burke and whispered, "You may have won this time, but we will beat you in 1900, if I have to run myself." It was at this same pageant that the English athlete-scholar George S. Robertson impressed the Greeks with the reading of his "Olympic Ode," a portion of which went this way:

> Up, my song!
>   An alien crowd we come
>   To this Athenian home—
> Yet not like Persian plunderers of old,
> But in frank love and generous friendship bold!
>
> See how, once more, from hills afar
>   Not now with arms and war,
> An Elander comes, of royal line—
>   Quitting his land for thine!
>
> Athens, all hail! Hail, O rejoicing throng!
> And from our lips receive the tributary song.

It was all very heavy; the contented but nearly forgotten Coubertin was practically assured that his city of Paris would host the 1900 Olympic Games, despite the American athletes' petition and the strong Greek lobby for a permanent Athenian site. At a Sunday breakfast honoring Spyridon Louis, the French correspondent, LeRoux, toasted the king of Greece, reminding all that, in that spontaneous outburst by the king's sons as they escorted the marathon champion to the royal box, "there were no more foreigners present in the stadium, neither were there any more Greeks; we were all only your subjects." The Athenian ambience had worked its magic. The crown prince invited Charles Waldstein, Thr. Manos, and Pierre de Coubertin to a private conference where an Olympic compromise was hammered out. Yes, there would be Paris Olympics in 1900, and American games four years later, but, every second year following these Olympics, "International Panathenaic Games" would be held in Athens. The perceptive young Englishman, Robertson, commented on this scheme, remarking that these games, if held continuously at Athens, "would be Olympic, but we fear, not international; if held elsewhere than in Athens, international but not Olympic."

No matter; in February of 1897, lurid reports reached Athens of Turkish soldiers massacring civilians on the island of Crete. The violently patriotic Greek society, Ethniki Etairia, which had gained such strength as a result of its country's splendid handling of the Olympic Games, induced a very weak government to start a war against Turkey. The Thirty Day War that ensued was disastrous in every way to the Greeks, and all thoughts of another Athenian Olympics were forgotten. "So much for Greece," said Coubertin. He knew that the Athenian Olympic outburst had made little impact on the sporting world and that another success, in Paris, was essential to the fulfillment of his dream—"to bring the youth of all countries periodically together for amicable trials of muscular strength and agility."

The fact that the IOC met in the remote French seaport of Le Havre in July of 1897 was Coubertin's way of turning his back on the Greek-Turkish War, of dismissing any possibility of Athens as the next Olympic site. No Greeks showed up at Le Havre, and thus Coubertin was left unencumbered by their brand of Olympic loyalty. The baron admitted that he felt more comfortable in an Anglo-Saxon environment during the Le Havre meeting which concentrated on the spread of educational athletics and Olympism throughout the world. "It was to Arnold that we turned for inspiration," he said. Right from the very beginning, the organizers of the Paris Universal Exhibition and Pierre de Coubertin were in deep disagreement on how to conduct the athletics portion of the world's fair. The former wanted a beehive of physical training exhibitions, including billiards, fishing, and chess. Coubertin insisted that it would all be "a vulgar, glorified fair" unless they adopted his idea of conventional athletic competitions of elite performers all under the rubric of "Olympic Games."

He did not have his way. So many things went wrong. Coubertin chose his life-long friend Viscount Charles de La Rochefoucauld as president of the games organizing committee, but he became unacceptable to the bureaucrats running the larger exposition. Coupled with French sporting club provincialism and even belligerence, La Rochefoucauld was forced to resign in April of 1898. A short time later, the beleaguered Coubertin wrote to President Charles Eliot of Harvard University asking if he would "please send good athletes, good sportsmen, and pure amateurs to the 1900 Olympic Games in Paris." Coubertin was rubbing almost everyone the wrong way, and he, too, was forced to resign. Twenty years later, Coubertin looked back at the spring of 1898 with the wry comment that "wherever public authorities undertook to meddle with any sports organization, they introduced the fatal germs of impotence and mediocrity." Of course, it was difficult for him to admit that which he knew only too well: international athletics, still in its infantile stage at the turn of the century, could not possibly be more than a mere side show of the Paris world's fair. He had been punished for attempting to place his brand of athletics in too prominent a role at what was, after all, an "Exposition Universelle Internationale," and not true Olympic Games. In Marie-Thérèse Eyquem's superb biography, *Pierre de Coubertin—L'Épopée Olympique*, she called these crippled Olympic Games of 1900 *"La kermesse heroique"*—"the country fair."

On the eve of the games, there was profound disorder with the organizing committee. What little communication existed with other nations was done by the dispossessed Coubertin. But it was too late. German athletes were fearful of showing up in Paris, the Americans were discouraged by the breakdown in communications, while the Danes, Bohemians, and Canadians complained bitterly about everything connected with these Games of the Second Olympiad. The influential American sportsman, Caspar Whitney, hinted rather simplistically that sinister forces were at work, and that Coubertin's expulsion and the horrendous confusion were the result of political intrigue. "Strangely enough," said Whitney in a 31 May 1900 issue of *The Independent*, "the Dreyfus case is at the bottom of the trouble." As for his grandiose plan of uplifting and generous physical culture for all—Olympism—Coubertin mumbled that most people considered it a "mere neologism," a new religious fad. Somehow, the strange cornucopia of games began. Besides athletics, rugby and association football, field hockey, cricket, lawn tennis, croquet, golf, pelota, baseball, lacrosse, gymnastics, fencing, boxing, equestrian and aquatic sports, target shooting, live- and clay-pigeon shooting, running wild-boar shooting, archery, cycling, and polo, there were scheduled angling, cannon-shooting, bowling, leap frog, three-legged races, and automobilism! There were more, but, mercifully, only some of the results are left for historians to study.

During the hottest day of the year, 16 July 1900, with the temperature at ninety-seven degrees Farenheit, an American ragtag team organized just the day before reached the finals in the tug-of-war competitions. They tossed their shoes and socks aside, grabbed the rope, glowered at their Swedish opponents at the other end, and pulled mightily, yelling all the time "like Darwinian deamons." They nearly won, and they set the stage for another Yankee Olympics, at least in those few events they chose to enter. The *New York Herald's* Paris correspondent, in his cablegram, "Americans Immeasurably Superior," was talking about track and field athletics. The British originators of modern track and field once again failed to bring a representative team to the Olympic Games, thus leaving wide open to the Americans the majority of medals in that sport. But, amidst the hodgepodge of pseudo-Olympic competitions that lasted several months, a surprisingly large number of sporting events were contested. Frederick C. V. Lane of Australia won the 200-meter freestyle event in 2:25.2, exactly 13 seconds faster than the world's record. It was not that impressive, however, for, as the foremost Olympic statistician Erich Kamper puts it, "The swimming events in Paris in 1900 were held in the River Seine and swum with the current, which explains the amazingly good times." This same Lane also won the 200-meter obstacle swim, a race in which competitors had to climb over a pole, clamber over a row of boats, and finally swim under another row of boats. It was the beginning of a long list of discontinued Olympic sports. John Jarvis of Britain won the

1,000-meter race, Ernst Hoppenberg took the 200-meter backstroke in 2:47.0, the Germans won the 200-meter team prize, while the Osborne Swimming Club of Manchester, England, won the water polo title, beating back Belgian and French teams. Frenchmen dominated the foil, epée, and sabre competitions, as well as epée for fencing masters, although Ramon Fonst of Cuba beat back a host of local athletes in the individual sabre. In a second competition for professional athletes, the Italians took 1–2 in the sabre for fencing masters.

French athletes won the single sculls and coxed fours, Dutchmen the coxed pairs, and the United States' Vesper Boat Club swept away from eight-oared teams from Belgium, Holland, and Germany. France's Masson won a 1000-meter cycling race, while Belgian horsemen won both the obstacle course race and the *saut en longueur* or "long jump." Crack shots from France won three shooting events, including the "running wild boar" affair, while a Swiss shooting-team won at 50 and 300 meters. Shooting at clay and live pigeons appeared to be a French and Belgian specialty, with the same two nations dominating archery. The lone gymnastic event, combined exercises, was an all-French affair, while the soccer final saw a British team beat the famed French UFSA. Unbelievably, this same French club produced the cricket champions over Britain's Devon Country Wanderers. Croquet honors were all French, while the English polo team, Foxhunters Hurlingham, beat the French and an American group of unknown players. A French rugby team overcame German and British contingents. And, finally, women made their appearance. Charlotte Cooper (Britain) defeated Helene Prevost (France) in lawn tennis singles. All the places in men's singles were won by the English, while Cooper and Reggie Doherty won the mixed doubles over Prevost and a certain Harold S. Mahony from Ireland. Yachting competitions on the River Seine and in the port of Le Havre were won by crafts representing Britain, France, Germany, and the United States. And lastly, to complete the strange mix of sports at the Paris Games, Charles E. Sands and Margaret Abbott, both from the United States, won top honors in golf.

The American patriot and iron-fisted boss of amateur athletics in his country James E. Sullivan was determined to send a great track team to Paris, despite IOC ineptness and the total disarray of the organizing committee. On the eve of battle, and despite horrible track facilities and a disconcerting announcement from half his American team that they absolutely would not participate in any of the many Sunday track-and-field events, Sullivan bluntly predicted that "we shall win 70 percent of all the prizes." He was remarkably accurate, his team winning seventeen of twenty-three events. The facilities at the Racing Club were very poor, attendance was even worse, and officiating was a discipline still being learned by the French. The Americans oozed self-confidence and probably arrogance. "None of them carries unnecessary lumber," said the *Herald* reporter; "All are finely drawn and models at getting off their marks like a shot."

The majority of athletes came from the universities of Pennsylvania, Michigan, Georgetown, Syracuse, Princeton, and Chicago; several were from the New York Athletic Club. They were all ahead of the world in technique and training, finding a French scientific questionnaire most amusing which asked questions such as: "Were you reared as an infant naturally or artificially?" "What was the state of health and physical strength of your grandfather?" "What is the color of your hair, beard, and eyes?"

It was a primitive track meet on the huge, soft, 500-meter track at the Bois de Boulogne, and yet some fine performances were posted. English distance-runners captured the 800-, and 1,500-, and the 4,000-meter steeplechase, and the 5,000-meter team race. Irving K. Baxter of the University of Pennsylvania won the high jump and pole vault. He had three second-place medals behind the incomparable Olympian, Ray Ewry, who dominated the three standing events: high jump, triple jump, and long jump. The long-legged wonder from the New York Athletic Club so overshadowed his rivals that an Ewry victory was looked upon as automatic. His standing long jump record of over eleven feet is still a nearly impossible feat for today's champion athletes. Francis Jarvis and Walter B. Tewksbury raced 1–2 in the 100 meters, despite the loss of Arthur Duffey, world record holder, "that wonderful little man from Georgetown University," who pulled a muscle as his feet became entangled in the space ropes along the ground dividing the lanes. American fans howled; French spectators called them "a bunch of savages." Tewksbury came back, winning the 200 meters, and his sprinting partner, Maxie Long, ran an Olympic record (49.4) 400 meters, with Americans Sheldon and John Flanagan taking the shot put and hammer throw. Rudolf Bauer of Hungary threw an Olympic record in the discus, with Janda-Suk of Bohemia and Sheldon close behind. Tewksbury of Pennsylvania did the job in the 400-meter hurdles, defeating France's Henri Tauzin—57.6–58.3. The talented Myer Prinstein of Syracuse broke the Olympic triple-jump record with 14.47 meters, and placed second in the long jump. George Orton, a Canadian studying at the University of Pennsylvania, won the 2,500-meter steeplechase in 7:34.4, with a cosmopolitan group from Britain, France, the United States, Austria, and Germany, trailing behind. On a particularly hot Paris day, 19 July 1900, France's Theatro Michel won the 25-mile marathon in 2:59:45. Spectators, in a rare mood of enthusiasm at these games, invaded the track and carried Michel off on their shoulders. Probably the single finest athlete in Paris was Pennsylvania's Alvin Kraenzlein, who sprinted 7.0 for

60 meters, a world record (Tewksbury was second), ran a record 15.4 high hurdles, leaped nearly 24 feet in the long jump (the wooden toe-board was 5 inches above ground level), and made another win at the 200-meter low hurdles in 25.4, the durable Tewksbury running home in third place.

The quality of the American track team plus some events on the expanded program saved the Paris Olympics from being an unqualified disaster. The games failed completely in drawing large crowds away from the sensational world's fair. The exposition hurt rather than helped the future of the Olympic movement. Baron de Coubertin was gloomy. His IOC was ineffective. He was sensitive about his nation's relative indifference to the Olympic Idea, and, of course, disappointed at France's thin layer of success in international athletics. At least, he surmised, the Americans would do better in their own version of the Olympic celebration during the summer of 1904.

A bitter and long intercity struggle between business and civic leaders of Chicago and the promoters of the Louisiana Purchase Exposition World's Fair in St. Louis was no way to prepare for truly representative Olympic Games. Students at the University of Chicago went wild when the IOC awarded the 1904 games to the Windy City in the spring of 1901. But James E. Sullivan of the A.A.U. and President of the United States Theodore Roosevelt felt strongly that the new Olympic Games should be celebrated in St. Louis on the grand occasion of the one hundredth anniversary of the nation's purchase of the Louisiana territory.

Coubertin was in a bind and turned to his committee for help. The IOC voted strongly in favor of St. Louis, and, at the "eleventh hour," 10 February 1903, President of the Exposition David R. Francis was informed that he had a year to prepare for the first American Olympic Games. Columbia University President Nicholas Murray Butler applauded the switch to St. Louis, reminding all that the Louisiana Purchase "commemorates the first great step in that expansion of the American spirit and its governmental forms. . . ." Exposition President Francis, successful grain merchant, mayor of St. Louis, governor of Missouri, and ambassador to Russia, had the new Olympic stadium on Washington University's campus named after him. An ambitious series of physical culture exhibitions under the direction of James E. Sullivan was a stimulus to many professional teachers, but added confusion to the Olympic Games. These activities, some of which were incorrectly called Olympic, began on 14 May with a city championship schoolboy track meet and ended on 24 November with a double-header football game and cross-country race. Sixteen Olympic events, indiscriminately spread over the St. Louis summer, didn't help the cause. Track-and-field took place from 29 August through 3 September 1904, and was totally dominated by athletes from the United States—to the dismay of those concerned with the future of the Olympic movement. President Coubertin didn't make it to St. Louis, nor did enough foreign athletes, to make these a good Olympic Games.

Japan struck at the Russians at Port Arthur on 5 February 1904, and a terribly costly war occupied the headlines of world newspapers during the summer months of that year. The Russian forces were inefficient and took a licking from the aggressive and well-organized Japanese. During the same week of 26 August, in which Olympic track events took place in the American heartland, two giant battles at Liao-Yang and Mukden cost the lives of tens of thousands of Russian and Japanese soldiers. With newspapers screaming headlines like "Kuropotkin's Army pressed in confusion toward unfordable river," and "Russian Army swept away," the games of the Third Olympiad failed to compete even with news of national baseball results, let alone rival bulletins about the murderous Asian confrontation.

The St. Louis Olympic Games track-and-field competition contained twenty-four events. All of them were won by athletes from the United States, except the Canadian victory in the fifty-six pound weight throw, and the modified decathon won by Thomas Kiely of Great Britain and Northern Ireland. Of the twenty-four events, containing 126 finalists, athletes from the United States won 112 places, the remaining 14 places captured by 4 Britishers, 3 Germans, 2 each from Canada and Greece, plus single-place winners from Cuba, Hungary, and Sweden. That was it, an essentially American track meet. And too bad, because the home team was a very good one and needed international testing. American Olympic and world records were tied or broken by Archie Hahn, Harry Hillman, Jim Lightbody, Charlie Dvorak, Myer Prinstein, Ralph Rose, Ray Ewry, Martin Sheridan, John Flanagan, while Nate Cartmell, Charles King, Arthur Newton, R. S. Strangland, William Hogenson, and George Poage won a great many second and third places. Poage, of the Milwaukee Athletic Club, sixth in the 400-meter flat race, and winner of two bronze medals in the 200- and 400-meter hurdles, was the first black man to win an Olympic medal. Thomas J. Hicks of Cambridge, Massachusetts, won the first Olympic marathon race ever held in North America. Fred Lorz of New York City crossed the finish line first, ahead of fifteen Americans, ten Greeks, two Kaffirs and one white man from Southern Africa, one Cuban, and one Frenchman, but he had disqualified himself by accepting an auto ride for nearly three miles. The heat and dust were horrible, and all suffered grievously. The staff correspondent of the *Chicago Daily Tribune* was at the twenty-mile mark and later wrote that:

> Hicks was running with mechanical exactness, slowly and with every motion of
> his body indicating by its regularity and apparent effort that he was suffering

from fatigue. But he was still full of grit. In answer to a question as to how he was feeling, he called back over his shoulder, "I want something to eat as soon as I get there. I'm nearly starved."

The mix of European and North American athletes was much better in the other sports: tug-of-war, swimming, water polo, boxing, weightlifting, wrestling, fencing, rowing, archery, gymnastics, soccer, golf, roque, tennis, and lacrosse. Of course, there were some good athletes among them. Canada's Etienne Desmarteau upset the legendary Flanagan and James Mitchel in the fifty-six-pound weight throw; Perikles Kakousis was in a class by himself in the two-hand lift, while Hungary's Zoltan von Halmay shared swimming honors with Charles Daniels. Fonst of Cuba was the fencing star of the Games, just as Julius Lenhart, an Austrian citizen working in Philadelphia, dominated gymnastics. The less said about the "Anthropological Days" the better. Misguided exposition officials, using the shallow pretense of scientific research, rounded up exotic ethnic groups from Africa, Asia, and the two American continents, inflicting on them running, jumping, throwing, climbing, and shooting trials. It was all bizarre, unforgivable, and, to Baron de Coubertin in far away Paris, "a particularly embarrassing part of the program. To Americans, everything is permissible," he said. This third Olympic experiment had not fared well; there seemed an urgency for quick repairs and the passage of four years was too long to wait.

A productive IOC meeting in London shortly after the St. Louis Games set the stage for the official formation of national Olympic committees in Britain, Germany, and the United States. Also, Rome was selected over Berlin for the next Olympic Games. The IOC next met at Brussels in June 1905 in connection with the Conference on Physical Education. In addition to redefining amateurism, Coubertin and his friends made it manifestly clear that Germany had acted incorrectly in replacing one of its own IOC members. The sovereignty of the IOC self-selection process was at stake, and the baron considered it "one of the fundamental privileges of the IOC, the basis of its strength and prosperity." According to Coubertin, the problem was resolved amiably. Most importantly, an Athens organizing committee was making strong overtures for another series of Olympic, or rather Panathenaic, Games which might take place at the same time as the proposed Rome games in 1908. Way back in 1896, and again in 1901, Coubertin had agreed, without enthusiasm, that the Greeks could have their own games provided they abandon their idea, irrational to Coubertin, of a permanent Athens Olympics. A somewhat more stable Greece now pushed for another festival. Coubertin, the crown prince of Greece, and others agreed on a tenth anniversary celebration of the original games— the Panathenaic Games of 1906. Two successive Olympic near-failures in

Paris and St. Louis had not convinced Coubertin of the wisdom of out-of-sequence, unofficial Greek Olympic Games. He was frankly relieved that an important Paris Conference on Arts and Letters was scheduled for the spring of 1906. "I would be able," he said, "to use this as an excuse for not going to Athens, a journey I particularly wished to avoid." Coubertin's antipathy toward rival games may have made it difficult for him in early 1906 to see that the Greeks were on fire to celebrate another series of Athenian Olympic Games, and would go to any lengths to insure their success. With little ability to accurately read the future, Baron de Coubertin could not know that these unofficial games of 1906 would give a boost to the whole Olympic movement and keep the modern Olympic Games from early extinction.

So keen were the Greeks for a first-rate games that they awarded the United States a gift of $1,500 for travel expenses. The dates 22 April to 2 May 1906, were poor for American college athletes, and many stayed home. "What kind of people are they," exclaimed one Greek, "when they can leave many champions at home and still win?" Sport czar Sullivan predicted a United States victory and the *American Review of Reviews* confessed that it is "our national craving to break the record" that led to Olympic domination—at least in track-and-field. Only *The Nation* of 7 June 1906, was critical of this success, calling it anti-intellectual and mere degeneration for medals—"something bordering on the brutal and animal side of human nature . . ."

By all accounts the pageantry, organization, enthusiasm, and British-Greek royal participation during the mid-Olympiad festival was of a high order. Twenty nations competed, bringing 887 athletes to the still new, gleaming Athens stadium. Twenty-three running, jumping, and throwing events were contested before daily massive crowds. Eleven other sports received lesser attention. Erik Lemming, a rangy, talented Swede, won three separate javelin throwing contests (a complete mystery to North American athletes), two bronze medals in the shot and pentathlon, plus fourth place in the shot. Familiar names like Ewry, Prinstein, Hahn, Hillman, Lightbody, and Sheridan were joined by American Olympic winners Paul Pilgrim and R. G. Leavitt. William Sherring of Canada was showered with praise for his marathon victory, Con Leahy, and Peter O'Connor of Ireland won in the high and triple jumps, H. Mellander of Sweden in the pentathlon, Georgantes of Greece in the fourteen-pound stone throw, Werner Jaervinen of Finland in the Greek style discus throw, Gouder of France surprised in the pole vault, and H. Hawtrey of England continued Britain's domination in the distance race of five miles. Daniels (United States) reversed the 100-meter freestyle swimming championships with a win over defending champion von Halmay of Hungary. George Dillon-Kavanagh (France) and Gustav Casmir (Germany) dominated fencing, while Francesco Veri of Italy cycled his way to victory in the 1,000-meter time trial, the sprint, and 5-kilometer track race.

Pierre de Coubertin had little to say about all this. He was busy with a Paris art conference at the Comedie Francaise which resulted in the eventual selection of architecture, art, painting, music, and lyric competitions at future Olympic Games. It was a project dear to him; like so many Coubertin creations, it was a provocative idea fraught with problems. Back in Athens, the celebrating crowds, especially the Italian contingent, were stunned by the news that Mount Vesuvius had erupted with the loss of 2,000 lives and $85 million. Italian economy had been devastated; the inevitable announcement came that Rome would have to withdraw as the Olympic Games city for 1908. The Olympic movement and the Olympic committee, in a perpetual state of crisis during this decade, moved to fulfill its commitment for the quadrennial games—now only two years away.

French Olympic Games historian Marie-Therese Eyquem called the games of the Fourth Olympiad "a tragicomedy." It was that and more, a bittersweet, extraordinary sporting competition of 1,999 men and 36 women, dominated by an American-versus-English athletic confrontation of quarrelsome excellence, boorish manners by many Americans, and a monumental panic on the part of English sports officials at the specter of American dominance in track-and-field athletics, the perpetual nucleus of the Olympic Games and the invention of nineteenth-century British athletes. The strangest part of this whole story never made the world newspaper sport-pages: the athletes from the British Isles won far more gold, silver, and bronze medals than did those from North America. It was not even close. Host athletes took the lion's share in tug-of-war, swimming, boxing, rowing and yachting, cycling, field hockey, archery, soccer, polo, rackets, and lawn tennis. The Australians beat the British in the rugby final, while the French motor boat *Camille* finished ahead of two British craft. Britain finished second to Canada in the latter's own sport of lacrosse, just as the British swept all places behind USA's ace, Jay Gould, in the French game of *jeu de paume*. Both Britain and America found combined gymnastics a mystery, leaving honors to the young men of Italy, Scandinavia, and Germany. Glory in the elaborate shooting competitions were split between Britain, Norway, and the United States. The remarkable hegemony of the Hungarian fencers began at these games; Enrico Porro of Italy won the lightweight Greco-Roman wrestling crown, while all the other division prizes were captured by Swedes, Finns, Hungarians, Danes, and Russians; in free-style wrestling, the Americans and British split the glory. At the spacious Prince's Ice Skating Club, experimental competitions saw English athletes hold their own against Germans and Scandinavians. Nikolai Panin-Kolomenkin, a Russian skater, became that country's first Olympic victor. Once again in the elemental sport of running, jumping, and throwing—now taking on scientific overtones in the United States—Yankee athletes beat back a strong British-Irish challenge. Even the *Times* of London found little solace in the fact that host athletes were winning almost everything in sight. What they did not dominate were the visible, stadium competitions in track-and-field, and, as one columnist said in a 16 July 1908 edition, "these competitions outside the stadium do not appeal to either patriotic pride or the imagination. . . ." Baron de Coubertin saw it all, and was torn between fascination and deep concern at what he called "a direct confrontation between the two Anglo-Saxon nations . . . a sort of muscular dual of champions."

By arrangement between England, Scotland, and Ireland, men from these three countries were entered as "Great Britain and Ireland." Their athletes did well in athletic competition, winning the bitterly controversial 400-meter dash, most of the distance races (5 mile, 3 mile team race, the steeplechase, the 3,500-meter and 10 mile walks), and the triple jump. Reggie Walker of South Africa sped a fast 10.8 in the 100 meters, Canada's Robert Kerr wining the 200 meters. Still, it was Peerless Mel Sheppard and his super team of runners and field men from the United States that stole the Olympic thunder, causing British bewilderment among spectators and secret anger among the all-British officials at the main stadium. The frequently abusive, sometimes gross, conduct of the American team, led by that embodiment of belligerency and efficiency James E. Sullivan, was to mark these games as extraordinary but imperfect. Sheppard won the 1,500 meters in Olympic record time, but his 800-meter win was a classic. He followed a fast English pace, burst to the front halfway through, was pressed very closely by two future greats, Emillio Lunghi of Italy and Hanns Braun of Germany, and won in a world record, 1:52 4/5.

The starchy English and the frequently overbearing Americans made for a near comic-opera scenario. For example, there were four heats in the semifinal of the 100 meters, and R. E. Walker, the South African, running very strongly, beat W. W. May of the United States by half a yard, in 10 4/5 seconds, equaling the record. In the second heat, Canada's Bob Kerr finished ahead of the United States' D. R. Sherman, prompting the London *Times* to say the next day: "It was rather refreshing to see the colonies coming to the assistance of the mother country in this way." It was like this all through the track-and-field competitions, with brouhaha following argument in the pole vault, 400 meters, tug-of-war, and marathon. Ewry iced his ninth and tenth medals in Olympic competitions with wins in the standing long and high jumps. C. J. Bacon and Hillman, American teammates in the 400-meter hurdles, easily outdistanced two Englishmen in a record-breaking 55.0 seconds. A chorus of "Rah, Rah, Rah," from the always noisy American spectators "made it quite clear," said the *Times* correspondent, "to what country the first two men belonged." E. R. Voigt of Britain followed the leaders throughout the 5-mile flat race, sprinting the last lap, winning by 50 yards over countryman E. Owen, with J. F. Svanberg, Sweden, 10 yards further back. Voigt's time was 25: 1 1/5.

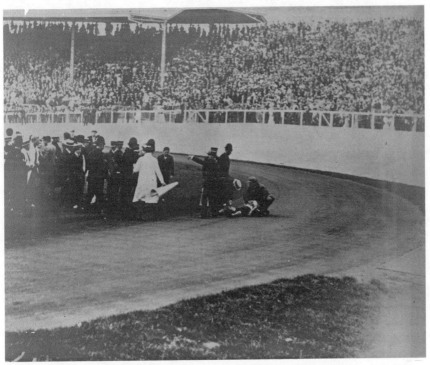

Dorando Pietri, Italy, drops from exhaustion, 1908 Olympic marathon. Credit John Lucas collection.

Anti-Yankee sentiment ran high in London during that July of 1908. Some of it may be accounted for by Rose's unaccounted failure to dip the American flag to the king during the opening-day parade. The giant Californian said he had never been given instructions on what to do that day. On the final Friday, 24 July, seventy-five marathoners lined up near the East Terrace of Windsor Castle, ready for the long ordeal of the Olympic Stadium. It was muggy hot, and the 5:01 2/5 first mile was too fast, even for the likes of Canadian champion Tom Longboat, the recent center of bitter attack by USA officials for his alleged professionalism.

Johnny Hayes, USA, winner of the 1908 Olympic marathon. Credit John Lucas collection.

Dorando Pietri of Italy and an elite group of South Africans and Britishers forced the pace, running 56:53, 1:15:13, and 2:02:26 at ten, thirteen, and twenty miles. The Americans, including 5'3¾", 125-pound, twenty-two-year-old Johnny Hayes, followed at a safe distance. Hefferon pressed on to Wormwood Scrubs Prison, within sight of the stadium. The tiny Pietri passed the South African, staggered into the packed and emotion-filled stadium, turned in the wrong direction, collapsed, was helped to his feet and pointed in the right direction, ran on, and collapsed within yards of the finishing yarn. He was helped again, this time to a short-lived victory, for the young American, Hayes, had entered the stadium and finished under his own steam in 2:55:18 2/5. The American protest was upheld, and Pietri was disqualified. He "lay between life and death for two hours," and became instantly world famous, the favorite of the English spectators, and the recipient of special prizes from the Queen, Sir Arthur Conan Doyle, and many others. Conan Doyle, master storyteller, was at the finish line and immortalized the "Dorando Scene" this way:

Thank God he is on his feet again, the little red legs going incoherently, but drumming, hard driven by the supreme will within. There is a groan as he falls again, a cheer as he restaggers to his feet. It is horrible, yet fascinating—this struggle between a set purpose and an utterly exhausted frame. . . . He has gone to the extreme of human endurance. No Roman of prime ever has borne himself better; the great breed is not yet extinct.

Pietri recovered rapidly, and, in late November of 1908 and through 1909, a marathon "craze" swept Britain, the Continent, and North America, making temporarily wealthy men of the Italian, Hayes, Longboat, St. Yves, Al Shrubb, and others.

A bizarre and memorable Olympic Games had come to an end; the Americans went home and were shepherded down New York's Fifth Avenue amidst a massive outpouring of national pride. The United States was at its bully-best during this first decade of the twentieth century, and very much at the center of this zeal was the president, Theodore Roosevelt, who greeted the Olympic heroes at his summer home at Sagamore Hill. The president, in his white duck suit on that last day of August, warmly greeted Sullivan, with whom he had exchanged victory telegrams several weeks before, and vigorously shook the hand of Hayes, repeating aloud, "This is fine, fine, and I am so glad that a New York boy won it. By George, I am so glad to see all you boys."

A somewhat more sober British Olympic Council and IOC president Baron Pierre de Coubertin tried to gauge the good and the bad that had been wrought by the extraordinary London fortnight. An all-English corps of officials might have worked perfectly had not the Americans showed up. They competed in great numbers in track-and-field contests, surfacing hidden animosities on both sides. Coubertin congratulated his friend and Games Director Lord Desborough, pointing out "the inevitability of some problems when 2,000 athletes gather."

The Council was wildly extravagant with its entertainment, hosting 500 to 1,000 party-goers at receptions and banquets on 11, 13, 14, 16, 17, 21, 23 July, several affairs in August and September, and a final banquet on 31 October 1908. When Theodore Andrea Cook, editor of *The Official Report of the 1908 Olympic Games*, added up all the bills for these entertainments, the total came to 5,271 English pounds, "the largest individual item of expenditure" and about $1/15$th of the total cost of the games. These "attractive and necessary" affairs, he said, were inestimably important opportunities for people of all races to mingle in the spirit of harmony and cosmopolitanism.

Coubertin attended most of them, although he excused himself from the October party because of the sudden death of his father. As always, whenever he witnessed Olympic Games, Coubertin was transported by the very best of what he saw. At a Grafton Galleries banquet, followed by a ball at the fashionable Holborn Restaurant, Coubertin reminded the audience that, at a recent service honoring the athletes, the bishop of Pennsylvania had pronounced "The importance of the Olympiads lies not so much in winning as in taking part." To this, Coubertin added, "The importance of life is not the triumph, but the struggle." He never missed a chance to preach the gospel of Olympism. The Americans and the English, he was convinced, were the only peoples that could significantly advance the cause of international sport, the litany of Olympic sportsmanship. He lamented along with his countryman Marcel Prevost that pervasive sport goes "against the French grain" and must come from other directions. Another Coubertin disciple, the Reverend Robert S. De-Courcy Laffan, called the twelve-year Olympic Games an experiment with unlimited physical, humanistic and even spiritual possibilities, "one of those great world movements which is going to develop itself long after those who are here have left this world." Coubertin, in a July 1908 *Fortnightly Review* article called "Why I Revived the Olympic Games" answered his own question with the observation "that there is nothing else upon which young men can employ their strength in their hours of recreation and liberty with such advantage both moral and physical."

The celebration of the Games of the Fourth Olympiad, despite excellent organization by the British, was muted by too many events and a chilling, sometimes senseless, animosity between the English and Americans. The best journalists from the two countries saw the larger picture, concluding that this new social experiment was capable of softening "the asperity [harshness] of national prejudice. . . ." It wouldn't be easy, and the experiment would be just that, an experiment lacking total fulfillment, for as long as the games existed. After the breaking of relations between American and British sporting authorities in the fall of 1908, the *Times* of 19 November whispered that one of the unrecognized reasons for the frequent hostility between the two nation's athletes was the great number of Irish-Americans who competed. "It might almost be said that the British athletes at the Stadium competed with Irishmen, not with Americans," complained the writer.

Coubertin's Olympian view attempted to look above and see beyond petty prejudices. New members of the IOC were selected. For the first time, Asia was represented, with the selection of Japan's famous judo innovator, Jigoro Kano, the IOC now composed of forty-three members from thirty-one countries. The IOC meeting in Berlin during the spring of 1909 was efficient and, according to Coubertin, for once "contained nothing the least bit political." The two contending cities, Berlin and Stockholm, presented their credentials for hosting the 1912 Olympic

Games, the Swedish city winning the most delegate ballots. It was generally understood that Berlin could begin serious plans for a 1916 celebration. Further preparations for the fifth Olympic Games took place in Luxembourg (1910) and Budapest (1911). The baron was perpetual motion during these days, and, at the 1910 Brussells Exposition, he repeated that the future of sport is assured, but only if the world understands the need to study its "psychological, cosmopolitan, and democratic implications." At an international architects' meeting that same year, he reminded the audience that athletics, art, and metaphysics dominated the scene at ancient Olympia. "It will be the same" in the modern version, he predicted. His message was the same in an *Olympic Review* article of April 1911 titled, "Pour l'honneur" in which he urged that the larger message of sport be disseminated to all peoples everywhere. He was maddeningly idealistic, but with a futuristic touch that may have to wait till the next century for fuller realization.

The Olympic world always seems to possess unreasonable patriots who place nation over the world community and efficiency over humanity. Such a man was James E. Sullivan—the American prototype leader at the London games. Outside of Oxford and Cambridge Universities, he said, amateur sports in England "is a joke." A little over a year later, in November of 1909, he traced his Amateur Athletic Union's best year, ending with the revealing injunction that "there can be only one organization and to have absolute control of sport, there must be obedience and loyalty to the dictates of the governing body." It is just conceivable that Coubertin might have wished to run his IOC with an iron fist similar to that of the America AAU boss. But the softer Frenchman was constitutionally incapable of such directness, preferring to use guile, persuasion, and appeals to sentiment and intellect in the execution of his Olympic business. The two men were different, both deeply involved in national and international sport. It was inevitable that the two giants would meet and clash.

4 • Early Olympic Antagonists: Pierre de Coubertin versus James E. Sullivan

International relationships between sovereign states cannot exist without elements of antagonism. Almost as frequently as the antagonisms, there exist singular common goals that tie the individuals together, and, sometimes, their countries. Such symbiotic relationships are not unknown in international sport. Probably the two most powerful sports leaders in the world during the period from 1900 to 1912 were France's Baron Pierre de Coubertin and James Edward Sullivan of the United States. They did not like one another, and this personal animosity contributed to the uneven harmony between the United States and the International Olympic Committee during the four official and one unofficial games of the century's first dozen years.

Men of extreme intensity, especially those with a singular life-purpose, frequently have little patience with countervailing forces. Coubertin's second visit to the United States was for the express purpose of creating an interest among its sports leaders for his grand idea of a world Olympic games. With the exception of Princeton University's William Milligan Sloane, Coubertin was met with massive indifference; America's sporting officials, he said, were too preoccupied with "the secret war between the colleges and the AAU." Sullivan was the young, hard-line secretary of the American Amateur Athletic Union at the time, and was persuaded by AAU boss Gustavus T. Kirby to meet with the French baron and form a United States Olympic Committee to send qualified athletes to the Athens games of 1896. Coubertin and Sullivan met for the first time at this November 1893 gathering in New York City's University Club; the American agreed to chair a committee made up of Kirby, Julian Curtis, A. G. and Walter Spalding, plus Caspar Whitney, the powerful, opinionated editor of *Outing* magazine. The precocious Coubertin was thirty years of age as he left for London and Paris to drum up Olympic interest. There appears no evidence that the thirty-three-year-old Sullivan did anything to stimulate domestic influence in what many viewed, at that time, an ill-inconceived idea. The tiny American team, privately financed by the Boston Athletic Association and Princeton University, did remarkably well in Athens, and yet Whitney strongly criticized Coubertin's newly formed International Olympic Committee as inefficient and mismanaged, incapable of informing Americans of "information vitally needed by clubs and colleges willing to join in the sending of American representatives." From its beginnings in 1894, the IOC had decided that the United States would host the games of the Third Olympiad, following those in Greece and France, "the original trinity chosen to emphasize the world character of the institution and establish it on a firm footing."

Paris and France were in total political disarray. The condemnation of Captain Alfred Dreyfus as an alleged traitor, the famous Emile Zola letter, Zola's arrest and trial after riots in Paris streets, and the imprisonment of Dreyfus, were all too much for Coubertin's Olympic committee during the unsporting years 1898 and 1899. European sporting organizations expressed their discontent at the lack of Olympic planning. A Colonel Louis Hamburger of the AAU and United States representative to the Paris Exposition attempted to see Coubertin in Paris, but returned home in disgust. His main purpose had not been American Olympic competition in the 1900 games, but, rather, his country's involvement in the Paris Exposition. Whitney, editor of *Outing* and American Olympic committee member, expressed his indignation at the Olympic status quo in an 11 October 1899 communiqué. The scholarly Sloane erupted by calling the Paris games committee "an organization of incompetents." Coubertin was in a poor position himself, having been summarily removed from the French Olympic Committee as one suspiciously aristocratic. On the eve of the 1900 Paris Exposition, and only incidentally the Olympic games, Whitney peevishly noted that "What this [French Olympic] committee does not know about sports would fill volumes." To say that the Paris Olympics of 1900 were poorly organized is to be repetitious. They were very much in the shadow of the world Exposition, and failed to fulfill the dream of Coubertin—the young idealist who was slowly maturing beyond the role of French patriot to that of world citizen. There was little danger of this kind of metamorphosis in the mind of the consummate American nationalist, Sullivan.

During the eleven-month period July 1900 to May 1901, a bizarre, ill-defined, but vaguely interrelated series of events occurred on both sides of the Atlantic that widened the ideological gap between the tough-minded plebeian Sullivan and the dreamy but effective aristocrat Coubertin. Sullivan was the power behind the American AAU and, as such, pushed for his favorite sport, track-and-field, to organize an international federation. Sullivan failed to gain this recognition on 27 July

James E. Sullivan, Director of the American Olympic Team at 1900, 1904, 1906, 1908, and 1912 Olympic Games.

1900 in a Paris meeting at the office of the Union des Sociétés Françaises des Sports Athlétiques. He would have to wait till 1913. In the meantime, he did all in his power to thrust athletics into a position of near total domination at the four Olympic games of 1904, 1906, 1908, and 1912. Coubertin disagreed with this approach, and he continued in the extremely difficult task of giving credibility and power to his self-appointed IOC. On 28 July 1900, the *New York Times* noted that the University of Pennsylvania had negotiated with British authorities for the 1904 Olympic games to be transferred to Philadelphia. No mention was made of Coubertin and his committee. It was stated that the American Olympic committee members, Sloane, Whitney, and Sullivan, favored the idea of a Philadelphia Olympics. Equally bizarre was Sullivan's unilateral announcement that the Buffalo, New York, Pan American Exposition would host Olympian Games in 1901—under AAU auspices. The news must have been surprising and unsettling to the baron. "The emphatic denial of the report," said Olympic historian Bill Henry, "silenced this attempt to interrupt the quadrennial sequence of the games. . . ." Coubertin's 1889 visit to Chicago, his return there for the 1893 Chicago World's Fair, and an engaging conversation with the brilliant University of Chicago president, William Rainey Harper, pretty well sold the Frenchman on the idea of a Chicago Olympic Games in 1904. "And it was beginning to receive a favourable press in the United States," Coubertin remembered, "when a furious letter written by James E. Sullivan was published."

The scenario of events in November of 1900 are complex and contradictory. On 11 November of that year, in Paris, Coubertin informed a New York *Sun* correspondent that the IOC had voted for either New York City or Chicago as a 1904 Olympic site, with the latter city his personal favorite. The *Sun* reporter stated that Coubertin had "received from President Harper of the University of Chicago an important letter which evidently makes the baron feel in favor of Chicago, . . ." President Harper immediately denied ever having written such a letter. Sullivan, who was in Paris at the time, called Coubertin a fake, a man stripped of all athletic authority by his own government, a pathetic figure in charge of an inept committee. The American AAU secretary censured Coubertin's announcement of the day before with this:

> The Baron de Coubertin or his associates have no longer any power to name the place at which Olympian Games or international athletic events of any character shall be held, as that will be done by the new union [the AAU/French alliance].

Sullivan went on to inform the world that international meetings would be held every year, the next one in Buffalo, New York at "his" Pan American Exposition. He ended his bombast with a reminder that, if President Harper wished to hold an athletic "meeting" at his Chicago University in 1904, there would be no problem, provided he obtained the International Union's permission. Sullivan's parting score reminded all that "Baron de Coubertin has no right to allot dates for such a meeting."

We know that Coubertin was deeply angered by Sullivan's aggressiveness; the Frenchman's two autobiographies discuss the matter at length. In his *Une Campagne de Vingt-et-Un Ans 1887–1908*, the baron stated that European sports leaders had not taken Sullivan seriously, and that American IOC member Sloane had written him on 12 December 1900, assuring Coubertin that there would definitely be some kind of athletic competition in Buffalo the next year, but, beyond that, "I can learn no more, as those who know the facts remain prudently quiet." We learn from Coubertin's *Memoires Olympiques*, that on 21 March 1901, Sullivan allegedly wrote him, "I am always willing, if I think I have made a mistake, to acknowledge it." The Frenchman could be forceful in his own way, and asserted that:

> At the end of 1900, the *Morning Telegraph* had written that "all this was a campagne [sic] against Chicago; . . . The freezing horror of the situation can only be fully appreciated when it is seen that James Sullivan is not the American member of the IOC."

Coubertin wrote this thirty years after the event, chortling that "The fight was on," and "The success of an idea is to be judged by the number of people who claim credit for it." We do not know if this was his attitude in the difficult days of 1900–1901.

Coubertin may have won this early skirmish, for, in January of 1901, Sullivan's close friend and fellow American Olympic Committee member, Caspar Whitney, found the IOC an organization of "high character," reminding all that Sullivan's AAU was not only without international jurisdiction, but that American college athletes, from which the great majority of the Olympic team would come, were also outside the control of the AAU. On 13 February 1901, according to Coubertin's recollection, in the city of Chicago, Dr. Harper presided over a banquet that formally opened the campaign to win for that city the right to host the Olympic games. Little is known about Olympic activities during March and April of 1901, but, on 21 May 1901, Coubertin and the IOC voted for Chicago, rather than St. Louis—sending two telegrams to the Windy City's Henry J. Furber, Jr., president of the Olympian Games Association. Coubertin's cable read, "Chicago wins." Henri Breal was even more dramatically succint. The single word, *"Oui,"* in his cable sent the Chicago press running to their desks; monster celebrations on the University of Chicago campus took up the entire week. "Joy in Olympian Games" and "Games baptized in fire," headlined the *Chicago Tribune*; Furber, Harper, Amos Alonzo Stagg, and others savored the victory. According to the baron, both Furber and Harper had written convincing letters in favor of a Chicago venue.

"Everything was off to a good start," beamed the Olympic *renovateur*. Two modern French scholars noted that "James E. Sullivan despaired at the choice," while contemporary Whitney dismissed Sullivan's abortive effort with a comment that "there really never was deviation from the original plans."

Chicago never got the Olympics. The reasons are so devious and labyrinthian as to almost defy historical accuracy. Olympic Chancellor Otto Mayer tried to explain it, but left enormous gaps. This research will deal with the St. Louis transfer only insofar as the Coubertin-Sullivan machinations are uncovered.

The vigorously efficient Sullivan ran a successful Pan-American Exposition at Buffalo in the summer of 1901. Furber revealed Chicago's details for the Games of the Third Olympiad. Coubertin asked Theodore Roosevelt if that vigorous new American president would accept the honorary presidency of the Chicago games of 1904. The powerfully financed ($1,000,000) Furber Committee made several European trips, talked to President Zemp of Switzerland, the king of Greece, England's Sir Thomas Lipton, and, finally, there was an "amicable talk at Munster, Alsace," between Coubertin and Furber. President Theodore Roosevelt pledged his support to the Chicago committee, although he voiced "regret that the United States cannot officially take charge or be responsible for the games. . . ." Coubertin never wavered in his conviction that a relatively disinterested IOC would always be the most effective ultimate arbiter.

The St. Louis World's Fair Committee exerted tremendous influence, and the site of the 1904 Olympic games slipped away from Chicago during the early months of 1903. The shoe was on the other foot; Coubertin now empowered Sullivan and the AAU to take charge of the St. Louis games. The Midwest was still very far away for Europeans. Besides, no one from the IOC would be making the trip. The St. Louis games were better than Paris in 1900, but neither pleased Coubertin, and he vowed never to hold Olympic Games in connection with a world's fair. Nevertheless, Coubertin must have felt some sense of gratitude toward his old antagonist, Sullivan, who did his usual fine organizational job in connection with the St. Louis Olympics. Sullivan received a letter from Paris from the IOC chief, dated 19 October 1904, awarding him a rare gold medallion. It was to be a very long time before Sullivan saw his medal, another source of irritation between the two powerful sports' leaders.

Two consecutive Olympic failures were sufficient motivation for the IOC and the Greek government to agree to the out-of-sequence Athens Olympics in 1906. Sullivan approved of yet another opportunity to prove the athletic superiority of the United States. There was unhappiness that the dates, 22 April to 2 May 1906, came while American college athletes were still in school. Sullivan went to Athens in late November of 1905 to make sure things were right. On 9 March 1906, at a White House luncheon with the president of the United States, Sullivan was appointed boss of the American team and pledged a strong showing. Coubertin, beseiged by French Leftists, rejected by many of his fellow aristocrats, and already in financial difficulty, was unable to attend the highly successful Athens games of 1906. Coubertin's first love was the Olympic movement, and he thanked the Greek Olympic committee for a job well done, assuring them that the games would continue to have a "salutary influence . . . on civilization." Sullivan was doing better; he had done his part in working "toward making honest and sturdy Americans." The Americans were "keen" for the 1906 competition, he said. "As is customary in our country," he boasted, "our men were trained scientifically. We go into athletic sport with an earnestness that the other countries cannot understand; . . ." Sullivan's temperament was reflected to an astonishing degree on the American teams from 1900 through 1912. Teddy Roosevelt was pleased, and sent Sullivan and his 1906 team a cablegram, "Uncle Sam is all right"; for Sullivan, "the athletic supremacy of the world was settled."

Sullivan was a "team" man all the way. Sport was a serious business to him, and international sport was a clear-cut manifestation of national strength. In a strong dictum to an American Olympian, Sullivan advised the young man to remember that "the team will go absolutely as an American team," and, if they do so, "this country will be victorious."

Immediately upon his return from Athens, Sullivan received a letter from Pierre de Coubertin, dated 27 May 1906. A month later, he replied with an astonishing 2,000-word outpouring, alternately praising the Olympic leader and roasting Coubertin mercilessly. "I propose to be frank with you," was Sullivan's initial comment. He mentioned conversations with IOC members at the recent games, resulting in a conviction "that you did not like me and that I thought the feeling between us was mutual." Sullivan quickly got to the sore point of his missing Olympic medallion of two years earlier. "I never received it," he said, "and I presume that the Baron is dissatisfied with something I have done." This personal note done, Mr. Sullivan got down to a castigation of the International Olympic

Committee and Coubertin, its inept leader. Why, he said, had Coubertin capriciously struck "my name from your membership"? A long-time hurt was revealed as Sullivan reminded Coubertin that a decade of loyal service to the Olympic Movement had not resulted in his appointment to the International Olympic Committee. "I lost all interest in the Olympic Committee," he said, in obvious self-deception. Sullivan continued his anger at Whitney's replacement on the IOC by the insurance agent James Hazen Hyde. The action was "a monstrous joke." Why does "the lovely gentleman," Professor Sloane, continue on the IOC, asked Sullivan? "He knows absolutely nothing about athletics . . .; I doubt if he ever attended an important athletic meeting in America." Sullivan thus dispensed with two of his countrymen, and in so doing, seriously criticized Coubertin's rationale for selecting IOC members. While in Athens, Sullivan had said several IOC members hoped he might join them in that select body. But, he told them "before I could accept anything like this I certainly would want a letter from you, . . ." Sullivan's preoccupation with his missing gold medallion returned mid-way through the letter. He lamented that:

> The letter which I received from you [27 May 1906] puts an entirely new tone to it. I did not know that it was necessary for you to hand me the medal voted. Had I known this you can rest assured that I would certainly have made arrangements so that you could have presented it to me on some one of my trips abroad.
>
> Yes, I did stop a few days at Paris on my way to Athens, and I would have been delighted to have called on you had I the slightest idea that such a call from me would be appreciated by you, as you have not recognized me in the slightest way in your organization, or, in your good work you have never asked me for my cooperation; you have gone along with the idea that you could get along without America.
>
> You say you do not understand my ways and manners. Perhaps not. I don't think you have tried to understand me thoroughly; if you did I think we could become firm friends.

Sullivan explained, to his own satisfaction, why he had attempted a rival organization to the IOC back in 1900. It was for the greater good of international sport, he said. Maybe, just maybe, said Sullivan, IOC membership for him might be unwise, "because I would disagree with you. I certainly will stand up for anything I think is right; . . ." In his concluding paragraphs, Sullivan had for Coubertin both "the greatest admiration" as Olympic innovator and also indirect criticism that the baron had never given him and his AAU even a vestige of recognition. Sullivan promised unqualified support in all future Olympic ventures. Share this letter with your friends, ended Sullivan. "It's immaterial whether you or I can get along together," he concluded. "You can always count on America as being with you when it comes to having international sports."

"My dear Baron," was Sullivan's salutation in another letter dated 31 July 1906. He was really angry at a recent Coubertin letter of 5 July which purported to cast doubt on Sullivan's motives in attempting to gain membership in the IOC. The exasperated Sullivan erupted with, "You pass my entire letter off by saying that there was not one single word of truth in any of my statements . . . well, I think that settles it! . . . I am thoroughly convinced . . . that we had better cease writing." There is a great deal of evidence that Sullivan, unfulfilled in several personal goals, was most effective—almost too much so—in marshalling his country's athletic muscle at three Olympic games. At a 1907 testimonial banquet, he was called "the greatest present force in athletics today." The next month, Sullivan practically demanded $100,000 for the 1908 Olympic Games expenses. "It is a question of national pride," said the new AAU president.

Whitney praised Sullivan to the sky as "a man who not only sees right, but has the courage to fight for it." And fight he did. While much was right about the 1908 Olympic Games in London, there was a near-disastrous, continual verbal battle between American and English officials. Some of the fault must lie in Sullivan's belligerency. "We have come here to win the championships in field sports," he muttered, "and we are going to do it, despite the handicap from which we are suffering." A week earlier, Coubertin once again had to defend the intergrity of the IOC selection system as well as the quadrennial rotation plan. Both men were in London at the time, Coubertin busy defending, Sullivan preoccupied with attack. The baron was deeply concerned about the vicious internecine struggle between England and the United States. Looking back at the success and turmoil that was London in the summer of 1908, Coubertin remembered the American Olympic chief with bitterness:

> I just could not understand Sullivan's attitude here. He shared his team's frenzy and did nothing to try to calm them down. This was followed on his return by a new betrayal; he persuaded the Amateur Athletic Union to appoint a commission for the purpose of forming a new International Olympic Committee and drawing up the statues of future Games. But this time, nobody listened to him. . . .

In a brief essay titled "American Ambitions," Coubertin recapitulated the three times in the previous ten years, 1899–1908, "that some American leaders have attempted to overthrow the Olympic organization." During these post-Olympic months, editor Whitney defended and criticized American Olympic and AAU leader Sullivan. The fire of misunderstanding and animosity between the two fifty-year-old sport giants smoldered during the intervening years, 1910–1912. Some mellowing may have taken place, for, in a letter dated 4 November 1910 addressed to Baron Pierre de Coubertin, 20 Rue Ouidinot, Paris, Sullivan commented on the progress of his Olympic history book, giving Coubertin his due as the founder. I am trying, he said "to keep away from the row we had in London, which was not a very nice row, as you will agree. It should never have happened."

The Olympic Games of 1912—the Games of the Fifth Olympiad—were the most successful and pacific since their inception. Coubertin, writing under a symbolic double French and German pseudonym, won a literature gold medal at these Stockholm games. His "Ode au Sport" was a romantic hymn in nine stanzas, praising sport as the messenger of beauty, honor, joy, progress, and, above all else, peace." Somehow, the anger had softened, and, in his new history of the 1912 games, Sullivan dedicated the book to Baron Pierre de Coubertin, "to whose perseverance and zealous work for 30 years is due the . . . final success of the Olympic Games." The Baron lived another quarter century of success and tragedy; Sullivan died of a heart attack while still young. His passing on 16 September 1914 was not without one final irony, for, in May of that same year, he had traveled to France for an IAAF meeting, and returned in July with a precious trophy presented to him in person by Baron Pierre de Coubertin "on behalf of the IOC . . . as a token of appreciation . . . in promoting the Olympic Games." Somehow, the two troubled giants had reached out and touched one another.

5 • The Olympic Idea in an Age of Rising Expectations

Despite wars somewhere in the world during the first dozen years of the twentieth century, most North Americans and many Europeans believed themselves headed for what historian R. R. Palmer called, "a kind of high plateau, full of a benign progress and a more abundant civilization. . . ." The concept of democracy seemed clearer and more nearly available to millions; nationalism and then national imperialism spread rapidly. It was, in short, a western world that took for granted the idea of change, that eagerly embraced national displays of strength, both military and physical. For many, it was an optimistic period; for a smaller group, it was an opportunity to work toward the brotherhood of man through altruistic international sport. The feverish, halting growth of the Olympic movement was only a challenge to improve and spread the gospel of Olympism. A new regime had arisen in Europe, a middle class that could afford to take their ease in leisured pastimes not only on a Sunday, but frequently on a Saturday afternoon, and at least one evening a week. In the United Sates and in several European countries, there arose educated and subtle-minded men who attempted to articulate the wisdom of cosmopolitanism over excessive national zeal. An even smaller group spoke of the possibility of the Olympic Games—a new kind of internationalism—as a vehicle for the partial fruition of the old concept of one world.

Modern-day American football players frequently react to a sideline chant that goes, "Keep the drive alive." In a quite different setting, but with similar intent, those who believed in the Coubertin altruism supported the Olympic idea and all that it meant to the baron.

Certain generalities do come through in attempting a universally accepted definition of Olympism. Few disagreed with the former American all-round champion and first-place silver-medal winner at Athens, Ellery Clark, that "the games were meant to reawaken an interest in manly outdoor sport the world over, and to bring back something of the spirit of the old Olympic Games." Undoubtedly, to many early disciples, the

Olympic revival offered something bigger and better than previous forms of international sport. The feeling runs unabated to the present day.

Coubertin never considered the sporting impulse that touched the lives of millions of people in the early years of the twentieth century as either spontaneous or irreversible. He said often that his life task was to nurture the new phenomenon and shape it in his own image. To say that he failed is also to admit that the proliferation of sport has infinitely outstripped in size and kind even his fertile imagination. As in early Christendom, the disciples actively shared their beliefs with all those they touched. Coubertin and his followers, in true Messianic fashion, spread the message of amateurism in sport. It was, to them, the only kind of sport. All the rest was display and gladiatorial entertainment. *The Century Magazine* of April 1896 put its editorial best foot forward, hoping that the new Olympic Games would reduce athletic brutality and excess, replacing them with "fairness" and "moderation." In an age breathing the last gasps of a century-old Western Romanticism, it did seem out of place for Olympic advocates to use words like, "honor," "sentiment," "peace, beauty, and joy." As long as he was editor of the *American Review of Reviews*, Albert Shaw supported that peculiar institution of international amateur sport with the Coubertin brand upon it, calling the Frenchman "the DeTocqueville of our day." A few days after the Athens Olympics were over, the famous archaeologist, Charles Waldstein, wrote that it was his hope that the temporary federation of nationalities so necessary at the games would eventually lead to a rise in the level of mankind's physical fitness and, especially, a kind of protracted *Ekecheiria* or "sacred truce." It was easier to accept such a concept in 1896 than today, but the idea persists.

No one was more critical of early Olympic Games ineptness than the influential sportsman Caspar Whitney, and yet, in 1900, he recognized that, with the rising concern for health, the growing preoccupation with sport "is not a craze," but a permanent manifestation of Western society, and the Olympic Games are an inexorable part of this growth. Even the usually critical editor of *The Nation*, in an editorial following the unofficial Athenian Olympic Games of 1906, admitted that at least the host nation's youth discovered "a new athletic life," and the masses, a vibrant, animated spirit. William N. Bates, Director of the American School at Athens that same year, agreed, marveling at how "deeply and seriously" all Greeks reacted to the new form of physical culture. Author, lecturer, and the first man to win a medal at a modern Olympic Games, James B. Connolly wrote in *Outing* magazine for April 1906 that "The Spirit of the Olympian Games" was real, and, he hoped, would "receive a fresh and lasting impulse." The 1908 Olympic Games were filled with controversy, prompting the *Times* of London to soberly conclude that the games could encourage international understanding, but only if they are extremely well organized, and so impartial "that every competitor, whether he has won or lost, goes away . . . feeling that every opportunity has been given and every courtesy shown to him." This ultimate standard has yet to be achieved, and represents a fundamental Olympic tenet.

Philip J. Baker, a recent graduate of Cambridge University in the year 1912, had placed sixth in the final of the furious 1,500-meter Olympic final. He reflected on the larger concept of the Olympic idea:

> Is it so fantastic to believe that the provision of a sane . . . rivalry of nations will help—slightly perhaps . . . in breaking up the absurd fabric of "routine thinking" on which the present system of international relations rests? If we can believe such a fantasy, if we can see in the future possibilities greater than the present shows, then we shall enter with redoubled ardor into the Olympic contest impelled not only by enthusiasm for the trial of strength itself, but also by devotion to the idea that lies behind it.

The perceptive twenty-three-year-old Englishman had, of course, captured the essential definition of Olympism. He won the silver medal in the 1920 Antwerp 1,500 and captained the British Olympic track team in 1924. He worked all his life in the international realm, and, in 1959, was awarded the Nobel Peace Prize.

War clouds were gathering in 1912; no one was more aware of the danger than the eminent American professor of European history, William Milligan Sloane. He had collaborated with Baron de Coubertin back in 1894, in the founding of the International Olympic Committee, and, as a charter member of that organization, wrote with some insight an article called "The Olympic Idea." He traced the brief history of international sport—especially the Olympic variety—calling it "a neglected means of international conciliation." Sloane admitted that the defenders of the Olympic dream must ever be alert to the evils of self-seeking patriotism and the base elements of human nature. But he saw this as no reason to abandon pursuit of the idea, a concept "which places honor above material reward," and one which would gradually expand the opportunity for play and for artistic and athletic competitions to every person on earth.

For thirty years, Sloane had basked in the reputation of a learned and dispassionate scholar. His essay on the Olympic Idea was learned, but certainly not dispassionate. There was the touch of the idealist, the flavor of the romantic; there was also a hint of the futurist in the article, especially his remark that the Olympic Games might benefit from a permanent site, "the main Olympia . . . in Switzerland, with a subsidiary one in America."

It was an era for such talk. In two remarkable speeches, the Canadian physician-sculptor-physical educator, Robert Tait McKenzie, spoke on "The Chronicle of the Amateur Spirit" (1910) and "The Quest for Eldorado" (1913). It was his own way of defining the Olympic code, a ritual which encouraged excellence with honor, and, at the same time, included participation and joy by all the people. In essence, what he tried to do was to define for a modern audience the subtle, complex Greek word *Aidos* and make it meaningful in a world where, even in his day, the salaried, professional athlete had a different viewpoint from the Olympic sportsman. In his second exposition, a presidential address at the twentieth convention of the American Physical Education Association, he echoed another Olympian principle: the servant of society is that person who best blends physical robustness with mental vigor, a moral code binding the two together. We must each find our personal "Eldorado," he concluded, and, when we do, "the crude ore of opportunity" shall be transformed "into the fine gold of opportunity."

G. Stanley Hall, first president of the American Psychological Association, sought sanity in sport through a clarification of goals and attitudes towards an individual "instinct for ideal conduct." His 1908 theme, "Elements of Strength and Weakness," was a repetition of one quite common among early twentieth century intellectuals.

In any case, Coubertin was not alone in attempting to define international sportsmanship or Olympism. The elusive concept tended to cluster about certain absolute standards, and, as the tendency toward relative morality grew stronger and more pervasive after the first World War, so, too, did the degree of difficulty in Olympism's universal acceptance and application.

Coubertin's cosmopolitan tendencies were formed early, as was his conception of the role of sport. The Olympic Games were to him, at least in the early days of the modern movement, the final test of the educative and ameliorative effects of competitive athletics. He felt that sport was a means to an end, "the upliftment of mind, strengthening of moral character and physical power." Sport on the scale and level conceived by Coubertin furnished a conspicuous example of fair play and international understanding regardless of race, religion, or political convictions. Such was his frustrating habit of asking too much of sport, an understandable sin in one steeped in romantic literature and constitutionally a visionary mystic.

It was his belief that no education can be good and complete without the aid of physical education and competitive athletics. But, if they are to play their proper educational role, he said, "perfect disinterestedness and the sentiment of honor" must always be included. The Olympic founder had unbounded faith in the power of the "pure amateur spirit" of Olympism, and saw in the new world of the future a supreme role for sport, "promoting progress and social unity." The idealistic baron always considered his form of sport a blending of the very best of ancient Athens, the idealized medieval knight, and the stuff from which the best of England's nineteenth-century leaders were made. Coubertin called this magic dust *Olympism*. The gradual spread of athletic interest throughout late nineteenth and early twentieth century Europe was, to him, a new "pedagogical revolution." Not for centuries, he pondered, had physical culture been looked upon as an instrument capable of increasing human happiness. To the baron, sport was one of the most effective means of strengthening human personality. "It was for this very purpose that I have revived the Olympian Games," he said, in the banner year of 1896.

The concept of unity dominated Coubertin's intellectual life and became part of his Olympic philosophy. His faith in the usefulness of amateur athletic training and competition was based on the ancient Athenian assumption that man's mind, body, and spirit, were somehow interdependent. It was his hope that modern societies might, in his lifetime, emulate the best that the Greeks had to offer. He called this "best" by the name Olympism. None of it must be done frivolously, he said. It must be organized, regulated, and yet entered into joyfully. He saw the necessity for reestablishing the Olympic Games as a supreme consecration of personal and unselfish motives. Anyone who studies the ancient Greek games at their best, he said

> . . . will perceive that their deep significance was due to two principle elements: beauty and reverence. If the modern Games are to exercise the influence I desire for them, they must in their turn show beauty and inspire reverence—a beauty and reverence infinitely surpassing anything hitherto realized in the most important athletic contests of our day.

Coubertin defined Olympism in scores of different ways. Three words continually emerged from his writings—religion, peace, and beauty—as he attempted to clarify the esoteric "mentality of Olympism," and, in so doing to create a new form of international education. Coubertin said many times that no philosophy and no religion preach loftier sentiments than those included in his version of sport altruism. He viewed Olympism as "a religion with church, dogma, and cult." Coubertin was, of course, its high priest. The whole Olympic movement, he said, encompassing much more than the Olympic Games themselves, must enlist youth "as adherents to the religion of sports." In the very early centuries of the ancient Greek games, religion was at the core of the sacred festival. Coubertin attempted to ignore the passage of twenty centuries and reintroduced the anthropomorphic concept into the modern Olympics.

It was Coubertin's everlasting hope that the Olympic Movement and its most glamorous emanation, the games, might promote a better and more peaceful world. A small nucleus of his friends jumped on the provocative bandwagon, essentially agreeing with his idea of Olympism as a medium of international conciliation and a precious opportunity for forging ties of friendship. Like many good men, Coubertin was incurably romantic; he loved what R. R. Palmer called "the mysterious, the unknown, the half-seen figures on the far horizon." He was sure that eventually his ideas would contribute to a grand internationalism, and would play an important role in what his friend Albert Shaw called "the supreme task of binding together rival nations, and relegating the barbarism of war to an evil past." All of this was said several generations ago, in less strident times, in a time period that prompted Alfred Nobel to award his first peace prize (1901), convincing many that the world was headed for unprecedented peace and prosperity.

The beauty of Olympism was Coubertin's third theme, and the most realizable outcome of sport participation. The Greeks worshiped physical beauty; so did Coubertin. Without athletics, Greek art and the Greek conception of beauty would have been impossible. During their best days, the ancient Greek games included rhythm, art, beauty, and balance. The French baron hoped that these things would be intrinsic to the modern games. His inclusion of art competitions in the 1912 Stockholm Olympic Games (and all Games through 1936) was his declaration of the inseparability of beauty from well-executed sport. To Coubertin, the Olympian qualities of religion, peace, and beauty, were fused in an "indissolvable marriage," tending to bring together "in a radiant gathering, all the principles contributing to the perfection of man."

At a 1901 Tufts College Phi Beta Kappa oration, Bliss Perry redefined "The Amateur Spirit" as a union of strict professional training with "that free outlook upon life, that human curiosity and eagerness, which are the best endowment of the amateur." One of Coubertin's closest friends, the Reverend Robert S. DeCourcy Laffan, called the London games of 1908 part of a great movement that would continue to grow for another century, dedicated to "the perfect physical development of a new humanity." Chivalry and mutual amity are legitimate goals of these games, he said. British Olympic Council member for that year, William Hayes Fisher, noted the rapid spread of the Olympic Games and the possibility of "bad blood" inherent in such growth. On the contrary, he said, the mutual understanding and respect engendered among athletes and nations will always outweigh ill feeling. Lord Desborough, one of England's greatest athletes, a scholar, and a member of the IOC, worked hard to overcome a British lack of interest in the early Olympic Games. He once wrote that the ancient Greek games were expressions of good-fellowship between Greek and Greek, a rare opportunity for Hellenic unity. "The same idea," he said, "of peace and unity in connection with international athleticism is capable of a modern application." A *New York Times* editorial, dated 15 July 1908, put its best foot forward and saw these Olympic Games as a "part of the new movement to promote the friendship of nations."

Grown men of this era hadn't seen a major war in their lifetime. They began to believe in the possibility of a world without war. The renaissance of the old Olympic Games was, to many of them, another proof that mankind was on the right road. The period was replete with great material gain and social progress, an era correctly called The Age of Progress. And yet, due to imperialistic tendencies on the part of all the major powers, expansion and military preparedness grew alarmingly. Amidst material plenty and liberal-democratic reform, each nation became convinced that, unless it armed itself to the teeth, its doom was sealed. The revival of the Olympic Games during the last years of the nineteenth century seems a logical outcome of a Western civilization caught between new wealth and optimism on the one hand and a growing alarm and need for armaments and physically fit men on the other.

Had Coubertin never been born, some other form of universal athletic competition would probably have emerged into the twentieth century. The European years following the Franco-Prussian War of 1870–1871 and the thirty years following Canadian confederation (1867) and the American Civil War (1861–1865) saw conditions ripe for the resurgence of physical education and athletics. The advance of sport also coincided with the height of the Industrial Revolution. The forty years of relative peace, 1871–1911, was a "Generation of Materialism" and, at the same time, a kind of enlightenment period. The idea of progress was becoming a general article of faith for millions. It was at this time that the popularity of British amateur and gentlemanly sport spread to the Continent, to North America, and percolated down to the middle classes. To those looking at what they wished to see, it seemed the millennium was at hand. On 18 May 1899, one hundred plenipotentiaries gathered at The Hague and pro-ceeded to discuss the possibility of permanent world peace. Coubertin was in Paris, musing on and working towards a home-town Olympic Games— one that would adequately reflect France's hope, and, above all, would realize his own dream for world peace.

Coubertin was schooled in an atmosphere of patriotism, "Christian ethics without Christian religion," an abiding love of ancient history, and all romantic literature. His philosophy combined Hellenism, humanism, and romanticism. The eclectic Coubertin preferred to be called a humanist teacher, prompting an associate, Louis Meylan, to conclude that "the integral humanism of Pierre de Coubertin, was his strongest personal characteristic." More than one critic pointed out the folly of having an incurable romantic at the head of the worldwide Olympic movement. And yet men like Reverend Laffan, Professor Sloane, Dr. Juri Guth, Colonel Balch, and most of that inner circle—the International Olympic Committee from 1894 to 1912—believed that the modern version would last as long and have far greater influence than the Greek games of antiquity. Significantly, they felt that it could all come about with leadership from Coubertin, or men similar in heart and instinct. A 13 July 1908 editorial in the *Times* disagreed about the relative impact of the two Olympic festivals, although pointing out connective links between ancient games, chivalric tournaments, and the modern revival. The writer concluded that the new games "seem likely to soften the asperity [harshness] of national prejudice. . . ."

At the very time that the youthful Coubertin was touring the college campuses of the United States, the remarkable president of the Massachusetts Institute of Technology, General Francis Amasa Walker, was delivering a daring Phi Beta Kappa speech called "College Athletics." The date was 29 June 1893, and the paper was controversial because Doctor Walker called for more leisured and competitive sport from his M.I.T. students and a reduction of the fifty hours per week of study so typical of the budding scientists. Disapproving of such overbalance, President Walker concluded that "sane athletics do wonderfully light up the life of our people."

We have no knowledge that Coubertin was aware of this Olympian view, but he frequently voiced similar sentiments. Twenty years later, on 8 May 1913, at Lausanne University, he convened a unique International Congress of Sport Psychology and Sport Physiology. A letter was read from Theodore Roosevelt expressing his strong feelings of support regarding sport and the vigorous life. Coubertin underscored a similar view to the uneasy assembly of scientists and medical doctors, echoing the ancient message of the integrated human and the resulting "intense view of life." The main speaker was Italian historian Guglielmo Ferrero, who reminded the audience that past civilizations had collapsed, in part, because of massive physical degeneration of its citizenry. A brief IOC meeting the day before had discussed the disqualification of Jim Thorpe, multiple Olympic champion. Letters were read, the case discussed, sympathy registered, but the American decision was upheld.

A year later, in June of 1914, the IOC met in Paris to celebrate its twentieth year of existence. For the first time, large numbers of national Olympic committee members were present. Coubertin threw a big party and, typically, paid for the whole affair. The symbolic, five-ringed Olympic flag—the flag of peace—was unfurled for the first time. The irony of the whole thing was that, at that precise moment, in the Bosnian capital of Serajevo, Archduke Francis Ferdinand and his wife, the duchess of Hohenberg, were murdered by terrorists. The catastrophe of universal war broke out. The world was shaken. Coubertin was shocked, especially so in remembering that, at another IOC meeting exactly twenty years ago, French President Carnot was assasinated in Paris. The baron was dealt still another blow that year of 1914. After writing a letter, tendering his resignation as IOC president (Baron Godefroy de Blonay was to replace him), Coubertin attempted to join the French army. "The captain cannot steer the vessel, especially in a tempest, if he is not present," he wrote. Coubertin reeled when told that, at fifty-one, he was too old to serve his country as a wartime soldier.

There was little to keep Coubertin in France. He had loved Switzerland ever since his first visit in 1903. On 10 April 1915, at Lausanne's city hall, papers were signed making that city the world headquarters of the Olympic movement. Berlin had been awarded the next Olympic Games. Their Imperial Olympic Committee, anticipating a short war, went ahead full steam with their ambitious plans for the 1916 Olympic Games. The general-secretary was Dr. Carl Diem, who also edited the publication *Korperkulter*. American Olympic champion Alvin Kraenzlein had already served two years in Germany as sport specialist. The German plan for a Berlin Olympic stadium continued into 1915. The huge horse racing track at Grünewald circled a deep excavation in which a 400-meter track was built and, within this circumference, a 100-meter swimming pool. Construction was stopped; the war took obvious precedence. The passionate Coubertin, in his Swiss isolation, addressed France's youth with a "1915 Decalogue" imploring sacrifice, total dedication, and the "saving of French civilization." He personally pledged his "total physicality to winning the war"; he pledged a new devotion to French history, culture, and the inevitable preservation of that civilization, thus "assuring my country's inevitable triumph. I pledge these," he concluded, "on behalf of a peace-filled future world." On 16 November 1915, he wrote his friend Baron de Blonay, "Things have been rough here since my inability to serve my country; I anticipate a long war." He also shared with Blonay his fear that Sweden's Sigfrid Edstrom, then president of the world athletics federation (I.A.A.F.), was plotting to replace the IOC with a committee of sport federations with himself as chief. The intense, little Coubertin submerged himself in reading, research, and publishing, at his own expense, a veritable Niagara of essays, monographs, newspaper editorials, and full-length texts. The November 1918 Armistice stimulated reactivation of the IOC, and, in Lausanne on 28 April 1919, the shattered city of Antwerp was informed that it had won the honor of hosting the games of the Seventh Olympiad. It had exactly a year to get ready.

THE OLYMPIC IDEA IN AN AGE OF RISING EXPECTATIONS • 83

Early in the war years, Couberton, the exiled IOC president, arranged for Olympic flags to fly at the first African games in Alexandria in 1914 and at the San Francisco modern pentathlon competition that same year. Contacts were made with sporting associates in Asia and South America about joining the Olympic family. In 1916, he founded the Olympic Institute for the perpetuation of those ideas he hoped would survive the holocaust around him. On 15 December 1917, unnerved by the severity and length of the war, he wrote of his desperate but still strong belief in cosmopolitanism. He echoed the same feeling, even more pronounced, in a 10 July 1918 note. Yves-Pierre Boulongne, in his Coubertin biography, *La Vie et L'oeuvre Pedagogique de Pierre de Coubertin 1863–1937*, is convinced that a profound and lasting change occurred within the restless baron during these war years. "Before 1914," Boulongne said, "the political concepts of Pierre de Coubertin were those of the classic French Left; he was generously humane, an internationalist, wise, opposed to the status quo. More and more, however, his habits and thoughts became reactionary." Possibly even closer to the mark was that constant and serious family problems plus a kind of intellectual exhaustion from having written too much, coupled with the universal trauma of World War I, conspired to make Coubertin a prematurely old man.

Coubertin wrote too much in his lifetime. Apparently, that's all he did in Lausanne during the war years. Several books, scores of monographs, pamphlets, newspaper essays, plus a blizzard of periodical articles flowed from the compulsive Coubertin during this painful five-year period. His eclectic habit touched on education, physical education, Olympic philosophy, psychology of sport, comments on war and peace, adolescence, morality, character building, and praises for the paradise that is Switzerland. His restlessness resulted in essays on pacifism, the neo-encyclopedists, French colonialism, French art, South America, Greek, and French history. He felt compelled to write articles titled, "Idealism in United States History," "Sport versus Alcoholism," "Athletic Specialization," "War and Peace," "The Founding of the Lausanne Institute," "Propaganda and Education," "Bonaparte and the Italian Republic," "The Coast of California," "The African Triumph," "A View of the Stars," and "The Mania of Nudity." Coubertin was curious about Theodore Roosevelt's skill as a boxer, the ancient Olympic Games as a Greek calendar, modern democracies, English history, Thomas Arnold—and wrote about them all. His *Lettres Olympiques* in October of 1918 touched on the restoration of Greek gymnastics, the concept of Olympism, bread and circus, the joy of sport, character building through sport, and the modern pentathlon competitor, the complete athlete. He wrote several texts, including a 659-page *Histoire Universelle* and *The Education of Twentieth Century Adolescents*. Several of his booklets were titled, *Leçons*

Dans le Gymnase D'Excelsior, Lecons De Gymnastique Utilitaire, A Travers L'Histoire Sud-Americaine, Pour Mieux Comprendre La France, Les Etapes De L'Astronomie, and *Amelioration et Developpement de L'Education Physique.*

When the IOC celebrated its twentieth birthday in the summer of 1914, Coubertin arranged one of the most elaborate parties seen in Paris for some time. Hundreds of guests were invited, including IOC members and their families, scores of Parisian elite, and selected French government officials. Receptions, artistic and dramatic productions, introductory remarks by the president of France, Raymond Poincaré, a Swedish choir, banquets, and, of course, Olympic business.

The British contingent, led by Reverend Laffan, opposed Coubertin's insistence that Berlin be retained as the Olympic site for 1916. With the war only days away, the Baron honestly felt that the power of the Olympic Movement was such that the Germans, who had wanted the games for ten years, would reduce their belligerent conduct and complete their plans for the Games of the Sixth Olympiad. Coubertin, in his 1931 *Memoires Olympique,* admitted how wrong he was. War came; the elaborate minutes of the IOC meeting and the details for the 1916 Olympic Games hastily put away, not to be looked at till November of 1919. Coubertin's consummate belief in the universal power of Olympism was still burning strong in 1914, but, like so many intellectuals in Europe and North America, the shattering years of the war modified an earlier mind set.

Olympism was, to Pierre de Coubertin, a way of thinking and, ultimately, a way of behaving. He channeled all this into an enormous amount of writing during the war years 1914–1919. Coubertin's personal and official vehicle of communication was the *Revue Olympique.* In a 1914 article called "Amoros and Arnold," these two great teachers of sport and classical education were applauded for their contributions to the Olympic ideal—a holistic approach to the unlimited capabilities of the well-educated person. In a newspaper article dated 9 August 1915, Coubertin discussed "The Origins of Sport," agreeing that there was a basic human play instinct, but insisting that this essence needed nurture, professional guidance, adult direction, and formal settings. In a letter from Coubertin to the editor of the *American Physical Education Review,* James Huff McCurdy, M.D., reproduced in the 15 December 1915 issue, the Frenchman lamented how little his sport philosophy was understood, and how Olympism, when better understood, might even blunt the war madness. McCurdy was quick to point out that Dr. Paul C. Phillip's use of the phrase "sport and international peace" was used solely in terms of preventing war. Coubertin's liason with South American nations resulted in a 1917 essay titled ¿*Qué es el Olympism?* When sport becomes fun and a way of life, not just competitive, he said, then it begins to contribute to the fuller realization of all mankind's redeeming qualities. This is Olympism. The following year, on 24 February 1918, at the Greek Liberal Club of Lausanne, Coubertin tried to answer the question, "What Can We Now Ask of Sport?" by tracing the recent history of sport, as it emerged from Britain and Europe, flourishing in the United States. But it was an educative and evolutionary process, he said:

> The United States at first remained indifferent to this movement. Noah Webster's assertion that "a fencing hall is as necessary to a college as a chair of mathematics" found no echo, and on the eve of the Civil War, American youth was steeped in the excesses of an unbalanced intellectualism. The fearful shock gave it a rude awakening. Gymnasia were built.

Coubertin was always careful to point out that the Olympic Ideal was more than physiological. In an 26 October 1918 "Olympic Letter," he reminded readers that "Olympism embraces spiritual and educative dimensions, as well as physical; it is essentially democratic in nature." The greatest of French physical educators, George Hebert, had addressed a letter to Coubertin on 2 May 1911 voicing his scorn for the saccharine-sweet ideology of Olympism. Its influence, he said, "is non-existent in exercising any influence on physical education in the family, at school or in the army." The games founder could handle such talk in the only way he knew how—to write refutations and to write such nakedly romantic poems as his 1912 Olympic gold-medal winning "Ode to Sport."

Fearing that one of his favorite ideas—Olympic competitions in the arts—might draw too few qualified artists and literati, Coubertin entered under the symbolic French and German pseudonyms, Georges Hohrod and M. Eschbach. Each of the poem's nine stanzas opened with the exclamation, "Oh, Sport," and then, one by one, linked it with "God," "Beauty," "Justice," "Boldness," "Honor," "Joy," "Imagination," "Progress," and "Peace."

He never quit in his variegated definitions of Olympism. He weakened, but never lost faith, and, when the war was over, at the twenty-fifth anniversary of the IOC, Coubertin exclaimed that, despite world collapse and the passage of five years, "Olympism is decidedly not one of the victims of the catastrophe." At this 28 April 1919 meeting, it was decided that Antwerp, Belgium, rather than the preferred city of Budapest, a member of the defeated Central Powers, would host the next games just a year hence. The nostalgic Frenchman, released from the agony of war, looking to the future but also looking backward, may have remembered the words of George Horton, United States Consul at Athens during the 1896 games:

> The King of Macedonia, it is said, was compelled to prove himself of pure Hellenic blood before he was allowed to compete at Olympia. The world is too big now for that sort of thing. All of us who love beauty, who have done no impiety or sacrilege, who believe in fair play, and who have stout hearts, are Greeks in the highest sense.

6 • The Phoenix Bird of Olympism Learns to Fly: 1912 –1927

"Of all the countries in the world, Sweden is at the moment best qualified to host a great Olympic Games," said the Baron de Coubertin at the Berlin International Olympic Committee meeting in May of 1909. Not always right in his prophesies, Coubertin was never more correct this time in predicting that the vigorous, physical-culture-conscious Swedes would bend every effort to conduct the best games up to that date. In several significant ways, the games of the Fifth Olympiad, celebrated in Stockholm, Sweden, were indeed the best organized and most pacific international games since the original Athens celebration.

To say this is not to intimate that this gathering of athletes (2,490 men and 57 women) from twenty-eight countries, hundreds of officials, and tens of thousands of spectators, was error-free or without gross conduct, misunderstandings, ill-feelings, and individual and collective temper tantrums. Such cantankerous behavior needs careful evaluation in contrast to the perceived benefits of such a festival. Human imperfections result in less than perfect institutions, but it is by comparing the progress of these institutions with that of the past, however difficult this may be, that some kind of scientific evaluation may be made. One French writer said the Olympic Games were no good; another called them one of the world's last great hopes. A British lord called the games a glorious manifestation of mankind's physicality, while several English editors called them sheer folly. Too many from the United States called the 1912 Olympic results proof positive that they were the superior people of the planet Earth. Others from that same country saw these mushrooming international games as a curious, even extraordinary form of human expression with obvious physical benefit, and with social and cultural attributes as well.

The Swedish government fully supported the Central Association for the Promotion of Athletics and the Olympic committee in their efforts to organize the 1912 Games of the first Scandinavian Olympics. The great Swedish trainer Ernest Hjertberg, on loan to the United States, was recalled in 1911 to organize the best possible national team. A small jewel of a stadium, with 30,000 seats, was built in the form of a medieval castle. English athletics specialist F. A. M. Webster was there, and was most impressed with its architectural design, the violet-gray Swedish bricks, granite dressings, all surrounded by an arcade

> in alternate arches of which were placed pedestals surmounted by symbolic figures. To the South the Stadium is entered under a massive entrance-arch flanked by castellated octagonal towers. . . . On the eastern tower are two figures rising upon a black mass. These two figures represent Ask and Embla, known to Northern folklore as the progenitors of the world.

The main focus of the Games—the central stadium's cinder track—was built under the supervision of Charles Perry, the same master groundsman who had worked the Athens games of 1896 and 1906, as well as Shepherd's Bush track in London in 1908. All footraces were photographed by a camera "so arranged that the breaking of the tape released the shutter of the instrument and recorded the photograph." So universal had these struggling Olympics become, and so rapid had technological change taken place, that photos were seen and results telegraphed all over Europe and North America.

On the 4 July 1912, Coubertin addressed the Swedish Parliament, assuring the members that he and fellow members of the IOC were totally devoted to the fruition of a successful Olympic Games—the culminating event of years of planning and the auspicious beginning of a new Olympiad. The king of Sweden, Gustave V, was presented with a commemorative Olympic medal at this session, which was also the fourteenth plenary meeting of the IOC. Olympic competitions had begun several weeks before, but the main attractions were about to begin. Colonel Robert M. Thompson of the New York Athletic Club and millionaire leader of the American Olympic committee, gave a dinner aboard his yacht *Katrina* for IOC members and their guests. Crown Prince Gustave Adolph was there, along with Coubertin and James E. Sullivan. Possibly for the benefit of the American and British ambassadors present, it was announced that their respective athletes "are training together in the most friendly way." In fact, correspondents were fascinated with the uninhibited carnival spirit on Stockholm streets as compared with the more solemn atmosphere of London in 1908, the former attitude considered "bad form" in the English capital. A *New York Tribune* reporter described the enthusiasm "as tumultuous as a college football game," the forest of flags and pennants "thicker than leaves on trees." Not to be outdone in literary expletives, a London *Times* observer was enthralled by the athletes as they trained inside and outside the stadium, filling the air with hammers, shots, javelins, and other "projectiles." But best of all for the man or boy in the street is the wrestling platform, he said.

> Here all day long, in the blazing sun, huge men, dreadfully uninviting and slippery with the heat, squat themselves down on the mat and tuck in their heads, until they look like something between a frog and a tortoise . . . making an entertainment better than any circus. It is an extraordinary display of the human form and muscles. And the Stockholm street-boy is getting a gratuitous education in athletics of the most cosmopolitan sort.

At 11 A.M. on 6 July 1912, the royal family entered their box seats at the stadium. Over 30,000 voices cheered, trumpets sounded, dignitaries, including IOC members in silk hats and frock coats, entered and stopped at the royal box. The choir sang a hymn just before the court pastor, the Reverend Oskar Clemens Aehfelt, preached a short sermon in Swedish. The Reverend Robert DeCourcy Laffan, an old rowing man, member of the British Olympic Committee and the IOC, stepped forward in his clerical robes and offered a prayer for world peace and friendship. Still standing, the assemblage sang the Lutheran hymn, "A Mighty Fortress Is Our God." The crown prince followed, eulogizing physical culture worldwide. His father rose and formally declared these Olympic Games open. A group of trumpeters in medieval costumes, stationed on the tower at the south end of the stadium, sounded a blast, which was responded to by another group of trumpeters. The prince waved his hat, and two hundred white-clad Swedish gymnasts performed a synchronized routine. The culmination of this spectacle, in part credited to Coubertin and so dear to him, was the march of athletes which featured nearly 600 Swedes. A new era of Olympic growth was about to begin.

Athletes from the United States, Britain, Sweden, and Finland displayed great superiority over competitors from the rest of the world at these fifth official Olympic Games. Finland emerged painfully and partially from under the yoke of the Russians to gain world recognition for her Olympic exploits, winning the 5,000 and 10,000 meters, the individual cross-country race, the javelin (combined hands), and both discus events, and she dominated Greco-Roman wrestling. Silver or bronze medals were also won in distance racing, field events, gymnastics, shooting, wrestling, and yachting. Finland's neighbor and host nation, Sweden, banked on a great sporting tradition and a monumental national effort just prior to the Games to emerge as the most dominant medal-winning nation. Swedish athletes, both men and women, were everywhere, and were winning. They succeeded in winning medals in one-third of all the track and field events, overwhelmed all opponents in tug-of-war, won the decathlon by default, set the standard in gymnastics, dominated horse-riding, and scored in lawn tennis. Swedes finished second in one rowing event and scored in every shooting competition except "clay birds." Olympic gold, silver, and bronze medals were won by Swedish men and women in swimming. The same was true of the Swedish men in wrestling. They also scored in the yachting competition and swept all places in the modern pentathlon.

Both Britain and the United States were obsessed with track-and-field athletics at these Stockholm games. Thus, Britain's good showing in this showcase sport was looked upon by many, especially those from England, Scotland, Wales, and Northern Ireland, as disgraceful. The fact that they won the 1,500-meter flat race and the 400-meter relay, won silver or bronze in the 200 meters, the 5000 meters, the 1600-meter relay, the 3,000-meter team race, the 8,000-meter cross-country, the 10,000-meter walk, and the tug-of-war was not enough for some British contemporaries. These same people were especially pained at Britain's backwardness in "scientific" throwing and jumping events, their nineteenth-century bastion of strength. Athletes from the United Kingdom did well in cycling, won the football finals, surprised everyone with their gymnastic skills, led the world in a variety of tennis competitions, picked up recognition and reward in all three categories of rowing, and did very well indeed at shooting and swimming. But, as will be seen later in this chapter, many British Olympic officials, bureaucrats, and newspaper correspondents perceived that the Union Jack was slipping badly. This is true in the pragmatic, Western sense: if one is not moving forward, one is actually falling behind.

Just as this was so of Britain in 1912, it was said of the United States's Olympic success in the 1970s. The United States has always been radically selective in its Olympic involvement. At Stockholm, the American Olympic committee concentrated all its monies, coaching expertise, and organizational skill into running, jumping, throwing, swimming, and shooting events. The results were spectacular within these parameters. Their track-and-field victories were breathtaking; Hawaii's Duke Kahanamoku dominated swimming, along with Canada's G. R. Hodgson. The American multiple victories of A. P. Lane and J. R. Graham in marksmanship led Caspar Whitney of *Outing* magazine to crow that "perhaps only in a frontier society can the ability to handle firearms be expected to take first place in the public interest."

The English athletic specialist at Stockholm, Lieutenant-Colonel F. A. M. Webster, called Hannes Kolehmainen's performances "incomparable" and "undoubtedly the sensation of that particular celebration of the Olympic Games." Eyewitnesses of the Finn's world-record, five-kilometer victory over France's Jean Bouin, called it a clash of giants. And yet, the *New York Times* sports reporter's poll of track authorities concluded that the 800-meter victory of teen-age Ted Meredith "was the greatest race they had ever witnessed." Superlatives were also directed at Ralph Craig's double sprint victories, at the world's record of Oxford University's A. N. S. Jackson at 1,500 meters, and at the Irish-American "Whales," Pat McDonald, Ralph Rose, and Mat McGrath. All agreed with King Gustave's assessment of Jim Thorpe: "You, sir, are the greatest athlete in the world." Sport historians soberly relate the first stirrings of Germany as a world athletic power. Notable marathon wrestling matches were recorded: the unresolved nine-hour Greco-Roman light-heavyweight clash between Anders Ahlgren and Ivas Bohling, both of Sweden, and the exhausing semifinal middleweight wrestling match between Martin Klein of Russia and Finland's Alfred Asikainen. A tradition of ultradistance running superiority was begun by the South African duo of K. K. McArthur and C. W. Gitsham who finished ahead of America's Gaston Strobino in the marathon. Hungarian domination of sabre fencing continued with a sweep by Dr. Jeno Fuchs, Bela Bekessey, and Ervin Meszaros. Ben and Platt Adams, angular brothers from the New York Athletic Club, won one gold, two silver, and one bronze medal in the standing jumps. Neither could beat the magnificent technique of Greece's Konstantin Tsiklitiras's 11 ft. 0⅝ in. jump. Lieutenant George F. Patton, the only American in the new, Coubertin-invented modern military pentathlon, and Avery Brundage in the classic pentathlon did well, finishing seventh and fifth respectively. Jim Thorpe's deeply regrettable banishment from Olympic history had moved Brundage up one notch from sixth place. Italian champions were Alberto Braglia in "combined gymnastics," Nedo Nadi in fencing foil, and Giovanni Pellegrini and Riccardo Barthelem in the experimental arts competition for painting and music respectively.

As soon as the track events ended, the entire infield was converted into a huge banquet hall for 3,000 athletes and officials, all accompanied by a 4,000-voice choir. The festival ended with fireworks. Then, within hours, the stadium underwent a complete transformation for the next day's equestrian finals. Hydrangea plants and a dazzling array of flowers, hedges, gates, and walls were readied for horse and rider. French, Swedish, German, and Belgian teams took all the honors.

There had been fewer disputes and better organization than at previous games; one pride-swollen reporter from the *New York Tribune* concluded that "The Olympian Games are justifying the ideals of their founders." However, a deep moan of dispiritedness arose from the British press as they correctly perceived America's aggressiveness and the greater involvement of foreign athletes in sport competition as the end of British athletic domination. Many of them were shamed by the relatively casual, unscientific air of many English athletes. Rare indeed was the *Daily News* declaration that Stockholm competitions were meaningless. What is of

*Jim Thorpe, USA, winner of the athletic pentathlon and decathlon at the
1912 Games in Stockholm. Credit John Lucas collection.*

real, national importance, it said, was "sport as a recreation of all-round character."

Generally speaking, Olympic athletes from every part of the world get along very well with one another. Competitive sport, especially the Olympic Games, however, are not the playground of athletes alone. Thousands of visitors, officials, national representatives, and members of the world newspapers press themselves on the public. This condition was more pronounced in Stockholm than in prior Olympic cities. The focus for many of the brickbats was the long-time rivalry between the United States and Britain.

The rhetoric was different this time. In 1908, American pugnaciousness was offensive to the British. In Stockholm, the Americans, even more successful in track-and-field athletics, were looked upon by many as an exotic racial mix, a semiprofessionalized army of gladiators, an overserious armada of recent immigrant stock, "red Indians," and Negroes that violated the spirit, if not the letter, of the Olympic ideal. All of the accusations were half-truths; all of them require scrutiny because, on both sides of the Atlantic, the racial innuendos, dire hints of degenerating Britain contrasting with a kind of muscular Uncle Sam were widely believed by the public. Sport headlines and editorials in the British Isles and in American publications exclaimed, "Why England Loses," "Race Questions and American Preeminence," "More Remarks on Our Athletic Supremacy," "Briton Must Wake Up," "Britain's Olympic Remorse," "Poor Old England," "Showing Shames England," and "The American Eagle Screams." It was all so much wonderfully inflammatory nonsense, calculated to sell copies, and, at the same time, reflect a growing malaise on the part of the once great British Empire, as well as an expanding Yankee national image.

Finley Peter Dunn, alias "Dooley," was extremely popular in the States. One of his sarcasms was directed at a July 1912 London daily that called American Olympians "Cheaters" and "Professionals." How unsportsmanlike are these Americans, said Dooley. Why they give up smoking, overeating, and train hard, scientifically, and on a daily basis. For shame, he said in his *New York Times* editorial for 28 July:

> These boys that you see hoppin' around th' thrack ar-re the rile represintive Americans. They are our ambassadurs, not the lords ye see makin' a ginuflixion befure th' king. Sports, Hinnissy, is like war. All the excuses an' all th' complaints ye hear come fr'm th' non combytants.

There was honest-to-goodness concern on the part of Englishmen about the slow demise of British athletic expertise and domination. Rational sportsmen like Lord Desborough and Theodore Cook wanted not so much to regain a recent supremacy, but rather "to give the best possible opportunity to our select athletes to show the best form, whether they win or lose." However, *Blackwood's Magazine* called the Americans "professional gladiators". The *Times, Mail, Standard,* and *Express*—all English newspapers—were angry at a "phony U.S. team" made up of Hawaiians, Indians, Negroes, and "the descendants of a hundred European nationalities." All of them agreed with the angry Sir Arthur Conan Doyle, who demanded that every nation and every people living under the egis of the British Empire should be represented at the 1916 Berlin Olympics by one flag and one uniform.

There was both envy and disgust in the British summation that "it is evident that the way to win in sport is to make it a business." There was a deep division. For every suggestion that British athletes and coaches—the lot of them—should be shipped to the United States for an extended leave of absence to learn the science of athletic training, there were countering warnings that the cure would be worse than the disease. The American win-syndrome was a sickness, some said, that could only be balanced by a serene, British sense of proportion and sensitivity to the physical and spiritual delights of rugged play. The tortured nature of much British commentary reflected the impossible dream—greater Olympic success without the loss of joy—the modern counterpoise of Grecian *sophrosyne* or "moderation".

All the American athletes had received coaching and encouragement in high school, college, and clubs. In little more than a generation, a national network of athletic competions had become an American tradition. By contrast, the centuries-old British tradition of sport was amorphous and overly individualistic. Large numbers of English athletes were uncoached and arrived in Stockholm by their own means. Several athletes offered that not a single British official told them what to do and where to go, and they added, "We would probably have been extremely annoyed if any one had presumed to do so." By contrast, the entire American team trained three to five hours a day aboard the *Finland* during the long ocean crossing, all under expert and specialized coaches. In an extraordinary, full-page article in the 25 August *New York Times*, Olympic committee chief Colonel Robert M. Thompson repeated that the whole object of the trip was to weld together a first-class team, an unbeatable team. The second generation of Americans, he said, so widely represented on the 1912 team, "no matter from what stock derived, is distinctly American. That gives a real American type, and that type is a fine one."

To say that many Americans were caught up in their successful Stockholm adventure is to understate the case. The *New York Herald* of 21 July 1912 roared that "America is near the ultimate goal of perfection and breaking of records will soon be of world-wide interest." The author, G.

W. Axelson, was wrong in the first instance and absolutely correct in the second. At this juncture in sport history, the American actors involved appeared incapable of sitting tight, of remaining moderately proficient; they were early participants in the passion for breaking world records, a compulsion that would soon become universal.

It was, of course, not the best spirit in which to play, but, even in 1912, the Olympic Games had ceased to be "games" or an ideal place in which to "play." Somehow the Americans grasped this idea more readily than Europeans, especially the English.

Pierre de Coubertin, in a rare moment of peevishness toward the English he so admired, criticized certain sport leaders that had vowed not to cooperate with the Germans at the 1916 Berlin Olympics unless British interpretations on amateurism were incorporated into the ground rules. "England will have to follow the international rules under the leadership of Germany, or give it up," said the baron on 26 October 1912. Quieting down, Coubertin admitted his visionary nature, proposing that he just "happened to have the enthusiasm and the luck to see the possibilities of international athletics on a big scale." In the next month's issue of *Revue Olympique*, he spoke of "England's duty" to fight back, restoring its "sacred tradition" of sport. But it was to no avail.

War hung heavily on the European horizon and what must have seemed like an interminable period of waiting following from 1912 to 1920. Of course, the Games of the Sixth Olympiad were never held. Before leaving Stockholm, the IOC president thanked the king, paid homage to the Swedish nation, and reminded his audience that the modern Olympic Movement owed much to the little-understood medieval tournaments, "whose only fault was sometimes to push beyond reason the elegant cult of honour, stoicism and generosity."

The great irony is, of course, that the one persistent criticism of the modern festival is what some consider their insufferable religiosity. Coubertin was frequently powerless in the grip of romance and tradition. For example, he was very much the apotheosis of the Victorian-Edwardian gentleman in his attitude toward women's athletic competition. The recent introduction of women participants at the games alarmed him, and he said so without too much eloquence or accuracy. Tennis and swimming for females were OK with Baron de Coubertin, but running, fencing, equestrian sports, and soccer put women in a compromising position. He would fight the inevitable for the remaining years of his life.

During his years of wartime exile in Lausanne, Coubertin was consumed with keeping the Olympic Idea alive. A torrent of essays flowed from his lonely Olympic headquarters. Somehow, as he said, Olympism failed to become a victim of the war, and the IOC was hastily convened in April of 1919, and Antwerp, Belgium, was selected for the games during the late summer of the following year. All mankind's forces must be harnessed to rise above the crushing damage of the world war, he said, and "Olympism is numbered among them." With more bravado than assurance that the immediate postwar Olympic Games would be a success, Coubertin and his small group of intimates traveled to the North Belgium seaport of Antwerp. Somehow, one can almost hear them say, "Let the games begin."

In an imperfect world, there can only be an imperfect Olympics. And yet, at certain precious moments, man is capable of transcending human defects, or at least it seems so in the world of art, music, literature, and sport. I think Coubertin caught a glimpse of this and hoped for the best.

Conditions were primitive at the Olympic site. Antwerp (Anvers) had been devastated during the all-to-recent war. The main stadium was not ready, there were no decent accommodations for the athletes, and the organizing committee ran out of money long before the first athlete arrived. But their agony was not unique. The American Olympic committee, helpless without adequate funding, had hired the USS *Princess Matoika* to transport its team overseas. The dreadfully tired military transport ship was grossly inadequate in every way, and a real mutiny broke out among the athletes. "You can't believe what we've been through," moaned one Olympian. Fred Rubien of the Olympic committee countered by saying that it was the very best they could do. Besides, he said, trouble began only as they neared Antwerp, and, hinting sinisterly, "There was an element of dissatisfaction in the team which assumed the aspect of a Bolshevic outburst. . . ." Somehow, they all made it through to the opening ceremonies and the beginning of competitions.

Coubertin, who had everlastingly believed that Olympism was not a system but a state of mind, invited the whole of youth, "patrician or plebeian—to select the quickest, the strongest, the most daring." The IOC's 1913 meeting had declared the keeping of point totals as un-Olympic; the Anvers gathering of correspondents immediately began telegraphing home a running point total of each day's results.

The American domination of track-and-field athletics was muted by sensational performances by the Finns and a partial resurgence by the resolute English. For example, in the sprints, England's Harry Edwards took two bronze medals behind Charlie Paddock, the first "world's fastest human" (100) and 200-meter champ Alan Woodring. Morris Kirksey and Paddock, both from the United States, were runners up in these short sprints. South Africa's Bevil Rudd won the 400 meters and was third in the 800 meters. The old warrior A. G. Hill caused joy in England by pulling off upset victories at 800 and 1,500 meters. The thin, enigmatic figure of Finland's Paavo Nurmi emerged at Antwerp, winning the 10-kilometer race over France's Joseph Guillemot and losing by an eyelash to the

Hannes Kolehmainen, Finland, winning the Olympic marathon at Antwerp, 1920. Credit John Lucas collection.

brilliant French war veteran at 5,000 meters. Nurmi prevailed in the 8,000-meter cross-country race. The 1912 10-kilometer winner from Finland, Kolehmainen, returned and won a fast marathon race (2:32:35.8) at Antwerp. The steeplechase was won by Percy Hodge of Britain, world records were set by Earl Thomson of Canada and Frank Loomis of the USA at 110- and 400-meter hurdles. Britain and America split victories in the 1,600- and 400-meter relays. In a remarkable concentration, all the field events were won by athletes from the United States, Finland, and Sweden. Helge Lovland (Norway) won the decathlon, Eero Lehtonen (Finland) the pentathon, and Ugo Frigerio (Italy) walked flawlessly at 3 and 10 kilometers. Sweden captured places one through four in the modern military pentathlon, while Britain's behemoths won the tug-of-war, the last time for that event at the Olympic Games.

Swimming stars at the 1920 Games were Hawaii's Duke Kahanamoku and Warren Kealoha, with the dominating figure of Norman Ross establishing a world record at 400 meters. American young women captured everything at poolside. For the first time, a significant number of American women were sent to the Olympics. The late James E. Sullivan had been opposed to such exposure, but he was gone. Women's suffrage in the United States was ratified by the required 36th state in 1920, and the climate seemed right for a new sport involvement. Ethelda Bleibtrey won the 100 and 400 meters, and anchored the 400-meter relay—all in world-record times. Boxing honors were divided between South African, Canadian, British, and American fighters. Frank Genaro won at flyweight, Samuel Moshberg at lightweight, and Eddie Eagan at light-heavy; Eagan returned a dozen years later, at Lake Placid, to another gold as a member of the American four-man bobsled team. Weightlifting honors were awarded athletes from Belgium, Estonia, France, and Italy, while tough guys from Finland and Sweden won most of the gold medals in Greco-Roman and freestyle wrestling. Only Italian and French athletes emerged victorious in fencing, the great Hungarians, regrettably, not being allowed to participate. Italy and Switzerland won rowing honors, but it was Jack Kelly at single sculls and the Kelly-P.V. Costello team that was remembered longest. The rowing sensation of the Games was the thrilling victory and world-record time (6:05.0) of the U.S. Naval Academy's eight-oared crew over a crack Oxford-Cambridge crew (6:05.8) rowing under the Leander Club banner. Norway and Holland won everything in yachting, while equestrian honors went to Swedish riders. Maybe the recent war had something to do with it, but, next to athletics, there were more rifle and pistol shooting medals awarded than in any of the twenty-two events at Antwerp. A reporter on the *Echo de Paris* observed that "not even at Verdun were so many rifle shots heard." Scandinavian and, especially, American shooters did remarkably well.

There were ten archery events; steady hands from Belgium and France won them all. Gymnastic prizes were won by Italian, Swedish, and Danish athletes. Water polo, polo, and field hockey laurels were all won by the British team, thus muting some of their bitter self-criticism. In soccer football, honors were divided between Belgium, Spain, and Holland, but there is a regrettable story here. Erich Kamper, in his very important *Encyclopedia of the Olympic Games* notes that the final match was between Belgium and Czechoslovakia. The match was abandoned in the fortieth minute

> because the Czech team walked off in protest against several questionable decisions made by the referee. As a result the Czechs were disqualified. Forty thousand spectators saw a very hard game right from the kick-off. The first goal was scored from a disputed penalty, the second from an off-side position. Furthermore, one of the Czechs was sent off, which unnerved the rest of the team.

The incomparable Suzanne Lenglen of France won the women's tennis in a meaningless walkover, while the rugby team from the United States surprised France with an 8–0 victory. Morris Kirksy and Dink Templeton, two American super stars traded their track uniforms to help their rugby team to victory. "American Athletes are Still Supreme," shouted the *New York Times*, although it acknowledged the fact that the rest of the world did not quietly concede to the Americans as they once did. It was a new age of wonders, one in which French scientist M. Edouard Berlin had managed to transmit a photographic image by telephone from Antwerp to Paris— that of the Swedish women's Olympic team.

Despite Coubertin's brave clarion call that "Sport is King" and his universal invitation to the whole of youth, "patrician or plebein"—to select the quickest, the strongest, the most daring—the 1920 Olympic Games were not a complete success. Very poor attendance, organizational lapses, and postwar money troubles had plagued the Antwerp organizing committee. Coubertin was determined to do better at the next games planned for Paris. At an important Lausanne IOC meeting in June of 1921, it was decided to look far up the road, with Amsterdam selected for 1928, and Los Angeles a strong possibility for 1932. Program reorganization went on in earnest, along with much needed IOC dialogue with the wildly variable, single-minded sport federations. The French educator R. P. Didon coined the Olympic motto, "Citius, Altius, Fortius"; Coubertin implored the world to put the bloody war behind them, to look to Paris for "the sweet struggle," where "friendship and courage will win out over tyranny and excess passion." At this same 1921 meeting, the committee decided that, at future Olympics, the names of all champions should be engraved in the stadium walls. More importantly, Justinien Clary, Melchior de Polignac, and Coubertin decided that a winter Olympic Games should be held at Chamonix, and that such a festival "could be conducted in a dignified and amateur manner." The twentieth and twenty-first IOC sessions were held in Paris in 1922 and in Rome in 1923. The semi-exile, Coubertin, was radiant upon returning home; in his address to the City Council, he reminded them "that Paris is my native town; long live Paris." It was the hottest summer in recorded Paris history. Temperatures of 45 degrees C (113 degrees F) were recorded, with week-long 100 degrees F days labeled a "cauldron" or "furnace." Nevertheless, forty-four nations sent 2,956 male and 136 female athletes to compete in eighteen events.

The host nation has always taken that extra measure in order to do well at the Olympic Games. French athletes, working very hard to overcome a national intellectual snobbery, did relatively well at the Paris games. Gold medals were awarded French athletes in fencing, cycling, water polo, shooting, wrestling, weight lifting, and tennis. Their young men and women were in the finals of track-and-field, diving, rugby football, equestrian sports, polo, the new winter games of bobsled, ice hockey, figure and speed skating. Of course, in the little-coveted arts competition, first and third prizes in literature and sculpture were awarded Georges Charles for his "Les Jeux Olympiques," and Leon Mascaux for "7 Medailles Sportives." Understandably, the French were caught up, for the moment, in these second world games held in their capital city. *L'Illustration* magazine was aglow with essays and photographs. *La Revue de France* devoted some space to "Les Sports." In it, Marcel Berger pointed with pride to the gains made by French youth in the field of sport, and, as a result, a boost to their manhood. "Just as significantly," he said, "Frenchmen of 40 are jogging along in tempo with autobuses!" The important French writer Henry de Montherlant's 1924 fictional *Les Onze Devant La Porte Dorée* deals with a foot race at the Colombes track. A similar work by Louis-Henry Destel in *LaRevue Universelle*, called "Le 10,000 metres," portrays the "agony and ecstasy" of physical effort and victory. Domanique Braga, in *La Revue de Genève,* compared the movements of a champion athlete to the rhythm of good poetry and music. Of course, the outpouring was not all so heavenly. Rene Besse's 1 September article in *Mercuré de France*, "La Leçon des Jeux Olympiques," called for greater sports participation by all the people, "but those activities must be native French games and not unnatural Anglo-Saxon imports."

Athletes from the United Kingdom were never really "out" of the Olympics. A track-and-field crisis during the first decade of the century had convinced many of impending athletic doom. At the 1924 Olympic Games, the British scored well in every flat race of 100 meters through the marathon, managed very little in the field events, did well in men's and women's swimming-diving, boxed their way to several gold and silver medals, gained honors in cycling, fencing, gymnastics, tennis, rowing, shooting, wrestling, riding, and made an impact in winter sports.

The patriot-millionaire and president of the American Olympic Committee, Robert Thompson, led another successful Yankee team to Paris. Track coach Lawson Robertson was from the University of Pennsylvania; his boys were in the top six of every single track-and-field event except the walk and the triple jump. Americans swam in awesome fashion, won two gold in boxing, dominated freestyle wrestling, won traditional honors in rowing and tennis, surprised again with an American football-like rugby victory, performed well enough for a rare victory in the long horse, and did their usual brilliant shooting. Of course, there were other successful competitors. Forty-four countries were represented; athletes from twenty-nine scored.

A brilliant tapestry of champions emerged from the enervating heat of Paris. It was "a renaissance of sport," cried the editorialist in a 6 July *New York Times* essay. Not even the American mania for baseball is comparable to the Olympic Games, he concluded. World records occur so swiftly and so regularly said *The Outlook* writer that they appear "like the telegraph poles from a fast-moving train." Anecdotes abounded by the hundred. The great multiple champion walker from Italy, Frigerio, requested the orchestra conductor to play a list of favorite selections while he walked a victorious twenty laps around the cinder track. The brilliant Scotch minister, Eric Liddell, refused to run 100 meters on a Sunday; instead, he won a gold and bronze medal at 400 and 200 meters. Wonder woman Helen Wills and legendary Hazel Wightman dominated women's tennis. On her last day in Paris, Miss Wills walked the full length of Champs Elysées, spent every French franc she had on fifteen pairs of "beautiful slippers, with spiked heels, delicate workmanship, and jewel-like colors." Benjamin Spock, a generation later the most famous doctor in the world, won a gold medal as a member of the eight-oared crew from the United States. To sport and Olympic aficionados, the names are legion. Tommy Hitchcock, the most famous American polo player, helped his team to second place behind the great gauchos from Argentina. Paddock, Jackson Scholz, Douglas Lowe, Harold Osborne, Bud Houser, and Edvin Wide of Sweden won double medals in track and field. The names Weissmuller, Kahanamoku, Kealoha, Arne Borg, and Andrew Charlton are legitimate swimming "greats." Little Aileen Riggin of 1920 fame was back in 1924, not only winning silver in her fancy diving specialty, but taking third in the 100-meter backstroke. English Channel swimmer Gertrude Ederle won two bronze medals and a gold before her famous marathon swim. French cyclist Armand Blanchonnet, Hungarian sabre specialist Dr. Sandor Posta, and tennis champions Vince Richards, Henri Cochet, Baron de Morpurgo, and Jean Borotra will long be remembered. The brilliant team of Kelly and Costello were memorable in a double sculls repeat. But possibly the most significant athletic phenomena of these Games of the Eighth Olympiad were the mighty Finns, the people of "Suomi."

"The superman has arrived at last," called Grantland Rice to the *New York Herald Tribune* office. It was, of course, Paavo Nurmi he was talking about, but he might have said, "supermen," referring to the entire Finnish team in Paris. The United States was its usual awesome self in the total number of medals won. Britain, Sweden, Italy, Switzerland, Norway, Belgium, and a surprisingly strong French team were prominent through-out the athletic program. But it was to Finland that the world turned at the completion of the games. In 1924, with a population the size of present-day Chicago, Illinois, the "men of Suomi" won thirteen gold, thirteen silver, and nine bronze medals, plus two first-place and a third-place team-championship in cross-country running, the steeple-chase, and clay-pigeon shooting (see table 1). Nurmi and Willi Ritola won nine gold and silver medals in the distance races. Greco-Roman and

Gertrude Ederle, USA, 1924 Olympic Games winner of three medals. She swam the English Channel in 1926. Credit Ronald Smith collection.

Table 1

Victories of Finnish Athletes at the 1924 Paris Olympic Games

Athlete	Event	Performance	Gold	Silver	Bronze
				Medal	
Paavo Nurmi	1,500 meters	3:53.6 Olympic record	●		
Paavo Nurmi	5,000 meters	14:31.2 Olympic record	●		
Paavo Nurmi	cross-country	32:54.8	●		
Paavo Nurmi	3,000 meters	8:32.0	●		
Willi Ritola	3,000 meters			●	
Willi Ritola	5,000 meters	14:31.4		●	
Willi Ritola	10,000 meters	30:18.8 Olympic record	●		
Willi Ritola	cross-country	34:19.4		●	
Willi Ritola	3,000 steeplechase	9:33.6 world record	●		
Albin Stenroos	marathon	2:41:22.6	●		
Eero Berg	10,000 meters	31:43.0			●
Elias Katz	3,000 steeplechase	9:44		●	
Vilho Niittymaa	discus	44.95 meters		●	
Jonni Myyra	javelin	62.96 meters	●		
Eero Lehtonen	pentathlon	14 points	●		
Anselm Ahlfors	Greco-Roman wrestling—bantamweight			●	
Valno Ikonen	Greco-Roman wrestling—bantamweight				●
Kalle Anttila	Greco-Roman wrestling—featherweight		●		
Aleksanteri Toivola	Greco-Roman wrestling—featherweight			●	
Oskari Friman	Greco-Roman wrestling—lightweight		●		
Kalle Westerlund	Greco-Roman wrestling—lightweight				●
Edvard Vesterlund	Greco-Roman wrestling—middleweight		●		
Artur Lindfors	Greco-Roman wrestling—middleweight			●	
Onni Pellinen	Greco-Roman wrestling—light heavy weight				●
Edil Rosenqvist	Greco-Roman wrestling—heavyweight			●	
Kustaa Pihlajamaki	free-style wrestling—bantamweight		●		
Kaarlo MaKinen	free-style wrestling—bantamweight			●	
Volmari Vikstrom	free-style wrestling—lightweight			●	
Arvo Haavisto	free-style wrestling—lightweight				●
Eino Leino	free-style wrestling—welterweight			●	
Vilho Pekkala	free-style wrestling—middleweight				●
Hans Dittmar	yachting—dinghy class				●
Lennart Hannelius	shooting—rapid-fire pistol				●
Konrad Huber	shooting—clay pigeon			●	
Finland team	team championship—clay pigeon				
Finland team	team championship—3000 meters				
Finland team	team championship—cross-country				
Medal total			13	13	8

freestyle or catch-as-catch-can wrestling were overwhelmingly the pre-rogative of these nickel-hard Finns. James B. Connolly, first Olympic victor back in 1896, and fervent Irish-American patriot, watched the parade of Finnish champions in Paris, and noted that, in the fervor of their competition, "the Finns are like the Irish. Pride of race stuck out all over the Irish athlete; and so, also, over the Finnish athlete." Nurmi won two gold medals and two Olympic records in a single hour; he seemed physically unaffected after running over six miles on a day when the temperature surpassed 110 degrees Fahrenheit. He ran machine-like in his 3,000-meter victory. Nurmi's countryman, Ritola, was almost as good, winning an unprecedented five distance-medals. When the "old one," Albin Stenroos, won the marathon, the *New York Times* correspondent was at a loss for superlatives, naively noting that "They never seem to lose their wind, and their hearts beat out distance as steadily as their legs."

Reams of newspaper and periodical essays were written about the Finnish "secret" of athletic superiority. Fascinating claims were made for native foods: raw, dried fish, rye bread "hard as biscuit," and sour milk. The magnificent introvert, Nurmi, added mystery by refusing to discuss anything about his private life and training regimen. Another theory forwarded by the half-educated was that the Finns, distinctly different kinds of people from the neighboring Swedes, were direct descendants of a physically tough "wild Mongol strain." The remote harshness of the land and the relative poverty of the people, 80 percent of whom lived in the country, were proposed as reasons for Finland's superiority over softer, technocratic societies. Truth and fiction were intermingled in descriptions (by non-Finns) of the *sauna* baths. Some said it was an ice bath followed by rolling in the snow that made them tough; others were sure that the peculiar heat of the sauna, accompanied by thrashing oneself with soft twigs and then the icy bath, couldn't help but breed tough men.

The reasons for Finnish success were all of these things and more. Finland's educational system received a big boost following its independence from Russia. Compulsory education, including a vigorous, daily, physical education program brought national literacy and a youthful mandate for rugged outdoor sport. The Finns are an enduring rather than quixotic people, due largely to climate and geography. K. P. Silberg, writing on *The Athletic Finn* in 1927, called his people fundamentally conservative, clinging "to the old and tried with unyielding tenacity." The unalterably harsh land produced men and women of "obstinacy and endurance." Very hard work followed by the daily reward of the sauna certainly must be considered a factor in the uniqueness of Finnish character. Lastly, the mystic element or *Suomalainen sisu*—"Finnish" *sisu* must be brought into the discussion as partial explanation of Finnish tenacity. For generations, though not widely understood in Finland today, *sisu* was revered as a national quality synonymous with endurance, perseverance, grit, and, as Silberg says, it is a coordinated "effort of mind and body to consummate a difficult task in the face of the most formidable odds." One writer, after watching Finnish toughness in the Paris Olympic arena, was convinced that Finnish success was the direct result of a small nation's patriotic unity, and the resolve of its people "to hold to one big idea with a bulldog grip and work long and hard for what it wants." Nurmi, Ritola and Stenroos, the amazing cadre of wrestlers, all became the instant symbols of Finnish sisu—archetypal Finns: honest, fearless, and stubborn. In just three weeks, much of the world's population became aware of these Finns and the Olympic Games theater upon which they had played so brilliantly a part. One person in particular—Coubertin—was pleased beyond measure by the whole thing. After all, he reflected, his Olympic Games had been rescued from a world war and a less than representative Antwerp Olympics in 1920.

The 1924 Olympic Games were not completely free of disagreeable "incidents," and it was not due just to the insufferable heat. There were more substantial criticisms of the Paris games than that of New York *Evening World's* Charles Parker, who called for a reduction in the number of distance events, in order to take something away from the great Finns. Olympic fans paid six million francs at the gate, but the host city and France's treasury had to live with a two-million-franc deficit. French spectators at their own Olympics were generally lacking in sports knowledge, reacting frequently in a discourteous manner. Citizen Doctor Bellin du Coteau, writing in *Echo des Sports*, criticized the ineptness of French officials, many of whom had wormed their way into the stadium through political influence. The respected English war correspondent Sir Harry Perry Robinson, writing in *the Times* of London for 22 and 23 July 1924, roasted the Coubertin experiment calling it a series of abusive confrontations. Disorders, fights in the stands, the shouting down of national anthems, booing and shouting by fans, bitterness in the boxing ring, a French-American rugby fight, quarrels in tennis, fencing, and at the water polo pool, all led Robinson to conclude that "To write this article is like delivering the funeral rites of the Olympic Games."

Coubertin's essential thesis that international sport tends to soothe intergroup misunderstanding and bitterness was challenged again by some English, French, and American observers. Little on this subject was heard from the athletes themselves. But then, as W. O. McGeehan of the *New York Herald Tribune* said on 25 July 1924, "The non-combatants always have been more ferocious than the men in the fight. . . ." For example, some British Olympic committee members demanded the withdrawal of their team from Paris rather than put up with what they perceived of as an unsportsmanlike atmosphere and the futile effort of

The Olympic Village, Paris, 1924, a far cry from the modern version. Credit Ronald Smith collection.

keeping up with "the American professionals." An immediate petition signed by English team members silenced any further action in this direction. The captain of the British team, the veteran middle-distance ace Philip J. Baker was convinced that the Olympic Games were a force for good, and that the Olympic movement was capable of meeting several of mankind's needs. The dean of American sports writers, Grantland Rice, reflecting on the 1924 Olympics, said he could think of nothing that brought so many of the world's people together in an atmosphere calculated to "develop a clearer mutual understanding." The *Literary Digest* of 2 August 1924, quoting an editorial from *The Christian Science Monitor*, predicted a great future for international sport, but just so long as the masses are educated to and the athletes reminded that "The chivalrous ideal of the true sportsman is to try his best to win, but to rejoice that the best man or the best side should carry off the prize."

Some refused to let go of the fact that ugliness had occurred during the Paris celebration. At a post-Olympic banquet, Coubertin answered his critics by pointing out "that in a crowd of 30,000 spectators, 50 hoodlums are sufficient to create incidents." In the September 1924 issue of *La Revue de Genève*, Coubertin, the recent Paris experience sharpening his sense of history and the future, assured all that the Germans would be welcomed once again into the Olympic family, and that their contribution would strengthen the next games in Amsterdam. "I dream of the twenty-sixth and twenty-eighth Olympiads in the years 1996 and 2004," he rhapsodized.

Although Paddock of the United States, the first "world's fastest human," may have had other motives in mind, he did accept Coubertin's 1924 invitation to tour the world in the name of "Olympism." After the Games, Paddock stopped at Coubertin's office on the Boulevard des Italien, talked with "the good old Baron de Coubertin," and was almost convinced that the transcontinental running tour might just do something for the world.

It seemed constitutionally impossible for Coubertin to accept sport as one of the purest and most delightful forms of occasional escapism. His concept of sport, by definition, included components of total education, character development, social service, moral training, patriotism, and health. The central core of a person's being was a conviction that sport represents something more than entertainment, more than escapism, more than mere play. In *The Official Report of the VIIIth Olympiad, Paris 1924*, the sixty-one year old Frenchman envisioned a future world in which international physical education demonstrations and athletic competitions might play "a supreme part in promoting progress and social unity." It was maddeningly idealistic, even irrational, and the IOC president continued to be the target of more sober minds—realists, whose study of history had convinced them that the Coubertin dream was just that, pie in the sky. But the dream persists to the present day. His insistence that the Olympic Games reflect a metaphysical dimension as well as remain world championship competitions remains today the central core of Olympic controversy. The Paris games closed with a new Coubertin wrinkle—the solemn ritual of raising three flags: that of Greece, symbol of the past, France, the host country, and Holland, rousing symbol of the next games and all those that would inexorably follow. It was Coubertin at his best—or worst.

In November of 1924, Coubertin announced that he would retire at the Prague Congress in May 1925 in order to devote his remaining years to "universal history and pedagogy." His last official suggestion, soon to be overlooked, was that both the summer and winter Olympics should take place in the same country.

The Dutch Olympic Committee, host for the 1928 games, was in big trouble all during the winter and spring of 1925. One million florins were needed, and the government simply refused to raise the money. Liberal and Socialist politicians supported the money expenditure; the Calvinist-Catholic faction condemned the Olympic concept as "Heathenish" and voted down the money. Finally, in late May of 1925, the Dutch East Indies Company, "as a matter of national honor," offered the million guilders ($400,000) to get the Amsterdam Olympics off dead center. A national subscription for two million guilders was started. In nearby Brussels, delegates to the Prague Congress were prepared to vote against German reentry into the Olympic picture. War memories and scars die slowly. Approximately 300 delegates from twenty-one nations were in attendance at the important Prague meeting.

At the town hall on 29 May 1925, the baron resigned as IOC president and delivered a lengthy speech, "a frank personal report rather than a flowery discourse." Organized, competitive sport, he said, is not natural to mankind. Neither is the discipline of physical education for the masses. A nation is neither virile or wise unless it supports both enterprises. He doubted (incorrectly) that those gathered at the convention could come up with an amateur definition applicable to every sport federation, although he supported such an effort. He went on for a long time and ended with the most provocative question possible for the future of the Olympic Movement. "Gentlemen," he concluded, "do you wish the Games to be a circus or a temple? The choice is yours." The old man had intimated in a dozen ways that the latter was preferable, the dream of forty years of hard work.

Count Henri de Baillet-Latour of Belgium beat out Monsieurs Polignac and Clary for the top Olympic job. The new IOC president was very wealthy, had a huge racing stable, rode well, and was president of the Brussels Jockey Club. The everlasting question of amateurism was his

Count Baillet-Latour, Belgium, President of the IOC, 1925-1942. Credit IOC Archives.

now, and he seemed no better able to handle it than the baron. The congresses of 1913 and 1921 had noted that each international sport federation might define amateurism as it saw fit. Such delegation of authority continued, although this 1925 Congress conceived "an amateur as one who devotes himself to sport for sport's sake without receiving directly his means of existence." A caveat with long-range implications was added. Not only were professional athletes denied Olympic participation but, more importantly, no amateur athlete was to receive "broken-time" payments for lost salary because of national and international sport competition. England's Reverend Laffan said it would be "a blow to poor people"; future IOC president, J. Sigfrid Edstrom of Sweden, was pleased with the decision. "Broken-time" money payments would "open wide the flood-gates." Clary of France would have preferred support, but just for the all-important Olympic Games. Coubertin returned to Greece in April, 1927—the fourth year of the eighth Olympiad—addressing, as was his custom, the unseen audience rather than the small gathering at Olympia. The Olympic movement is both a practical and idealistic effort to uplift mankind, he said. All of us need to embrace "Olympism" and become "converts to the religion of sport," he concluded.

Back in Paris, the French Olympic Committee was in trouble, for the government refused to allocate even a single franc to send athletes to Amsterdam. In late July of 1927, the perfume king, François Coty, donated a million francs, or one-third the amount needed. Months of haggling continued until, on 15 November 1927, former Premier Edouard Herriot, then Minister of Education, made "a short but spirited oratorical sprint which took the senate's breath away and brought applause and a large majority to his project" of an additional 2,000,000 francs.

Money and politics were never far from the Olympic Games. The latter motivated the Soviet Union, on 28 November, to announce that it would have its own sporting festival rather than attend the games in Holland. The Russians would miss the new entry of women in track-and-field competition, and the reentry, after sixteen years, of Germany. All was merely a repetition of history in these pre-Olympic months. The host city was burdened with near insurmountable problems, the Americans wrestled with their quadrennial dilemma of raising hundreds of thousands of dollars through public donation, the British were sorely vexed at the alleged tacit approval by the IOC of "broken-time" to European soccer players, and the French continued to doubt the wisdom of such nonintellectual enterprise. The baron was ill and unable to attend the games; he sent a message asking that the Olympic flame not only be kept alive, but that it be understood everywhere. "Once again," he said, "I beg to thank those who have followed me and helped me to fight a forty-year war, not often easy and not always cleanly fought."

7 • The Games Become a World Phenomenon 1928 –1944

The new winter Olympic Games, although restricted to athletes from a very few countries, proved very popular, and the second series took place at St. Moritz in January of 1928. Norwegian and Swedish skiers swept the two cross-country races, while Norway's Alf Anderson and Johan Gröttumsbraatan won the jumping and Nordic competitions. Norway's amazing child star, Sonja Henie, outskated Austria's Fritzi Burger and the United States Beatrix Loughran. The men's figure-skating version went to Gillis Grafstrom of Sweden, while the popular "pairs" belonged to France's Andrée Joly and Pierre Brunet. The Finns and Norwegians dominated speed skating, with Clas Thunberg, Ivan Ballangrud, Bernt Evensen, and America's John O'Neil Farrell winning honors. The United States team just beat out Germany in bobsled competition, while Canadian, Swedish, and Swiss ice-hockey teams won gold, silver, and bronze medals. The Coubertin-inspired arts competition, never successfully integrated into the modern Olympic Games, nevertheless produced some skilled artists from Germany, France, Holland, Denmark, Switzerland, Austria, Britain, Luxumbourg, Poland, and Hungary. Adolf Hensel's "The Nuremberg Stadium" won him a gold medal in town planning, while Jan Wils's "Olympic Stadium in Amsterdam" was judged best in architectural design. Sculptor Paul Landowski's "Boxers" won top honors, just as Edwin Grienaur's special "Medals" was deemed the best art entry. In painting and graphic art competition, Isaac Israëls's "The Red Rider" was considered best, just as Jean Jacoby's water-color, "Rugby," was awarded a gold medal. Graphic art, music, lyrics, and epic works competitions made in 1928 Olympic arts display the most impressive effort in this direction. Gold-medal winner Dr. Ferenc Mezo's *History of the Olympic Games* was the definitive work in the field until it was supplanted by the even more accurate 1972 *Encyclopedia of the Olympic Games*, the result of thirty years of research by Austrian journalist Erich Kamper.

The prominent *New York Sun* journalist George Trevor wrote a provocative essay, "The Good and Bad in the Olympic Games," that received wide publicity in the United States just before the summer games of 1928. His message was simple: The Olympic Games are a great sporting event, but why must they everlastingly be viewed as the Pollyanna "sure-cure" for international ill will? Surely one would think they could stand or fall upon their own merits, he said. But no, Trevor continued,

> . . . we must confuse the issue with irrelevant chatter about "international amity," "bringing the millennium a step nearer," "hands across the sea," and all the rest of it. To read some of the pre-Olympic blurbs you would suppose an Olympiad was a cross between a Billy Sunday revival and an international love feast.

Trevor's implication that the Olympic Games are no more than a gigantic world's championship was just as wrong as Coubertin's thirty-five-year sermon that carefully orchestrated, international sporting competitions offered the world a chance for perpetual peace. We have Pierre de Coubertin to thank for a very special kind of athletic experience. The precious personal and collective participation in these games in any capacity, including vicarious television viewing, can be extremely rewarding in several possible physical-psychological dimensions. The very nature of the games contains ingredients of drama, pathos, and exhilaration unlikely to be found in local or regional sport. A Paavo Nurmi, a Johnny Weissmuller, or a Sonja Henie absolutely needed a world stage to play upon. The Olympic Games have been and continue to be a unique, important forum for personalities of this magnitude to reach something close to the ultimate human physical achievement.

Everyone can take something away from the Olympic Games. No cynic can argue this small but precious gift. No evangelist for the games would refuse this modest offering, but he might think twice before demanding too much from them. It may have been, in the early days of the Olympic Movement, that overstatements and superlatives were necessary for the survival of a concept radically new in the world. International sport on a large scale and the Olympic Games have now been with us for nearly a hundred years. An evolution, rather than a revolution, is in order regarding the definition of Olympism. The concept lives. The possibility of collective, and, especially, individual betterment is possible through involvement in the Olympic movement—an idea incorporating universal health, world physical education, sport for all, and, for those at the top of the athletic pyramid, a chance at being Olympic champion. This chapter will deal with the gifted—the very best nonprofessional male and female athletes gathered in Amsterdam, Holland, for the summer games of the ninth Olympiad.

Forty-six countries sent 2,724 men and 290 women to compete in fifteen sports. Athletes from the United States, Finland, Germany, Sweden, France, Holland, Italy, Britain, Canada, and Norway dominated the festival, but men and women from an additional twenty-three countries also won medals. Track-and-field was center stage again, the Yanks and the Finns winning fully fifty percent of the first-place honors. Sober-faced American track coaches, while pleased with the over-all success of their athletes, were disturbed in retrospect that only Ray Barbuti (400 meters) and Elizabeth Robinson (100 meters) won gold medals in individual

Assembly of nations, Opening Day Ceremonies, 1928 Olympic Games, Amsterdam, The Netherlands. Credit John Lucas collection.

running events. The long boat trip, inadequate housing aboard the "floating hotel" *President Roosevelt,* and the almost total lack of training facilities in Amsterdam were forwarded as reasons for this radical departure from American Olympic domination. The rise of European strength, due in part to the dissemination of American coaching techniques, was another reason for the changing in fortune. But the American coaches said unanimously that the exhausting, lengthy series of trials and eliminations leading up to the traumatic final trials at Harvard Stadium on 6–7 July 1928, three weeks before the games began, left many of the athletes exhausted. They were "peaking" early; the American system, with its hundreds of world-class performers, seemed to require weekly eliminations.

Eddie Farrell of Harvard echoed the other coaches in recommending having an Olympic trial one year prior to the games, selecting half the numbers for each event, and then, quietly, and selectively during the Olympic year, adding or dropping athletes from the team. Then the athletes would arrive at the all-important Olympian final refreshed and in top form.

More than half a century after Coach Farrell's sound ideas were published in the *American Olympic Committee Report 1928*, the selection system remains inadequate. No system would have convinced Chimoney, the fastest of the Zuni Indians, to compete in one of the 1928 American regional marathon trials. He had already run an accurate 2:30.0 for a carefully measured forty-two kilometers, the fastest time ever recorded.

Willi Ritola and Paavo Nurmi, both of Finland, followed closely by Sweden's Edwin Wide, in the 1928 Olympic Games 10,000 meter finals. Credit Ronald Smith collection.

Chimoney's religion forbade him from entering white men's competitions or from crossing "the great sea." A good team of ultra-distance runners did, nevertheless, represent the U.S.A. in Amsterdam: William Agee, Harvey Frick, Jimmy Henigan, Al Michelson, and the three-time Olympians Clarence DeMar and Joie Ray. Ray ran a courageous, up-front marathon (2:36:04), finishing fifth behind the French-Algerian dispatch-bearer, Mohamed El Ouafi (2:32:57). Miguel Plaza (Chile), Martti Marttelin (Finland) and Kanematsu Yamada (Japan) finished ahead of the American, thus exemplifying the cosmopolitan nature of these Olympic Games, the first that were somewhat representative of all the continents of the world. Paavo Yrjola and Akilles Jarvinen, strong-arm boys from Finland, took 1–2 in the Olympic decathlon. Finnish athletes Harri Larva, Willi Ritola, Paavo Nurmi, and Toivo Loukola, won all the distance races in the stadium, capturing nine of the twelve medals. Nurmi was not invincible, but his two silver and one gold reconfirmed him as the greatest of all distance runners, "a marvel of fleetness and grace." John H. Finley, writing in the *New York Times*, compounded the Nurmi legend, comparing him to the hero-god in the Finnish folk epic, the *Kalevala*, extolling the twelve-medal winner "who runs as if air was his road."

Writ large on the walls of the Amsterdam stadium are these additional athletics gold-medal winners: Percy Williams (Canada), Douglas Lowe (Britain), Sidney Atkinson (South Africa), David Burghley (Britain), Mikio Oda (Japan), Patrick O'Callaghan (Ireland), Erik Lundkvist (Sweden), Lina Radke (Germany), Ethel Catherwood (Canada), Halina Konopacka (Poland), and the Canadian women's victory in the 4 × 100-meter relay. American men won both relays in record-breaking times. Americans Charles King, Ed Hamm, Carr, John Kuck, and Clarence Houser won the high and long jump, the pole vault, shot, and discus.

The Swedes continued the tradition of victory in the modern pentathlon. Swimming was very big at Amsterdam with more than its share of stars: Johnny Weismuller, Alberto Zorilla, Andrew Charlton, Arne Borg, George Kojak, Buster Crabbe, and the superb double winner in diving, Peter Desjardin. Germany won at water polo, India in field hockey, and the smashing repeat victory of Uruguay over Argentina before mammoth crowds proved, among other things, that soccer was the most popular sport in the world. Weight-lifting honors were divided among men from Austria, Germany, France, and Egypt. The Italians did very well in boxing, as did Argentinian fighters. In the two styles of wrestling, honors were divided between lads from Germany, Estonia, Hungary, Finland, Egypt, Sweden, Switzerland, and the United States. French and Italian fencers dominated foil and épée work, while the Hungarians owned the sabre skills once again. Helene Mayer, German Jewess, not only won the ladies' foil, but would gain an additional measure of fame and controversy at the 1936 Olympic Games. Paul Costello won a third gold medal in rowing in three consecutive games. The Germans, Swiss, British, and Italians also did well in this sport. In the American speciality of eight-oared crew, the University of California crew rowed so fast that according to the *Herald Tribune* correspondent W. O. McGeehan, their time "made them not only the greatest of the crews, but the greatest athletic unit ever developed within my knowledge." Sweden won in yachting; Denmark, Italy, France, and Holland were traditional champions in cycling, while the Dutch, the Germans, the Czechs, and the Spanish won at exotic equestrian sport. Georges Miez of Switzerland was the star gymnast at the 1928 Games, with Dutch, Czech, and Yugoslav men and women displaying championship form in this traditional mid-European sport. A greater orderliness in the selection of events to be contested at the Olympic Games was countered by the growing strength of the many international sport federations and their insistence that more events and greater prominence be given them at the quadrennial festival.

Amateurism being more a state of mind than it is compliance to painfully contrived rules, the arguments dealing with athletes' motivation raged with particular fury during the Olympic year of 1928. The problem was vexing because the American definition of amateurism included massive subsidization of college athletes, while the continental version condoned "broken-time" salary payments to special athletes. The English athlete, and especially the British Olympic establishment, representative of an upper-middle and affluent class, rejected out of hand both the American and the European model.

For almost the entire history of the International Olympic Committee—until the late 1970s—nothing was done to settle the much-debated controversy. The English press, in perpetual anger at amateur and Olympic abuses, echoed the London *Daily Express* with the comment that "The British nation, profoundly interested in sport, is intensely uninterested in the Olympic Games." The thoughtful American journalist John R. Tunis thought the Olympic Games was a good idea gone sour. The grim road to gold medals sacrifices opportunities for friendship or sportsmanship; the "unnecessary ballyhoo" adds nothing to the games, he said. For some, an ever-growing number, the quicksilver of world peace was certainly not to be won by staging quadrennial Olympic Games. Coubertin, always quick to respond to critics, wrote in the 7 November 1928 *Sport Suisse* that "Sport, at its very best, has the capacity to contribute to human progress." He enjoyed the view from Mount Olympus, almost always talked in terms of ultimates and ideals. It was always his great strength and great weakness. The next year, on 6 March 1929, in Paris, Coubertin delivered one of his most passionate lectures,

"Olympie," ending with a reminder that the best of ancient societies has been transferred to a modern Olympic setting and that this "essential sap" is needed to revitalize world societies. "Nations are only slain when they wish to die," he cried, and Olympism may some day contribute some of the essential yeast to national upliftment.

Major General Douglas MacArthur, president of the American Olympic committee, an admirer of Coubertin, and a totally involved spectator at the Amsterdam games, wrote a memorable report to his commander-in-chief, Calvin Coolidge. MacArthur repeated a familiar ideology that "we must build athletically not only for health but for character," that the athletic code (Coubertin called it Olympism) is a kind of religion embracing ethics and the highest moral law. He was proud of the American Olympic team and their successful coupling of skill with honor. " 'Athletic America' is a telling phrase," he said. "It is talismanic. . . . If I were required to indicate today that element of American life which is most characteristic of our nationality, my finger would unerringly point to our athletic escutcheon." From out of Berlin, at the same time as the general's report, and with a similar patriotic ring, the *Boersen Courier* reminded the world of the twenty-nine medals won by Germany at the recent Olympic Games "despite war, hunger, blockade and inflation. . . ." The old linkage of national virility with Olympic medals began in earnest and would continue escalation for the next half-century and more.

A long time ago—nearly fifty years—President Robert Gordon Sproul of the University of California spoke to 105,000 people at the inauguration of the Games of the Tenth Olympiad of the modern era. The date was 30 July 1932, and the new Los Angeles Memorial Colosseum was the place. At 2 P.M., immediately preceding the administration of the Olympic Oath to the assembled contestants, the remarkable Sproul said he hoped the games would lift the life of men and women to higher physical, spiritual, and moral values, that the love of and dedication to sport displayed would be an inspiration, and that the reciprocal good will and sportsmanship might help "wash away the immemorial feuds of mankind." President Sproul was then, and would continue to be for another generation, one of the nation's great educators. He reminded the vast audience that the ancient Olympic games were religious experiences, and, during their best years, "a solemn reunion in Greek energy, the totality of human activity, physical, mental and spiritual, . . ." He hoped that all present, with one heart and one voice, might embrace this ancient sporting philosophy—a kind of universal sportsmanship that the modern games' founder, Baron Pierre de Coubertin, called Olympism.

The main responsibility for the success of the games was in the hands of William May Garland and journalist Bill Henry, the sports technical director. But thousands of men and women shared in the success of this most pacific of all Olympic Games. Future International Olympic Committee president J. Sigfrid Edstrom was concerned about the oppressive heat in the city of Los Angeles during an earlier summer visit. During the two-week period of 1931, corresponding to the games period a year later, careful records were kept to prove that Los Angeles had good weather. "It was the committee's misfortune, however, to have a real heat wave in Southern California during the first two weeks of August 1931, and the traitorous readings, hovering around the one hundred-degree mark, were hastily suppressed." Happily, fifteen days of seventy- and eighty-degree days greeted the 1932 athletes. Some 50,000 fans were outside the stadium, unable to see the "Tribune of Honor," the "Parade of Nations," and the 2,000-voice choir celebrate: "Now sing of virile games by which the body's beauty is made to live once more. . . ." After Sproul's speech and one by Vice-President of the United States Charles Curtis, 2,000 doves were released, the symbolic Olympic flag raised, and Lieutenant George C. Calnan, USN, an American fencer, gave the Olympic Oath, repeating it "as though he meant it." The chorus followed with "Lest We Forget." A *Los Angeles Times* correspondent noticed that "wet eyes in the stands above were dabbed at in a surreptitious way."

Paavo Nurmi, silent, with thin lips clamped tightly, sat glumly in the stands, barred from competition for having taken excessive travel expenses. But he was gracious when Douglas Fairbanks and Amelia Earhart came over to shake his hand. Jim Thorpe, at first denied admission to the stadium, sat in the press box weeping silently, remembering past glories and tragedy. Puckish Will Rogers attended every day's activities, allegedly never recovering from seeing the entire American men's team wearing French berets as they entered the stadium. "Those 'boudwoir caps,' " he cried, "are bad enough on a Frenchman, but on an American they are a scream." Society columnist Alma Whitaker was shocked that the enraptured crowd never even gave a passing glance to the likes of Joe E. Brown, Tallulah Bankhead, Ethel, Lionel, and John Barrymore, the Marx Brothers, Gary Cooper, Bing Crosby, Cary Grant, and Buster Keaton—all sitting in the stands watching another kind of superstar.

The radiant California sun, unapproached facilities, and another world generation of talented, disciplined athletes disposed of most Olympic records. Eddie Tolan, Ralph Metcalfe, Billy Carr, and Stella Walsh owned the sprints; Luigi Beccali, the Finns, and Zabala dominated distance events; Edward Gordon, Chuhei Nambu, William Miller, Jarvinen, Leo Sexton, and Ireland's Patrick O'Callaghan wrote their names large in Olympic history. The French and Italians dominated cycling and fencing, and the Americans, surprisingly, won heavily in gymnastics. The Swedes Johan Oxenstierna and Bo Lindman carried on

Mildred "Babe" Didrikson, three-medal winner of the 1932 Olympic Games. She was the first great female track and field star. Credit Ronald Smith collection.

that country's pentathlon tradition. In swimming, Buster Crabbe won the 400 meters, but the Japanese won everything else. America swept both diving events. Middle Europeans were strong in weight lifting and wrestling while the provocative trio of American girls, Helene Madison, Eleanor Holm, and Dorothy Poynton, captured swimming and diving gold medals.

Olympic protocol allowed the organizing committee to arrange two demonstration sports. Football players from Yale, Harvard, and Princeton, the East team, played a vigorous game against a West team from California, Stanford, and Southern California. Three games of exhibition lacrosse were played on 7, 9, and 12 August. A Johns Hopkins team beat a Canadian all-star group 5–3 in the opener, played before 75,000 spectators. In the second game, "the Americans showed notable skill and teamwork and were victorious 7 to 4, thus winning the series two games to one, with a total score of 16 goals to 12."

Another kind of Olympic games—art competitions and exhibitions— occupied the Los Angeles Museum. General Charles H. Sherrill was in charge of 1,100 exhibits by artists from thirty-one nations. Painting, sculpture, architecture, literature, and music prizes were awarded. Blue-ribbon juries as well as artists were on hand. For example, selecting the best of the literature were William Lyon Phelps, Thornton Wilder, Hugh Walpole, and André Maurois. They thought Avery Brundage's essay, "The Significance of Amateur Sport," good enough for honorable mention.

Coubertin did not attend these games. Retired since 1925, the Olympic *renovateur* was celebrating his seventieth birthday in 1932. In a Lausanne, Switzerland, speech that year, he repeated himself by calling for a world recognition of an old Grecian theme of joy through physical effort, intellectual and spiritual balance acting as catalyst for "honest, complete, and unremitting altruism." He said it a hundred different ways, this hymn of Olympism. The actions of most athletes at Los Angeles spoke of Olympism with equal eloquence and far greater clarity to the "man on the street." Coubertin was often very little understood. Only radical educational reform, he said, can save mankind, and that education must include salubrious sport for all men and women from childhood to old age. Coubertin enjoyed rowing and moderate exercise in his last year. For the person trapped in a technocracy, lifelong exercise is a must. Olympic sport is only the tip of the iceberg, he felt; all of us must view personal involvement in sport as did the Greeks—"in a spirit of almost religious reverence."

Coubertin founded one of the most important social and sporting institutions, the modern Olympic games. The universal philosophy of these games he named Olympism, a blend of the very best Greek, chivalric, and English sporting traditions. In every case, this code placed personal and community pride, all-around excellence, the rational development of the competitive instinct, and a sense of joy above making a profit from athletics.

William May Garland, the organizational genius behind these 1932 games, was fortunate to have on his executive council Zack J. Farmer, Gwynn Wilson, H. O. Davis, Bill Henry, and J. F. MacKenzie. They did their job so well that every succeeding Olympic organizing committee has looked back at Los Angeles as a model and as the beginning of massive technological innovations into the movement. The idea of an Olympic Village was born in Los Angeles; the daring use of a stadium seating in excess of one-tenth of a million people had proved successful; public information, not only at the various stadia but worldwide, reached new heights; a thousand policemen were specifically assigned to the games to help avoid major confrontations; photographic, medical, and press arrangements were models of efficiency. Eight months of scientific artistry by Switzerland's finest watchmakers went into the production of the thirty stopwatches used at the games. The twenty-one jewel Omega watches were tested for accuracy by an electric chronograph connected to an underground astronomical clock, the latter enclosed in a pressurized vault kept at an even fifty-nine degrees. The performance of this clock was "regulated by the stars with a meridian telescope and checked against radio reports from other observatories."

Of course there were problems—some small, some humorous, some serious. The substitute lap-counter made the steeplechase runners do eight and three-quarters instead of seven and three-quarters laps. Volmari Iso-Hollo of Finland won anyway. Lord David Burghley, defending champ in the 400-meter hurdles, was disappointed at his fourth place finish and angry at a front-page photograph of himself, the caption calling him "the poorly conditioned ex-champ." There were "incidents" in the women's high-jump, in the men's 5,000-meter final, with the Brazilian water-polo team, and at the disputed 100-meter-dash final; there were disquieting rumors of oxygen administered to the Japanese swimmers.

And yet, when it was all over and the joy filled closing ceremonies of the Games of the Tenth Olympiad took place on 13 August, most agreed with the famed sport journalist Braven Dyer that this was indeed "the greatest show in all history." Grantland Rice, doyen of correspondents, called it the "greatest sporting pageant in world history." "Citus, Fortius, Altius"—the Olympic motto had become a metaphor for swifter, braver, better in international relations. The spellbound 100,000 spectators listened to the great chorus sing the Hawaiian farewell, "Aloha." "Taps" was played as the standards, standard bearers, flags, and flag bearers, disappeared through the tunnel. The torch faded in its great bronze bowl. Coubertin's words remained emblazoned on the scoreboard: "The main issue in life is not the victory but the fight." The 1932 games had passed into history.

Coubertin was seventy years of age in 1932. He was failing, but always rallied when it came to making a speech. At a birthday ceremony in Lausanne, he recalled great bygone days in that city, commanded his seen and unseen audience to lives of "unremitting altruism," and then, paraphrasing Goethe, petitioned all to "strike boldly through the mist." In his 1934 "Message to American Youth," he reminded them of their greatest leader, Theodore Roosevelt, with whom he shared the same philosophy of morality, mind, and muscle—and definitely in that order of importance. Finally, in a message broadcast from Berlin on 4 August 1935, Coubertin repeated for the hundredth time the reverential compo-

nent of Olympism, the exquisitely aristocratic and yet egalitarian character of Olympism, and, finally, the peace potential of Olympism.

Few listened to the old man in this bellicose year of 1935. Massive
unemployment in Europe and North America, the angry and provocative
voice of Chancellor Adolf Hitler, in Germany and Mussolini's murder of
Ethiopia all drowned out the voice of the French baron. His message
appeared hopelessly outdated. As the Carl Diem-inspired Olympic torch
relay wended its way from Olympia to Berlin's great stadium, Coubertin
repeated to the athletes that the "cult of athletics" at its noblest level
teaches toughness and instills within individuals the capacity to solve
problems. His Olympian litany would be severely tested as Hitler and his
lieutenants came close to wresting control of the 1936 Olympic Games
away from Count Henri de Baillet-Latour and his International Olympic
Committee.

The huge, half-built sunken stadium in Berlin, unused since the
abortive 1916 Olympic Games, was enlarged to accommodate 110,000
persons. With Los Angeles as a high model, the German sports, military,
and political establishments threw themselves into the great enterprise.
Everything was planned with superlatives in mind; almost all were
intoxicated with the emerging glory of the German Fatherland. Make no
mistake, the I.O.C. knew that it was in a dogfight with Hitler, Goebbels,
and the inner circle. As late as fall 1935, Baillet-Latour warned that, if the
Olympic statutes were not observed in every way, "we possess the power to
remove the games from Berlin." However, all seemed well with him, and
with American Olympic Committee President Avery Brundage, despite
significant European opposition and a powerful anti-Nazi, anti-Olympic
Movement in the United States. In the Bavarian village of Garmische
Partenkirchen, in an opening-day blizzard, the fourth winter Olympic
Games began. Although twenty-seven countries were represented by 266
competitors, all the gold medals were won by Scandinavians, Germans,
Austrians, Swiss, Americans in two-man bobsled, and a Canadian-
dominated, British ice-hockey team. Some of the names were familiar—
repeaters from Lake Placid and St. Moritz. Karl Schäfer, Henie, Birger
Rudd, and especially Ivar Ballangrud, dominated. Adolf Hitler showed
up, along with tens of thousands of other curious spectators—comfirming
these nontraditional Olympic sports as an integral part of the games.

To the north, in Berlin, the most complete facilities for Olympic Games
were nearing completion. Money was no problem, and Sports Com-
missioner Dr. Diem forged ahead with the world's largest swimming pool,
a stadium seating 18,000, separate venues for most of the events, and a
festival ground where a million spectators might watch gymnastic displays. Perfection in every detail was his goal. Electrical and chronometric
devices of the highest sophistication were used everywhere. And, of

course, there was the Olympic Village (for men)—a massive affair modeled after the one in Los Angeles, consisting of 160 buildings, each housing twenty-four to twenty-six athletes, and 38 dining halls catering to national tastes, which prompted someone to say that "the best place to eat in Berlin is at the Olympic Village." All possible training facilities, including a brand new 400-meter track, a lovely artificial lake, and natural wooded surroundings were available and served as a hard-to-match model for all future Olympics. Diem organized the relay of runners from Olympia, Greece (20 July 1936) to the Berlin stadium for the opening day ceremonies (1 August). Three thousand youths, each running one

Dr. Carl Diem, Germany, pioneer physical educator and Olympic Games administrator. Credit Frau Liselotte Diem.

kilometer while holding aloft his own 1,300-gram torch donated by the Krupp Steel Company, raced through Athens, Sofia, Yugoslavia, Budapest, and Prague into Germany, where a relay team of 267 young people ended on the Via Triumphalis, guarded by 10,000 storm troopers.

Everything centered at the stadium: 110,000 expectant, almost mesmerized spectators, the airship *Hindenburg* hanging overhead with the Olympic flag trailing behind, the ranking officers of the Hitler regime, the IOC members, and diplomats from every continent were there. Coubertin was in Lausanne, too ill to attend. It was all surrealistic: Richard Strauss and the Berlin Symphony Orchestra, a chorus of 3,000, the tolling of the ten-foot, ten-ton Olympic bell, the presentation of flowers to Hitler by Diem's five-year-old daughter, and the long, emotion-packed march of the athletes. There was much more. The recorded voice of Coubertin filling the stadium with his canonical Olympic code, an overlong, pompous speech by Dr. Lewald, and Hitler's perfunctory sixteen words opening the games, continued the much-praised, much-criticized opening day ceremonies. The raising of 100 national Olympic flags, a trumpet flourish, the booming of cannon, the release of 20,000 doves, the singing of a new Olympic hymn, and, finally, the entrance of the ultimate relay runner, that paragon of German youth described by Richard Mandell in his definitive *The Nazi Olympics* as "a polestar, a fabulous, newly minted figure of mythology!" With right hands upraised, the ocean of athletes listened in silent agreement to the reading of the Olympic oath. Handel's "Hallelujah Chorus" burst forth, there was the awesome presentation of an olive sprig to Hitler by the living Olympic legend, Spyridon Loues himself. Orchestral music followed the joy-filled crowd as they left the stadium, unaware that the Olympian link with the future had been consummated that day by an IOC telegram to the mayor of Tokyo, informing that happy gentleman that the Games of the Twelfth Olympiad would take place in his city in the summer of 1940. Tens of thousands of overjoyed Japanese shouted "Banzai," and the Olympic flag was hoisted in 600 Tokyo schools. Back at Berlin's stadium, the perceptive *Tribune* journalist Jesse Abramson called it all "a tumultous sixteen hours of military, religious and fervid nationalistic celebrations." The impatient athletes would be released the following day.

The games had been streamlined to sixteen days and would continue this pattern through the Moscow Games of 1980. On Day two, 2 August 1936, Ilmari Salminen, Arvo Askola, and Iso-Hollo swept the twenty-five-lap, 10,000-meter race, beating back the courageous Kohei Murakosa; the fabulous Jesse Owens sped a world-record 10.2 seconds for a hundred-meter trial; Cornelius Johnson, David Albritton, and Del Thurber dominated the high jump, and Hans Woelke surprised everyone in the shot-put final. Tilly Fleischer's 45.18 meters broke "Babe"

Didrikson's Olympic javelin record, while Tony Terlazzo and Anwar Mohammed Mesbah won gold in featherweight and lightweight lifting.

Earlier in the day, Hitler had greeted each of the first three champions, but he had left his loge long before the two black high jumpers completed their task. Baillet-Latour quickly reminded Hitler that Olympic protocol demanded he congratulate every winner or none. He chose the latter for

Jesse Owens, USA, winner of four gold medals in Berlin, 1936, voted greatest sprinter of twentieth century's first fifty years. Credit Track and Field News, Inc., California.

the remainder of the games. A perceptive editorialist in the next morning's *Herald Tribune* wondered whether the great festival "really belongs to the realm of sport or of diplomatic history." The Olympic fathers were sure, but remained uneasily vigilant for the next two weeks.

Day three, 3 August, was filled with trials and a meteoric final in the 100 meters by Owens, the "Buckeye Bullet." Karl Hein beat the world in the sixteen-pound hammer, won his country's first athletics gold medal, and received the warmest (although unofficial, behind-the-stadium) greetings from Der Führer. Louis Hostin earned gold and an Olympic record for his three-lift total of 372.5 kilograms.

Day four, 4 August, was a memorable one for freestyle wrestling champions Kustaa Pihlajamaki, Karoly Karpati, Frank Lewis, Emile Poilve, Knut Fridell, and heavyweight Kristjan Palusala—six gold-medal winners from six different countries. At center stage, Owens beat Luz Long with an Olympic long jump of 8.06 meters; the still-uncontrolled talent of John Woodruff won the 800 meters; smooth Glen Hardin raced to victory over ten barriers at the 400-meter hurdles; the brilliant Helen Stephens's 11.5 seconds was a world record for 100 meters; and Gisela Mauermayer's discus record, although primitive by today's standards, was a dozen feet ahead of the 1932 Olympic record. The Italian tradition continued as the Italians won the men's team foil honors. The impressive victories by American blacks so early in the games prompted one editorialist to wonder with tongue-in-cheek "how Nazi ethnologists will rationalize this one." On this same day, the famed Swedish explorer and Asiatic geographer, Sven Hedin, congratulated all Olympic champions for their "boundless energy, iron will, and intense training," hoping that this combination of qualities would aid them personally and collectively to a more universal fulfillment. It was his own definition of Olympism.

Day five, 5 August, saw Owens run 200 meters in 20.7 sec. and Harold Whitlock walk 31 miles in 4½ hours—both amazing feats, world and Olympic records. Ken Carpenter from the University of Southern California won the discus, while schoolmate, Earle Meadows edged Shuhei Nishida in the vault. Another wrestling title was settled by Zombori, Ilona Elek won the ladies' foil crown, while El-Touni and Josef Manger won gold at middle- and heavyweight lifting.

All the way across the sea in New Orleans, Louisiana, Ernest Lee Jahncke, former assistant secretary of the Navy, was fighting to keep his seat on the IOC. A powerful coalition had demanded his resignation; Jahncke replied: "I shall not resign solely because of my opposition to America's participation in the Berlin Games." Summarily, he was relieved of his position and soon replaced by Avery Brundage, the driving force behind the United States's presence in Berlin.

It was all track-and-field on day six, 6 August, as Jack Lovelock beat Glen Cunningham and a super 1,500-meter field with a world record; Naoto Tajima won another world best in the triple jump; Forrest Towns, the world's best high hurdler, made first place; a popular Gerhard Stöck won a popular javelin victory, breaking the Scandinavian monopoly. Valla's 11.7 seconds in the 80-meter hurdles final was one-tenth slower than her Olympic heat, but she won both races. In the military pentathlon, Lieutenant Gotthard Handrick scored fewer points (31½) than Lieutenant Charles Leonard (39½), thus winning the gold medal in a harsh contest of shooting, fencing, swimming, riding, and cross-country running.

Nothing could stop the German spectators, and unprecedented num-

*Glen Cunningham, USA, silver medalist in 1936 Olympic 1500 meter run.
Credit John Lucas collection.*

bers of visitors jam-packed almost every venue every day, prompting one observer to note the "almost hysterical Olympic spirit that has gripped this nation's capital." There are those that would argue with Mr. Abramson's use of the word Olympic in this context.

Day seven, 7 August, saw relatively obscure Olympic events compete in vain with track-and-field. At least in the States, Archie Williams's 400-meter victory and that of Gunnar Hockert in the 5,000 meters were much more publicized than the equally precious gold medals won by pistol-shooters van Oyen and Ullman (559 perfect shots out of 600), by sprint cyclist Toni Merkens (in unprecedented fashion, fined 100 gold francs but not disqualified for an obstruction), by canoe specialists Ludwig Landen, Vaclav Mottl, Zdenek Skrdlant, Gregor Hradetzky, Sven Johansson, Eric Bladström, and the uneven 11–0 polo victory of Argentina over Britain.

Willy Rogenberg won a rifle gold medal on day eight, 8 August, with 300 out of 300 shots in the bull's-eye. The Italian épée team, cyclists Arie van Vliet, the tandem-cycle team of Ernst Ihbe and Carl Lorenz, plus the French pursuit cycle-team showed traditional European strength. Four canoe finals were settled this day in relative anonymity, while, close by, the entire sport world heard of the dramatic decathlon sweep by buddies Glenn Morris, Bob Clark, and Jack Parker. Iso-Hollo repeated as Olympic champion in the 3,000-meter steeplechase.

Day nine, 9 August, was Greco-Roman wrestling day as six gold medals were awarded, while the tough, little one-hundred-pound Kitei Son won the 42-kilometer marathon; the Americans and British shared honors in the 400-meter relay (39.8 seconds, a world record) and the 1,600-meter relay. The German team, the best women's relay team in the world, dropped the baton on the last exchange, the huge partisan crowd groaned, the Americans swept to victory, and the four German girls wept uncontrollably. Eyewitnesses noted that not one of the young women dared look up at Hitler's box seat. Stylist Ibolya Czak won the women's high-jump, while countryman Ferenc Csik won the 100-meter freestyle in the nearby Olympic pool. Owens collected his fourth gold medal this day and left immediately with a group of Americans for Cologne and another international competition.

Day ten, 10 August, saw the dominant female swimmer of the world, Hendrika Mastenbroek, collect the first of her four medals (three gold, one silver). Yachting finals were held in Kiel Harbor, while the brilliant Robert Charpentier won the individual 100-kilometer cycling road race, his French team winning the collective title. In Cologne, Owens was agonizing between keeping his well-publicized commitment to tour Europe with the American track team or returning home immediately to become a very wealthy athletic entertainer. Caught in the cross fire, this greatest sprinter of the century sailed for New York, was soon drummed out of the amateur athletic ranks, and, maddeningly, made very little money as a pro.

Day eleven, 11 August, saw the finals of the 4 × 200 meter freestyle relay (Japan, in a world-record 8:51.5), springboard diving for men (Richard Degener), "200"-breaststroke for women (Hideko Maehata), épée winner Ricardi, and the gymnastics final dominated by the superior skills of Georges Miez and Albert Schwartzmann.

The next day, 12 August, gave the German women an opportunity to finish just ahead of the Czech team, and well in front of Hungarian, Yugoslav, American, and Polish gymnasts. Jack Medica broke Crabbe's Olympic 400-meter swimming-record with a 4:44.5 sprint, while thirteen-year-old Marjorie Gestring, Katherine Rawls, and Dorothy Hill-Poynton dominated springboard diving. What amused the world press, however, was the American exhibition baseball game, played at night before 100,000 bewildered spectators. One newspaper headline chuckled: "Baseball Planned to Enlighten Berlin Puts 100,000 in the Dark." The massive crowd never did fathom the purpose of third base, or, as they called it, third location, nor did they understand why the fielders "spent most of their time caddying in the shadows for the elusive ball. Even the Americans in the dark." Everyone cheered everything, in a kind of mindless human festival.

Dina Senff beat Hendrika Mastenbroek in the 100-meter women's backstroke on day thirteen, 13 August; as usual, the Hungarian sabre team was superior; equally impressive was Heinz Pollay in the individual dressage, and his German comrades in team competition. The Olympic Games were nearly over, and it was obvious that the organizing committee and the German athletes were doing a brilliant job, a job, some astute observers pointed out uneasily, that was "too good."

On day fourteen, 14 August, eight-oared crew finals were settled, the blue-ribbon event won by the University of Washington over Italy and Germany; only one second separated the three shells. The usually efficient Germans had decided to contest Olympic basketball in the out-of-doors. With the game's inventor watching the finals in a heavy downpour, the U.S. quintet managed a 19–8 win over Canada on a mud-filled clay court. The Germans, Austrians, and Swiss had their way in team handball.

As if in anticipation of the end of the games, 15 August, day fifteen, was crammed with finals, including eight boxing finals and the same water polo (Hungary versus Germany) results as in 1932, the Magyars coming out on top. Endre Kabos won individual sabre, and the Indians continued their domination of field hockey with an 8–1 decision over Germany. Adolf Kiefer dominated backstroke competition with a 1:05.9 Olympic victory; Noburu Terada finished 21 seconds ahead of Medica in the swimming

1,500, while Marshall Wayne proved to be the best platform diver. The impressive closing ceremonies on the last day, 16 August, were preceded by equestrian finals. Outside the stadium, the three-day riding event became a Pyrrhic victory for Ludwig Stubbendorf. The course was much too tough, dangerous to horse and rider. Veteran sport journalist Peter Wilson saw it this way:

> Three horses had to be destroyed. . . . Of the fifty horses, twenty-seven completed the cross-country course and the notorious pond took heavy toll. Here the horse had to jump a fence into water and the depth was clearly uneven. Of the forty-six who attempted this, eighteen fell and ten horses unseated their riders.

Stubbendorf, aboard "Nurmi," led the Germans to an easy team-victory over the Poles. Some said as many as 120,000 people jammed the stadium on this lazy, warm Sunday afternoon.

To say that the closing ceremonies were impressive is to understate the magnificent finale. Mandell's *The Nazi Olympics* devotes an entire chapter, called "Farewells, Conclusions," to the quite extraordinary closing ceremonies. It took several hours of high drama and theater, of pageantry and symbolism, before the "holy fire" was finally extinguished and the games of the eleventh Olympiad of the modern era were finished.

The jury has been out ever since these Berlin Olympics became history. Mandell judged them to be an essentially Hitler-inspired "Nazi Olympics." F. T. Birchall, writing in the *New York Times* about that memorable Sunday closing ceremony was terribly impressed by the whole Olympic spectacle that he had just witnessed for sixteen days. And yet he was observant enough to see that this particular set of games was unable to emancipate itself "from the goose-stepping tradition." Ralph Barnes' column in the *New York Herald Tribune* found little to cheer about, suggesting that the astonishing success of male and female German athletes might significantly aid the maniacal Nazi cause. He was alternately amused and made uneasy at the wildly rapturous victory celebrations of the German audiences followed by silent, glum dejection when a German lost. For reasons difficult for him to explain, he didn't like the supercharged, contrasting atmospheres, noting that, in the English translation, the lyric " 'Take your discus in your hand, throw it for your Fatherland' . . . seemed slightly ridiculous, but in the German original they didn't seem so to those who competed for the German Fatherland."

Four and one-half million tickets were sold in Berlin that fortnight; nearly eight million marks were spent by visitors; 160,000 television viewers in twenty-one Berlin locations watched the spectacle via this new media. William L. Shirer saw it all and admitted it was very, very good—too good, for

. . . Hitler and his Nazi thugs had succeeded in making the XIth Olympiad the most colorful in history and, what was more important, had used the Olympics to fool the world into believing that Nazi Germany was a peaceful, civilized and contented nation.

The president of the IOC, Baillet-Latour, disagreed with this veiled assessment that the games had been taken away from him. At any time up to the eve of the competitions themselves, he said, the IOC could have cancelled the games. Opinion vacilated from "splendid achievement by a new and energetic German people" to a Berlin atmosphere "odiously chauvinistic and military." Oddly, both feelings were correct. Bill Henry, Olympic historian, was preoccupied with something else—the "living denial of the purely Nazi racial theories." Men and women of every color, from scores of nationalities, and from every continent had won Olympic medals. Regardless of the Berlin magnificence, he says in an *Approved History of the Olympic Games,* these games

. . . by their very enormousness, were getting away from the ideal of the ancient games, in which the individual athlete's victory was personal, surpassing in every way the surroundings, the spectators, the officials; even the nation he represented was proud to honor him, rather than seeking to claim his glory for itself.

Adolf Hitler was transported by the success of the 1936 Olympic Games. His mad dream of a great Germanic empire seemed possible in the spring of 1937 when he visited Albert Speer's Berlin showroom. The official Nazi architect and genuine intellectual showed him a seven-foot high model of a stadium for 400,000. Hitler was gleeful, and announced that, after the Tokyo games of 1940, the Olympics "will take place in Germany for all time to come, in this stadium." Another star in the Hitler firmament at this time was the brilliant film-maker Leni Riefenstahl. All during 1937, she was absorbed in editing her Hitler-commissioned "Olympia," a block-busting, 220-minute, supremely artistic film of the 1936 Olympic Games. The heavy impress of German youth depicted in the award-winning film has been alternately viewed as (1) Nazi propaganda, (2) a near-perfect film re-creation of Olympic Games that were, in truth, dominated by German athletes, and (3) a visual manifestation of Leni Riefenstahl's sensual-artistic preoccupation with the athletic human body—especially the male physique. The three interpretations come through clearly in the film. Her one hundred cameramen took 1,300,000 feet of film at a cost of $7,000,000. She took two years to edit every foot, and, in 1938, "Olympia I—Festival of the Nations" and "Olympia II—Festival of Beauty" emerged as her own personal testimony. One of her biographers, Glenn Infield, pointed out that "The threat of war, the

Jewish problem, the brutal policies of Hitler—all were ignored. Art, not moral responsibility, was her goal." She was driven by some inner compulsion, and drove her crew mercilessly. Her word was law. During the filming inside the Olympic Village—restricted to men—Miss Riefenstahl directed the film crew in martinet fashion, handing dreaded pink slips to any cameraman in the wrong place at the wrong time. Receipt of two such slips, which said, "Remove yourself immediately from where you are—Riefenstahl," meant permanent removal of the offender. She was a tough, talented, sensuously attractive woman; she had a restless, searching, experimenting mind that was obsessed with the beauty and grace of the human body.

As a member of the Nazi inner circle, the worldwide success of "Olympia" failed to keep Riefenstahl a heroine after World War II— except among the artistic community. A political exile, the indomitable film-maker made it clear that she never took a political position. "I have always been a romantic and loved beauty," she repeated after fifteen years of film making in central Africa during the 1960s and 1970s. A vigorous woman in her seventies, Riefenstahl published a remarkably illustrated book, *The Last of the Nuba* (1973). In several ways, the text as well as the Nuba warrior-wrestler photographs are reminiscent of her "Olympia" film. Hymns of praise for the athletic human body, manifestations of individual and collective pride, permeate the film and the book. Over thirty-five years separate the two as her cameras linger on the panther-grace of Owens and the skill of the Nuba wrestling champion. "The strength of the wrestlers vitalizes the rest of the community," she says. Thus, wrestling transcends sport and becomes the supercharged Nuba way of life. Psychological, social, and religious significances are attached to this level (wrestling) of sport competition and is, she concluded, "the expression in the visible and social world of the invisible world of the mind and of the spirit." Three more years in the African Sudan produced another Riefenstahl special, *The People of Kau,* an even more visually startling book of glistening, perfectly sculptured male bodies. Paul Zimmerman's essay in the 29 November 1976 *Newsweek* called her a photographer almost without a rival—a woman whose "very genius lies in the ability of her art to stir passions, to serve a vision and to capture 'beauty' in its most romantic sense." The ancient Greeks might well have appreciated Leni, for her anthropomorphic philosophy—one that conceived physical beauty and inner goodness as inseparable—was shared by both.

Things did not go well for Baillet-Latour and his IOC—mostly because the world itself did poorly for the decade following the Berlin games. Inevitably, worldwide sabre-rattling and frenetic political rhetoric drowned unsteady Olympic Committee efforts for the realizable 1940 games. The perpetually complaining British, again unhappy at their

Olympic showing, lamented their lost glory in sport. *The Spectator* of 21 August 1936 treated its audience to the ultimate rationalization, concluding that "When to win the Olympic Games becomes an object of British, as it has German, policy, we shall really have reached the stage of senility, the true decadence." Larger matters were brewing, and, in October and November of that year, the Berlin-Rome Axis was formed; Hitler denounced the Versailles Treaty, and the German government recognized the insurgent Spanish General Franco. The hard-headed Brundage addressed 20,000 German-Americans in Madison Square Garden on 4 October 1936, defending the decision to send the American team to Berlin as an anti-Communist, pro-American act of patriotism. Jahncke, still bitter about his July expulsion from the IOC for leading the battle to keep the U.S.A. out of the Olympics, lashed back in an 11 November 1936 "Letter to the *New York Times*" in which he denied being a traitor to the Olympic Ideal; he quoted from a copy made by the International Committee for the Preservation of the Olympic Ideal allegedly proving German repression of churchmen, racism, military-political control of the Berlin Olympics, and "extraordinary chauvinism."

The year 1937 opened uneasily on a destitute, Lausanne-bound Coubertin. Although receiving financial help from the German Olympic Organizing Committee, he felt honor bound to refuse 50,000 Swiss francs from a newly-created Coubertin Educational Fund. Baillet-Latour hoped that the baron would reconsider and accept the money on 1 January 1938, Coubertin's seventy-fifth birthday. But on 2 September 1937, the famous old man collapsed and passed away while walking in a Geneva garden. "The world has lost a genius," lamented Baillet-Latour.

Coubertin's *Bulletin du CIO* ceased publication, but was resumed in April of the following year as a result of a Coubertin letter dated 16 March 1937, urging Dr. Diem and his associates to "carry on the cause." Diem published the letter in a new *Olympic Review* for April 1938:

> I wasn't able to complete what I wanted to accomplish. What would be dearest by far to me would be the creation of a very modest small institute in Germany, in memory of the Games of the XIth Olympiad, to which I would leave all my papers, documents, unfinished projects concerning the whole of modern Olympism in order to dispel previous inaccuracies. I think that an Olympic Study Center, not necessarily in Berlin, would more than anything else support progress of this movement and preserve it from ideological deviation, of which I am so fearful.

During Coubertin's 1927 visit to Olympia, he and the IOC member from Greece, John Ketseas, talked in a general sort of way about a permanent, annual sport festival at the sacred site. Ketseas and Diem, rolling the idea around in their thinking, never forgot this unfinished mandate to create some meaningful institution, and, many years later in 1961, in their own old age, the two Olympic leaders founded the International Olympic Academy, a brave effort for athletes, students, and scholars from every country in the world to come live together, and to discuss and debate the viability of the Olympic movement.

These were the "lost years" of the Olympic movement. Moving in quiet desperation against the background of the Japanese conquest of China and never-ending European military rumblings, the IOC suffered through the years 1937 and 1938. American IOC member Garland, upon returning in June of 1937 from an inspection of the progress of Tokyo's building for the 1940 Olympics, announced that the only problem was "whether to build a coliseum seating 100,000 or 150,000." A few weeks later, at the Marco Polo Bridge near Peiping, Japanese troops clashed with Chinese and a large-scale war began in the north of that country. Mr. Brundage, recently elected to the IOC, grimly announced on 12 January 1938 that the next games would be held in Japan or not at all. Japan's military policy is of no consequence to us, he said. "Sport transcends all political or racial considerations," he reiterated in language identical to that used prior to the Berlin games. He reminded Judge Jeremiah T. Mahoney, leader of the 1936 American Olympic boycott, and all new foes of perpetual games participation that the host city does no more than carry out IOC orders, and that its narrow but essential role is to provide a good facility for the athletes. Tokyo "has no more to do with the judges, referees, timers, or with the conduct of the events than any of the visiting nations," rumbled Brundage as he quoted from the *Olympic Rules and Regulations*.

On the same day, 12 March 1938, that IOC members, meeting at their thirty-seventh session in Cairo, were listening to the venerable Jigoro Kano assure everyone that Tokyo Olympic plans were on schedule, German armies were invading Austria. The IOC meeting forged ahead, accepted 1944 Olympic Games bids from London, Athens, Helsinki, Budapest, and Lausanne; that same day, in Berlin, Adolf Hitler told the Reichstag that his action in Austria saved many lives. Page one of the *New York Times* for 15 April 1938 screamed "42,000 Japanese Slain in China Fighting." Buried on page twenty-four was a note of Brundage's return from Cairo, of his awareness of the serious Asian situation, but also a reminder that the Olympic Games, once awarded, cannot be taken away. The venue can be changed, he said, only if the host city voluntarily gives it up. This is exactly what the Japanese cabinet did on 16 July 1938, announcing to the world that holding Olympic Games in their country would weaken "the essential Japanese spirit." Baillet-Latour immediately released a bulletin awarding Helsinki the 1940 summer games. An editorialist extended "all good wishes to the people of the Thousand Lakes."

A track meet, billed as an "Olympic Preview," took place in London on 7 August 1939. Two weeks later, Hitler signed a nonaggression treaty with Russia. This "diplomatic bombshell" led inexorably to the 1 September bombing of Warsaw, the invasion of Poland by German troops, and an official declaration of war by France and Britain. The second European war in a generation, soon to be a world war, had begun. With the hindsight given us in looking back in history, we may think it seems bizarre that the IOC refused to give up plans for the 1940 and 1944 Olympic Games. Finland discontinued stadium construction in December of 1939 as massive Soviet armies invaded that unhappy land, leading one angry journalist to view Russia's intent as "an obscene hypocrisy" as they carried "chains into Finland in the name of liberty." Back in the States, Judge Mahoney was urging an Olympic boycott until world conditions changed. They did not.

Nonetheless, during a Paris IOC meeting in mid-February of 1940, plans were discussed for a grandiose torch relay from Mount Olympus to Helsinki. The French Olympic Committee replied that it would be unable to cooperate, as all France's young men were at the war front. Grave Finnish casualties during these early winter months of 1940 made the Helsinki Olympic Games an impossibility, and, even when the "Hundred Days War" between Russia and Finland was over by April, Erik von Franckell, Finnish Olympic Committee chairman, declared that any sporting festival at this time "would be a mockery of the Olympic Ideal." He added, on 23 April 1940, that his country would not host the summer Olympic Games. Both Sapporo, Japan, and Garmisch-Partenkirchen, Germany, had already given up opportunities to host winter games for that year.

In those tremulous months prior to Pearl Harbor, Brundage kept busy supporting Charles Lindberg and the "Citizens-Keep-America-Out-of-the-War Committee." In Chicago's Soldier's Field, on 4 August 1940, 40,000 people heard them both oppose "foreign entanglements." Brundage, the most singleminded of men, was howled down by his sports associates, when, amidst the very deepest American war-involvement, he announced on 11 December 1944 that it was his sincere hope that both Germany and Japan would be invited to the next Olympic Games.

Illogical bravery of this sort marked the man, and the International Olympic Committee he served. The history of the IOC—that organization which combines rationality and irrationality in bewildering combinations—needs careful study. The next chapter will try to do this, although doomed to incompleteness from the beginning.

8 • Entangling Alliances—The International Olympic Committee Structure

The International Olympic Committee is one of the world's most unusual organizations. It has no legal status and is accountable to no higher authority. More than 310 men have served on the committee since 1894, but never a woman. In order to retain "absolute independence", the IOC has never accepted a delegate member from any nation, but has steadfastly maintained a policy of selecting or co-opting members from the world sporting community that would be acceptable ideologically to the remaining membership. The IOC insists on recruiting its members in order to create a climate of uniform and universal agreement on Olympic policy, rules and regulations.

For about half its eighty-five year history, approximately during the time of Baron Pierre de Coubertin's influence, the effort for a like-minded committee was very successful. Coubertin said repeatedly that the democratic process, most laudable as it was, should not govern every single human institution. The long-time director of the IOC, the perceptive Monique Berlioux, once commented that Coubertin did not always admire parliamentary government, and that the committee was conceived to be "dependent on nothing," answerable to nobody other than an idea, and thus, hopefully, would insure its incorruptibility. As Jean Leiper said in her 1976 doctoral dissertation on IOC history: "The privileges and responsibilities attending membership have altered only in minor details between 1894 and 1970."

The dictionary definition of the word *fabulous* as something "almost unbelievable" must certainly encompass the controversial IOC history. The remainder of this chapter will look briefly at the temper of the seven IOC presidents, at several significant events that helped shape the tenor of the organization, and will review the present hierarchical structure of the IOC, its satellite national Olympic committees (NOCs), and the highly independent international sport federations (IFs).

136

IOC Presidents 1894 – 1925

Right from the very beginning in 1894, Coubertin perceived his creation, the International Olympic Committee, as independent, international, sovereign, and assured of permanence. It was Coubertin's dream and responsibility to select, as often as possible, members more loyal to the Olympic idea than to any earthly institution. The culmination of the 1894 Congress was the selection of Athens, Greece, as the site of the New Olympic Games, the selection by Coubertin of a twelve-man "Comité," and his choice of Dimitrius Bikelas as the IOC's first president. The distinguished Greek man of letters played an indispensable role in the success of these first modern Olympic Games. His work done, Coubertin took over, serving till 1925. The baron and his IOC associates recognized that they had something unique—the first multisport and multination athletic competition.

Absolute independence in selecting IOC members rather than accepting delegates to the committee was perceived very early as the only way the institution could survive, let alone supervise the universal structure of the Olympic movement, promote the games, decide in what city they should take place, and help the national Olympic organizing committee to bring the games to successful fruition. As IOC expert Leiper said, "The IOC was intended to be, and became the policy-setter for the Olympic movement, concerning itself with translating philosophy, principles, and goals into action guidelines for those who would undertake the tasks of preparing Olympic contestants and competitions." For much of the history of the IOC, no person or faction thinking differently from the main body, was capable of gaining admittance, let alone usurping power. Differences of opinion always existed on the committee, but only during the 1960s and 1970s have serious ideological disputes disturbed the relative tranquility and "club-like" atmosphere of this gathering of sportsmen.

The single-minded idealist Coubertin was the acknowledged leader of the IOC, even during his seclusive World War I days, when he asked Baron Godefroy de Blonay, a Swiss, to take over the presidential duties. Although he resumed his power in 1919, Coubertin could never dispel a desire to retire, which he did on 29 May 1925 at the event-filled Prague IOC meeting. Speaking at that meeting, Coubertin might be forgiven some degree of exaggeration when he said that "the very fact that this committee is self-recruiting makes it immune to all political interference, and it is not swayed by intense nationalism nor influenced by corporative interests." Without so much as a degree of deviation, all through his long tenure as the Olympic Movement's dominant figure, Coubertin mistrusted the "selfish and gigantic figure of the State" as potentially destructive to the Olympic mission. He felt that the best way to serve democracy did not always consist in a wholesale surrender to the electoral system. Had the IOC been chosen on the same principles as other governing bodies, Coubertin felt, it would have soon disappeared after unending bickering. He believed that the games would be a battlefield of ideologies if nations were allowed to send delegates to the Olympic Committee. IOC members under the Coubertin scheme, it was hoped, could never be preinstructed by their countries. The first American IOC member, William Milligan Sloane, put it succinctly when he said that "every man, as it were, is an ambassador to his own country from the committee."

IOC Growth 1925 –1952

During the Coubertin years of leadership, the IOC was, in a sense, searching for an identity, a common purpose, and a set of rules or criteria under which it could more effectively administer the Olympic Games and advance the larger concept of the Olympic movement and its philosophical equivalency, Olympism. Necessarily, during these years, abrupt IOC changes rarely occurred. While the next period, 1925–1952, was certainly not marked by revolutionary fire, the process of IOC evolutionary changes gained some momentum, especially during the leadership of the Belgian, Count Henri de Baillet-Latour. Two energetic projects met with limited success. The first was creation of a fair, universally understood, and wholly acceptable definition of an amateur athlete. The second task was equally difficult and unconsummated—the integration of the growing number of national Olympic committees (N.O.C.'s), and the international sport federations IFs), with the parent organization, the IOC.

An executive board of the IOC—originally a small group of six men—had been formed in 1921 to add greater efficiency to the gradually enlarging main committee. Both Baillet-Latour and J. Sigfrid Edstrom of Sweden were on Coubertin's first executive board, thus signaling a tradition that future IOC members be selected from this group. The growing triangle of tension between the IOC, the NOCs, and these IFs. resulted in the steady increase in national Olympic committees, the first criterion for membership in the Olympic family.

Also, during this quarter-century, a similar burgeoning of specific international sport organizations called federations (basketball, judo, boxing, biathlon, handball, volleyball, and archery) created an ever-growing triangle of tension between the IOC, the NOCS, and these IFs.

The other vexing problem, defining the words "amateur" and "amateurism", was incapable of solution during this period as the ever-growing Olympic movement increasingly included athletes, not only from the upper middle and well-to-do socio-economic classes, but also from the poorer. In addition, divergent life styles and cultural and religious attitudes of a rapidly widening Olympic membership made a universally accepted definition of amateurism an impossibility. Baillet-Latour was a brave man and an effective leader of the Olympic movement from 1925 to 1942. The resolute Swede, Edstrom, was active in the movement since before the first world war, and served as president of the IOC from 1946 to 1952. He passed away in his ninety-fourth year between the Innsbruck and Tokyo games of 1964. The flint-hard Avery Brundage began his twenty-year leadership role, retired in 1972, and died on 8 May 1975, at age eighty-seven. These two decades following World War II were, of course, the Olympic movement's greatest growth period, as it also saw the most accelerated expansion of all nonprofessional, professional, and mass sport participation. The tumultuous Olympic years since 1972, volatile and sometimes unmanageable, have been in the able administrative hands of Michael Morris, Lord Killanin.

Contrasting IOC Leadership 1952 –1980: Brundage and Killanin

Avery Brundage was, in several important ways, the most effective of all IOC presidents, the most obdurate Olympic leader, the most uncompromising defender of the "amateur code." And yet his personal strength, dynamism, and unflagging single-mindedness was not enough to hold together in a single ideological commitment the minds of all his Olympic committee members. The IOC method of membership self-selection—for a long time an effective guarantee of overwhelming support for the original Olympic idea—finally, during the last years of Brundage, was unable to quiet the strident, opposing voices from within the organization itself. Unprecedented world political discontinuity during President Brundage's twenty-year reign (1952–1972) created a near-constant state of crisis within the IOC, putting a strain on the unanimity that had been more marked in earlier times. The political problems of the two Germanies, the two Koreas, the two Chinas, the Hungarian revolt, the tragedy of Viet Nam, war in Ireland, the Middle East, and confrontations all through southern Africa were reflected in IOC issues and edicts.

It seemed that Brundage and the committee were continually fighting uphill battles against what many societies espoused as radically changing attitudes in a nonabsolutist, situational world. For example, Brundage was unmoved by journalist's rationalizations that the public demand for Olympic Games point-keeping was met by day-to-day point totaling, and, therefore, it was OK to keep score. It was wrong, against the Olympic rules, and no amount of rhetoric could change that, he said in 1952:

The IOC deplores the practice in the newspapers of the world, of attributing and publishing tables of points showing national placings in the Olympic Games. This is entirely contrary to the rules and spirit of the Olympic Games, which are contests between individuals with no points scored.

At the Athens IOC meeting in 1954, President Brundage chided the membership for their preoccupation with technical questions and for being "neglectful of the moral side of our task." This was always his way—brutally direct and undiplomatic. The year 1956 was constantly punctuated by international crises in Hungary, at the Suez Canal, and between mainland China and Formosa. Ensuing withdrawals from the Melbourne games predictably angered Brundage, and he hoped that those national teams would reconsider. He reminded them:

In an imperfect world, if participation in sport is to be stopped every time politicians violate the laws of humanity, there will be few international contests. Is it not better to try to expand the sportsmanship of the athletic field into other areas?

The seventh president of the International Olympic Committee, Michael Morris, Lord Killanin, took office on 12 September 1972, shortly after the extraordinarily well-planned Munich Games. The holocaust of Israeli Olympic athletes dying at the hands of terrorists during the games overshadowed all, and gave a somber greeting to the new IOC president. The very success of the Olympic movement, especially the Olympic Games, had enlarged old problems, created serious new ones, and raised the possibility of future crises of grave proportions. All problems were dumped in the lap of Killanin and his Olympic committee. The autocratic and pugnacious Brundage had given way to a quite different man—a cooler head, a man sensitive to the media, a person always ready to at least discuss arbitration on the serious Olympic problems of the 1970s.

IOC Director Berlioux is convinced that her organization is capable of resolving these problems, and thus, as she has said, allowing the Olympic movement and the Olympic Games to help "in forming the complete and munificent man of tomorrow." Bulgarian IOC member Alexandru Siperco agrees, adding that the IOC, the NOCs, and the I.F.'s should all work harmoniously toward Olympic Games which can be a contribution "to the deep aspirations for international brotherhood." Inflationary costs of building Olympic facilities, the accelerated growth of international ultranationalism, and an abysmal lack of public understanding regarding Olympic philosophy, aims, and objectives plague the whole Olympic movement and its central organ of communication, the IOC. James Worrall, Canadian IOC member, suggested in 1974 that sport idealism was not dead or even dying. In fact, he said, it was growing among youth, and he suggested that "the doddering, old-fashioned members of the IOC are closer to the modern youth than the generation or two that seems to separate them."

Obviously, the work of the IOC is only as good as the cooperation received from 135 NOCs and 26 IFs around the world. The symbiotic relationship between the IOC and the NOCs and the working arrangements between these organizations and the 26 IFs form a triangle, or, as the IOC calls it, a tripartite of great importance in international sport harmony. Mutual trust, understanding, and a significant degree of cooperation among the hundreds of men and women involved in this Tripartite form the basis of Olympic success.

The next section will deal with the movement's rules and regulations—the *Olympic Charter* (1978). A closer look at certain of its mandates may give some insight into what Jean-Paul Courant meant when speaking at the 1969 Olympic Academy: "I feel there is . . . a trace of childishness in the Olympic Spirit, and this is perhaps the surest warrant for its continuity."

The Structure and Character of the *Olympic Charter*

The contents of the 1978 *Olympic Charter* are divided into five rules (subdivided into sixty-eight paragraphs), thirteen bylaws, three instructions, six conditions necessary for the organisation of the Olympic Games, and two brief definitions, one of IOC commissions, and the other of Olympic awards. The aims of the Olympic Games and the larger Olympic movement, strongly influenced by Coubertin's writings, are highly altruistic and aim heavenward toward the creation of international goodwill, the promotion of universal physical and moral qualities, and the education of youth, "thereby helping to build a better and more peaceful world." It is pure Coubertin—idealistic overstatement, and yet difficult to criticize as laudable goals for the world community. No Olympic Games discrimination is allowed against any country or person on ground of race, religion or politics. Throughout, "the supreme authority of the IOC" and its rules regarding all matters Olympic is underscored. The IOC selects the host games city, but that city and its NOC "shall assume complete financial responsibility" for their organization. Discussion continues regarding two nearly contradictory statements—one stating clearly that only citizens of a nation-state may represent that country in the Olympic Games, the other reminding the world that "The Games are contests between individuals and not between countries."

Paragraphs 12 through 23 deal with IOC membership (89 members from seventy countries in the fall of 1978), emphasizing that each is a representative of the IOC in his country and not that nation's delegate to the IOC. Retirement is set at age seventy-two, while expulsion is possible if a member "has betrayed or neglected [IOC] interests or has been guilty of unworthy conduct." The president of the IOC is elected for eight years, with the possibility of reelection for successive terms of four years. Three vice-presidents are elected for four years, while the executive board is composed of the president, the three vice-presidents, and 5 additional members. Quite in concert with the original Coubertin master plan, the powers of the executive board continue to grow in rough proportion to the increased growth in numbers and personal persuasions of the larger committee itself. There appears little support for the proposal from several Soviet and Bulgarian members that the IOC be composed of 135 members, or the same number as there are national Olympic committees. The recent proliferation of new NOCs from socialist and Third World nations make the rationale for such a move rather transparent. The frequency of meetings or tripartite sessions, mandated by the rules, among the IOC, the NOCs, and the twenty-six sport federations is an encouraging sign. And yet, it is clear that the International Olympic Committee is the final authority on all questions concerning the Olympic Games and the Olympic movement.

Rule 5, "Organisation of the Games," deals with the duties of the organizing committee, comments on the host city, the program, publications, advertising, emblems, music, tickets, the Olympic flag and flame, all formal ceremonies, plus the IOCs patronage of regional sports competitions such as the Pan American games, the Asian games, etc.

The NOCs select their own athletes for competition at the games, and thus have great power. They must remain politically neutral, devote themselves to their youth, and work closely with the national sport federations. NOCs must recognize but one IOC-approved federation in each Olympic Games sport. This has posed no problem except in the United States, whose unique university-oriented system of athletics has frequently clashed with internationally-connected governing bodies.

Rule 26, the eligibility code, no longer contains the stipulation that an Olympic competitor be amateur. After nearly ninety years of agonizing definitions of an "amateur athlete," the latest charter simply states that salaried, full-time-employed professional athletes are not eligible for Games competition. It is safe to say that, for the past one hundred years, various forms of financial subsidization have been awarded to most of Britain's and America's top amateur athletes. Since the inception of the modern Olympic Games, the same may be said of France, Germany, Italy, and other Western countries. Since 1950, the three Scandinavian countries and the socialist and communist countries all have supported, on a massive scale, a small cadre of outstanding male and female nonprofessional athletes. The Coubertin ideal of self-support by the amateur athlete was a concept borrowed from eighteenth-century English aristocracy. The concept was a wise one and worked nicely as long as well-to-do English gentlemen played against one another; but the rude intrusion of all the lower classes into national and international sport competition without an accompanying modification in the amateur code only begged for widespread abuse. Coubertin knew all this, recognized the futility of such a dual standard, and said so in print. However, he and his IOC successors consistently supported a code which, by the 1920s, was hopelessly outmoded. Pressure for changes in the *Olympic Charter* mounted during the 1960s and into the next decade. IOC President Killanin and some of his liberal collaborators worked hard and successfully introduced a radical change in rule 26 of the 1978 *Olympic Charter*.

Byelaw 26 disallows professional athletes or coaches admittance into the Olympic Games. Advertising monies paid to famous athletes must be turned over to the athlete's federation or NOC. However, for as many years as individuals are effective in their sport work, the NOC may support them with: food, lodging, full cost of transportation, pocket money, insurance costs, all equipment and clothing, full medical care, plus that once-illegal ancient, "broken-time," or, as the rule states:

> Compensation, authorized by his or her National Olympic Committee or National Federation . . . to cover financial loss resulting from his or her absence from work or basic occupation, on account of preparation for, or participation in, the Olympic Games and international sports competitions.

There it is, the single most liberal piece of legislation ever passed by the IOC—legislation that undoubtedly would not have received the approval of all previous IOC presidents. Times change, and Killanin reminded his colleagues of the basic inequity of the old rule and the massive disregard of it in post-World War II Europe.

The modern Olympic athlete in most European countries is certainly not a professional in the American sense, nor is he an amateur in the British-Brundage sense, either. Following the passage of byelaw 26 in the mid-1970s, the United States Olympic Committee, under enormous pressure from athletes, started a campaign to find monies from the public and private sector in order to financially aid deserving athletes. Despite a quarter-century head start, the always optimistic USOC thinks its athletes have the talent and "moxie" to catch and surpass the rest of the world. Both Robert Kane, president, and F. Don Miller, executive-director, of the USOC have announced in the most vigorous manner that government monies have been requested, donations from private industry solicited, and their own funds earmarked—all to better prepare their athletes for the

1980 and 1984 Olympic Games. None of this would have occurred in the United States without the passage of Olympic byelaw 26.

The third division of the Rules of the *Olympic Charter*, section C, "Instructions," is divided into eight subsections. "The Political use of Sport" is categorically rejected as antithetical to the high principles of the Olympic ideal. "National exaltation" must never be valued above the concept of friendly internationalism, concludes this first instruction. "The Olympic Games are not for Profit," and all monies amassed are to "be used for the promotion of the Olympic Movement or the development of amateur sport." Protocol and ceremony are important IOC traditions and are included in every one of their meetings.

Subsections 3 and 4 deal with seating arrangements, hotel accommodations, authorized guests at IOC meetings, the exact arrangements of the conference hall, the detailed program, simultaneous translation, the media, security, the introduction of new members, and a detailed "Questionnaire for Candidate Cities Holding I.O.C. Sessions." Of greater importance are subsections 5, 6, and 7, the "Organization of the Games—Conditions Laid Down for Candidate Cities." Fifty-two questions must be answered affirmativly by city leaders in order to be given Olympic Games consideration. Respect for IOC rules, general and cultural information, organizational matters, finances, and radio and television items dominate this section. Honest answers immediately eliminate almost all of the world's cities. The few remaining must answer "yes" to such questions as:

> Can you guarantee that no political meeting or demonstration will take place in the stadium, or any other sports ground, or in the Olympic Village during the Games?
> Can you confirm that the full receipts for television, less the proportion due to you as Organizing Committee, will be handed over when received, in conformity with the I.O.C. formula for division between the I.O.C., International Federation and N.O.C.'s?

Subsection 8 deals with "The International Olympic Committee Commissions," or sixteen subcommittees to deal with the Olympic academy, eligibility, culture, rules editing, emblems, finance, legal, medical, press, program, publications, awards, rule-book review, solidarity (funding for talented athletes and scholars, and the all-important tripartite-commission membership of ten (three each from IOC and NOC, the Federations), under the leadership of the IOC president.

Section D of the *Olympic Charter* deals with "Regional Games," the proliferation of games on the various continents of the world, and the stipulations under which the Pan-American games, African games, Balkan games, Asian games, etc., must work in order to "enjoy the patronage of the IOC." Section E, "The Olympic Awards," and section F, "Publications of the IOC," are self-explanatory and somewhat of an anti-climax to the rich, discussion-filled, and frequently controversial material in the previous sections of this important *Olympic Charter*. A helpful interpretation and elaboration of some of these rules is a 1969 text, *The Administration of an Olympic Games* by Sandy Duncan (Britain), Marcello Garroni (Italy), and Yukiaki Iwata (Japan).

The strongest opponents of the International Olympic Committee consider that organization's deliberations the machinations of a fascist-like clique, while its ultradefenders never find fault in any IOC decision. Both sides are wrong. Born an aristocratic, conservative, male-oriented organization, the IOC has been slow to change. And yet Coubertin was very perceptive in noting that survival would have been impossible for the IOC had he based its structure on totally democratic principles. Democracy is not forever, for everyone, and for all institutions the best method of governance, he once said. The 1973 Varna, Bulgaria, Congress of all NOCs, all IFs, and the IOC—a rare happening—was the beginning of a greater understanding of the role and function of each organization, and, above all, consideration for the needs of aspiring Olympic athletes—rich, middle class, and poor.

The single greatest criticism leveled against the IOC has been the unfairness of its unceasing, eighty-five year vendetta against the professional athlete. Nineteenth-century English elitism lingers on well into the eighth decade of the twentieth century. The deep cleavage between the old amateur English gentleman-athlete and those working-class athletes who also enjoyed their sport but profited from individual and collective skill has been consistently reflected in Olympic rules since 1894. Byelaw 26 does not reverse Olympic history and allow salaried, full-time professional athletes entry into the games, but it does take into consideration the modern-day necessity for amateur athletes, rich and poor alike, to devote thirty hours a week to hard training, often supervised and frequently scientific in nature, in order to have even a chance at Olympic success. The gifted, natural athlete, or the primitive, Rousseauian figure can only on rare occasion win an Olympic medal. For the rest, unrelenting hard work added on to his or her regular job is the route that must be taken.

And it is all very expensive. The IOC has been realistic and generous in its present posture, and liberal subsidization of nonprofessional athletes, finally made legal under byelaw 26, is a real step forward. The IOC needs to institute several other progressive measures, including the liberalization of its membership criteria. Highly qualified men and women who are not independently wealthy should be invited to serve as members of the IOC on a salaried basis. The International Olympic Academy at Olympia, Greece, has been operational for nearly twenty years. The IOC should throw its full weight behind the idea of expanding this educational-philosophical concept to many nations around the world.

Lastly, and most importantly, the IOC must abandon its unworkable dream of sponsoring a different Olympic site every four years. A rotating Olympic site at three already established facilities would be far better. Best of all, I think, would be the creation of a single, permanent Olympic Games site in either Switzerland, Finland, or Greece. This site could be ready by 1996, the hundredth anniversary of the modern Olympic Games.

The true idealist is not simply a dreamer. As David Gunston said in an 11 April 1978 *Christian Science Monitor*, the true idealist "seeks always to pursue what his hope leads him to long for, what his heart tells him is right, in a way his head says will work." The International Olympic Committee has absolutely no political axe to grind. It continually seeks to find the common denominator which, as the practical Lord Killanin hoped, would "bring those divergent views which have wholly arisen for political and historical reasons, and gather them together on the field of sport."

9 • Prelude to Olympic Gigantism
1945 –1959

Count Henri de Baillet-Latour, President of the International Olympic Committee, died at his home in Brussels on 7 January 1942. Only a few months earlier, his son, Guy, an assistant military attaché of the émigré Belgian government in London, was killed in a transatlantic plane crash. The IOC was without a leader. Coubertin was gone, and Baillet-Latour's thirty-nine years with the Olympic movement was ended. J. Sigfrid Edstrom of Sweden was the IOC vice-president, but the European war prevented his assuming leadership until 1946. During this Olympic vacuum, 1942–1946, Dr. Carl Diem attempted to transfer the intellectual center of Olympism from Lausanne to Berlin. Madame L. Zanchi, IOC secretary from 1927 to the mid-1960s, told the author, in a series of interviews in August of 1960:

> At the height of the War, I was left alone in Lausanne. When Professor Diem attempted to remove the Olympic headquarters to Germany, I hid the most important documents in the cellar, and convinced the community that Diem was a spy. I alerted Mr. Edstrom of Sweden.

There is ample evidence that Coubertin had requested Diem to continue publication of the *Olympic Review* and to seek in every way possible the continuation of the ideals of the Olympic movement. No one in the world was as well qualified to do this as Diem. But he was German and probably posed a dreadful figure to Madame Zanchi and her Swiss friends in 1942. It was also possible that that kind and genteel lady had taken on at least one of Coubertin's habits, for, as she concluded her talk with this writer:

> Coubertin was always fighting with someone. He saw enemies where there were none . . . a sort of persecution complex. He believed so strongly in Olympism that he was willing to make concessions in writing and in action to anyone . . . as long as the Games continued.

Regrettably, the games did not continue; both the games of the twelfth

147

Olympiad (1940) and Thirteenth Olympiad (1944) were cancelled. but somehow, during this interminable period of human madness, the idea of the Olympic Games and the humanist concept of Olympism survived. Waving a small flag of idealism in 1942, IOC member Count Alberto Bonacossa wrote an essay in volume 18 of the *Olympic Review*, entitled, "L'Idea Olympica e la Realta Politica." War, he said, tends to alienate people and athletes, "but the common bond shared by all dedicated and spiritually-minded athletes shall survive even the war itself." In 1945, following the armistice, Edstrom called a meeting of the IOC Executive Board, but only Britain's Lord Clarence Aberdale and Avery Brundage were able to join the aging Edstrom in discussing the reestablishment of the long-quiet Olympic Games.

London, England, in 1948 was very much like Antwerp, Belgium in 1920—still bleeding from war but reluctantly agreeing to host Olympic Games. St. Moritz, Switzerland, hosted the fifth winter Olympics with athletes from Sweden, Finland, Norway, Switzerland, the United States, and Austria dominating the meet. Competitors from France, Italy, Canada, Belgium, Hungary, Czechoslovakia, Britain, and Holland rounded out the scorers in the first six places. The summer Olympics—the games of the fourteenth Olympiad—opened on 29 July 1948.

Twelve days earlier, at Olympia, Greece, an olive branch kindled into flame by a magnifying glass was touched to a torch, "a torch of brotherhood across an anxious world." Avoiding hostile Albania, Yugoslavia, and Bulgaria, the torch sailed the Adriatic to Italy, torch runners crossed the Simplon Pass to Lausanne, Switzerland, where the widow Coubertin was presented a gift, through France, across the Channel to Dover by British destroyer, and on to Wembley Stadium. Stopping at Buckingham Palace, the relay runner presented Princess Elizabeth with a 2,300-year-old Greek earthenware lamp. Long an advocate of the Olympic Games, the former champion, Lord David Burghley, the Marquess of Exeter, looked forward to a festival that had not been celebrated in a dozen years. It cannot fail, he said, because "when a great cause marches hand in hand with sincerity and enthusiasm, none can stop its progress."

There was absolutely nothing grandiose about these Olympics. As little money as possible was spent. There was no Olympic village and no new stadia were built. Athletes from the West and athletes from Eastern countries were housed apart in army camps and converted school rooms. The Soviet Union, Japan, and Germany did not compete. However, 4,009 athletes from fifty-nine countries did participate in seventeen sports, not including the twenty-five nations that competed in the last of the arts competitions, held at the great Victoria and Albert Museum. Although massive London absorbed the games with hardly a ripple, and despite the traditional sangfroid of the English and much poor weather, the festival must be considered successful.

There was opposition, of course. Stanley Frank, writing in *Cosmopolitan* prior to the games, said, "Let's Ditch the Olympics," and predicted more ill will as, in his words, pampered, overfed athletes would descend on a British population still living under the most austere wartime conditions. Ronald Stead's editorial in the 10 July 1948 *Christian Science Monitor* saw it differently. Unfortunately, he said, if one competitor slaps another in the face, it makes big news in the sensation-seeking newspapers, "but if a thousand competitors slap each other on the back," it goes unnoticed. However, the English held these games and did a good job, considering the handicaps. The president of the IOC, Edstrom, attributed the success of this "project in the Grand Manner . . . to the British genius for improvisation." The Right Honorable Philip Noel-Baker's assessment of these London games was that they had met Coubertin's threefold Olympic criteria: to raise the standard of skill, strength, speed, and endurance; to spread sport knowledge and awareness worldwide; and "to touch the hearts and stir the imaginations of the athletes." A touch of realism was added by the romantic-idealist, Edstrom, who said that the Olympic Games cannot enforce peace in the world, but they do afford youth the opportunity "to find out that all men on earth are brothers."

In reflecting on why the host nation, his own English people, did not perform well at the 1948 Olympic Games, the medical doctor, Sir Adolphe Abrahams, proposed that apathy and its accompanying inability to deal with athletic minutia was partly the cause. He suggested that British athletes attend American universities and get some real training. Regrettably, said Sir Adolphe in the *Times* of London, 13 August 1948, British athletes might respond unkindly to such a suggestion "with the classic phraseology of the young lady in Mr. Bernard Shaw's *Pygmalion*—'Not bloody likely.' "

Harrison Dillard, denied the opportunity to race his hurdle specialty, switched to the 100 meters and edged out American teammate, thirty-year-old Barney Ewell. At 200 meters, Ewell was edged out again, this time by Southern California's Mel Patton. The 400-meter struggle was a classic as six feet, four and one-half-inch Arthur Brying Wint, medical student and son of a West Indies parson, beat fellow Jamaican Herb McKenley in Olympic record of 46.2 seconds. Wint met his match at 800 meters in Ohio State University's Mal Whitfield—1:49.2 to 1:49.5. Henry Eriksson won a muddy 1,500 meters with three Swedes in the top six. Little Gaston Reiff, also splashing through a London rain, outsprinted Emil Zatopek in a classic five-kilometers. It was a different story at double that distance as "The Czechoslovakian Train," Zatopek, beat the favored Finns in a runaway. His upper body contortions were terrible; he ran "like a man who's just been stabbed in the heart." Three Swedish steeple-chasers had perfected their art during their country's neutral war years and swept that event. Bill Porter, Clyde Scott, and Craig Dixon swept the high hurdles; Roy Cochran ran a record 51.1 intermediate hurdles, and the United States won both relays. Eighty thousand spectators stared in disbelief as Belgium's Etienne Gailly staggered into the stadium with only a lap to go in the 42-kilometer marathon. But "his heart demanded things which his stilts of legs could not obey," and the twenty-nine-year-old Buenos Aires fireman, Delfo Cabrera, caught him, winning in 2:34:51. The ancient Welchman, forty-two-year-old Tom Richards, finished third. Swedes John Mikaelsson and John Ljundggren won the two walking races. Willie Steele, Arne Ahman, John Winter, Guinn Smith, Wilbur Thompson, Adolfo Consolini, Imre Nemeth, and Tapio Rautavaara won the men's field events, while the precocious boy, Bob Mathias, won the coveted decathlon title. Micheline Ostermeyer of France was a double field-event winner, but the superstar of the meet was the thirty-year-old Dutch mother, Fanny Blankers-Koen, "5'7½" of streamlined femininity," and winner of four gold medals. Jerry Nason of *The Boston Globe* noted that she seemed unimpressed by her own exploits, and predicted, with amazing accuracy, that

> Women athletes are just coming into their own. It is only a matter of time when women will be high jumping six feet, broad jumping 23 feet and running 100 yards in 10 seconds.

The United States dominated basketball, beating France 65–21 in the final. Boxing gold-medals were distributed to athletes from the Argentine, Hungary, Italy, South Africa, and Czechoslovakia. Cycling took place at Herne Hill and Windsor, the Italians, French, and Belgian teams dominating. Olympic football took place between 31 July and 13 August; the well-balanced Swedes won over Yugoslavia, 3–1. At Empire Pool, the American men and women captured twelve out of sixteen events, Italy winning the water-polo gold over Hungary. Freestyle and Greco-Roman wrestling took place at Empress Hall and Earl's Court, the gold medals being distributed to tough guys from Turkey, Sweden, Finland, Italy, Hungary, and the United States. The "Miniature Hercules," sub-five-foot tall Joe de Pietro, started the parade of weight-lifting gold-medal winners from Egypt and the United States.

Fencing at these games of the fourteenth Olympiad attracted a larger entry than at any previous Olympics, and the Palace of Engineering was busy for two weeks. In the men's events, there was no serious challenge to the French and Italian supremacy, nor to Hungary at sabre. Ilona Elek of Hungary, the Berlin winner, beat everyone in London, retaining the ladies' foil championship. The Finns, Swiss, Hungarians, and Czechs won the highest awards in gymnastics with Karl Frei, Josef Stalder, Veikko Huhtanen, and Walter Lehmann dominating.

Wretched weather greeted rowers from twenty-seven countries at Henley-on-Thames, with honors being distributed among individuals and crews from Sweden, Czechoslovakia, the United States, and the women's single-kayak award went to Karen Hoff of Denmark. The British crews had been forged in less than a year, and their success, according to the British *Official Report*, "did them great credit." John Scott Hughes, writing in this same *Report*, thoroughly enjoyed the yachting competitions at Torbay in South Devon where sailors from Norway, Britain, Denmark, Sweden, Cuba, Portugal, Argentina, and the Netherlands won gold, silver, and bronze medals.

The all-powerful Indian hockey team beat England 4–0 before 25,000 spectators on soggy ground in Wembley Stadium. Cook (United States), Emil Grünig (Switzerland), Cam (Peru), and the remarkably ambidextrous Karoly Takacs (Hungary) were the shooting stars of this Olympics. Equestrian events and the modern pentathlon took place on the Aldershot area at the Royal Military Academy. Swiss, Swedish, French, and Mexican riders won, while the dominant figure in the military pentathlon was the great Swede, William Grut. His record low score of sixteen points may never be broken: first place in shooting, swimming, and riding; fifth in fencing; and eighth in cross-country running.

There is absolutely no scientific evidence to show that anything positive or permanent emerged from all this physical and emotional agitation. But there is nothing "hard" in the other direction, either. The ancient Greeks never attained political unity; there was massive uneasiness among nations in this 1948 postwar Olympics. At ancient Olympia, for the briefest period of time, the Greeks met as brothers in a sanctuary where no arms might be borne. The brother-and-sister modern counterpart does exist; natural aggressions are released without destroying each other, and the opportunity to make many and long-lasting friends does surely exist.

Dr. Willy Meisl, British sport authority once said that "the hallmark of faultless organization is that everything should run smoothly but unobtrusively." The jewel of them all, the seventh Olympic Winter Games held in Oslo, Norway, 14–25 February 1952, approached this standard. Over 700,000 people watched superb performances from Dick Button, Stein Eriksen, Zeno Colo, Othmar Schneider, Andrea Mead Lawrence, Trude Jochum-Beiser, Hallgeir Brenden, Veikko Hakkulinen, Ken Henry, Hjalmer Anderson, Jeannette Altwegg, Ria and Paul Falk, Simon Slattvik, Arnfinn Bergmann, L. Wideman, the German bobsled champions, and the Canadian ice-hockey champions. The attention of the Olympic sports world now shifted to nearby Helsinki, the smallest city ever to host Olympic Games. Surprisingly, when the final verdict was in, eyewitnesses from many disciplines called these summer games superior to those in Berlin and Los Angeles and to any of the previous festivals.

When news reached Finland on 17 June 1947 that the IOC had once again chosen Helsinki to host the Olympic Games, the national flag was hoisted everywhere. Newspapers published special Olympic editions, and, possibly for the first time, an entire people was caught up in an Olympian fever of joy. President of the Republic J. K. Paasikivi gave the successful fruition of these fifteenth games the highest national priority. For the first time, over 5,000 athletes participated in Olympic Games, representing sixty-nine nations. Indoor, outdoor, and sailing facilities were in close proximity, and the very best that money and technology could produce were on hand. And yet, those that were there consistently pointed out that the Berlin kind of gigantism, the uncomfortable feeling of being visually overwhelmed, was not present during the Helsinki summer of 1952.

Over 2,000 paid and volunteer workers spent a year of special training to prepare for what they hoped would be flawlessly efficient games. The Swiss watchmaking firm Omega carried out all timekeeping free of charge. The Kapyla Olympic Village for men, a much smaller women's village, and a separate housing development at Otaniemi for men and women from the Eastern Block countries, comprised unique, pleasant living-quarters. The new tradition of a torch relay was continued, with the "sacred flame" transported from Olympia to Athens, flown in a miner's lamp to Copenhagen, ferried over to Malmo, Sweden, from which runners, motorcyclists, and bicyclists carried the torch to the stadium where the magnificent Paavo Nurmi circled the track, kindled the Olympic Flame, and handed the torch to the great, old Olympian Hans Kolehmainen, who carried the flame up the 72.71-meter stadium tower, lighting another symbolic bowl. Finnish sporting immortal Matti Jarvinen had thrown the javelin exactly that distance in winning the Los Angeles Olympics twenty years earlier. For those that love ceremony and pageantry, the almost-four-hour festivities on opening day were impressive. Dr. Heikki Savolainen, veteran of five Olympic gymnastic competitions, delivered the Olympic Oath, and symbolized the reverence with which this small nation of Finns accorded their athletes. Eddie Eagan, American two-time gold-medal winner (1920 in boxing; 1932 in bobsled), was typically effusive about the Helsinki games and the Olympic movement's creator. "The spirit of Pierre de Coubertin steps forward," he said, . . . to take curtain calls as one of history's heroes and supermen."

The dominating personality of the 1952 Olympic Games was Emil "The

Zatopek leads Mimoun and Shade into home stretch of 1952 Olympic 5000 meters, with Chataway lying on curb after fall. Credit Track and Field News, Inc., California.

Magnificent" Zatopek. No one since the magnetic Nurmi and Jesse Owens had so captured the world sporting imagination. His tortured style of running (Jesse Abramson of the *Herald-Tribune* said Zatopek made "more faces than Lon Chaney") won him gold medals and Olympic records in the 5,000- and 10,000-meter runs and in the classic marathon. His Czech wife, Dana, won the women's javelin championship to make theirs an unrivaled Olympic combination. Ninety-five track-and-field athletes, only a few of them gold-medalists, beat the Olympic record in their event, with eight world records falling. It marked the modern reemphasis on record-breaking, a Western, century-old tradition that placed infinitely greater value on the quantifiable mark rather than on the ritualistic or intrinsic value of the performance.

In large measure, responsible for this were the reappearances of Germany and the Soviet Union at the Olympic Games. Many European socialist countries, measurably recovering from the war, embraced a kind of political realism which placed high priority on international sporting success, especially at the Olympic Games. For example, Hungarian women won four of the five swimming events, while Soviet male and female gymnasts took home twenty-one gold, silver, and bronze medals. The United States officials, aware of their nation's brilliant Olympic heritage, put on their furious, once-every-four years Olympic team recruiting, and did a great job in those areas that interested them (athletics, swimming, boxing, weight lifting, freestyle wrestling, eight-oared crew, yachting, shooting, and basketball). Athletes from the U.S.S.R., Hungary, Sweden, Finland, and Turkey were strong in Greco-Roman and freestyle wrestling; the French, Italians, and Hungarians maintained their traditional domination of foil, épée, and sabre fencing; Sweden was very strong in equestrian sports and the modern pentathlon, while canoeing and rowing honors were divided among athletes from the United States, the Soviet Union, Sweden, Finland, France, Argentinia, Yugolslavia, and Czechoslovakia. The cycling gold medals went to specialists from Australia, Belgium, and Italy, the basketball title to the United States in a low-scoring 36–25 win over the USSR. The four best teams in soccer were Hungary, Yugoslavia, Sweden, and Germany; in field hockey, India, Holland, Britain, and Pakistan; and in water polo, Hungary, Yugoslavia, Italy, and the United States. A dozen different countries produced gold-medal winners in shooting competition, but Takacs's repeat victory at the 25-meter rapid-fire pistol-shooting was most notable, the Hungarian having switched to his left hand after a permanent disability to his right.

Another games were over, and no one knew for sure what had been accomplished, other than the obvious production of a small international cadre of super athletes. *Blackwood's Magazine,* in a rare deviation from its snobbish tradition of no comment on sporting matters, cynically noted that the Olympics and hunting were both forms of war, "without its guilt, and only five-and-twenty percent of its danger." Veteran sport correspondent Sydney Skilton marveled at Finnish efficiency and the harmony of the Helsinki Games, and was convinced "that sport could succeed where politicians had failed." A *Boston Globe* reporter was fascinated by the huge scoreboard inside the Russian camp at Otaniemi, prominently displaying the daily point-total of the USSR over the United States. However, on the last day of the games, the United States won in basketball, swimming, and boxing, giving them the strictly unofficial team title. "There were more red faces than red banners at the Iron Curtain Camp," the reporter chortled. Another Western newspaperman entered the Russian camp without permission. "The board was still up. But the points were down," concluded the article.

The essence of news is conflict. Members of the press have always sought it out and reported it. Most of the strife at the Helsinki games was on the athletic fields. The perceptive Red Smith of the *New York Times,* a frequent critic of the Olympic Games, called the Helsinki affair "The Quiet Olympics." He wrote that:

In spite of irresponsible predictions of a throat-cutting match between communism and the free world—specifically between Russia and the United States—this has been up to now the most companiable international quilting bee ever promoted.

When it was all over, Erik von Frenckell, president of the organizing committee for these Games, the fifteenth of the modern Olympic era, congratulated the athletes, the IOC, the sport federations, and NOCs around the world, but, most of all, he thanked "the entire Finnish nation for the helpfulness and skill shown in the promotion of a common cause." Edstrom retired, and American multimillionaire sportsman Avery Brundage was elected president of the IOC. He called the Helsinki Games "the best ever" and devoted the next twenty years to keeping the games small, controllable, and amateur. He was doomed to failure. But for the moment, at least, even the *New York Times* was euphoric and agreed with Mr. Brundage that the dream of international friendship and fair play was brought a little closer to reality by the recent Olympic Games. "This dream is far more important than winning a race," said the editorialist, and "whatever happens in the world, the dream does not wholly die."

In the year 1956, global politics was especially topsy-turvy, and, with the summer Olympic Games occurring in the southern hemisphere during November and December, the accumulated international conflict and disorientation had a profound impact on them. President Brundage grumbled more than usual, repeating that "if we held up the Games every time the politicians made a mess of things, we would never have them."

The Olympic year began with the winter Games in Cortina, Italy, in late January. Uncooperative weather failed to keep the resourceful Italian organizing committee from consummating another glittering winter festival. Cross-country skiing was dominated by athletes from the USSR, Norway, Sweden, and Finland. The Finns refused to give up their domination of jumping events, while the host nation's athletes divided bobsled honors with the Swiss. The Russian, Americans, and Canadian ice-hockey teams won a dozen games with but three losses among them. Anton Sailer of Austria won three gold medals in downhill skiing, his brilliant athletics and handsome features making "Toni" an instant world celebrity. Scandinavian, Swiss, Austrian, and Soviet women were the class of downhill cross-country skiing, while Soviet male speedskaters won seven of twelve medals. Hayes Alan Jenkins, Ronald Robertson, David Jenkins, Tenley Albright, Carol Heiss, all from the United States overwhelmed the figure skating scene, while the Austrian pair of Kurt Oppelt and "Sissy" Schwarz outskated couples from Canada and Hungary. Between these winter and summer games, tension in the Suez Canal zone, ideological conflict between mainland China and Taiwan, and the

vicious military aggression against Hungary reminded some folks of the
months just prior to the Berlin Olympics of 1936.

Fainting spells were contagious in the sweltering mass of 103,000 at the
summer opening ceremonies, one victim being Russia's Galina Zybina,
shot-putter and "the strongest women in the world." On the second day of
these Australian Olympic Games, 23 November, the Russian sailor,
Vladimir Kuts, ran a ruthless 10,000-meter final in a record 28:45.6.
"Kuts murdered me," confessed Gordon Pirie, who fought gallantly for
twenty-one laps. World Champion Charlie Dumas became Olympic

*Glen Davis, double gold medal winner at 400 meter hurdles, Melbourne and
Rome, 1956 and 1960. Credit John Lucas collection.*

champion with a high jump of 6'11 ¼", while the statuesque Czech, Olga
Fikotova, set a new Olympic discus record. Americans Chuck Vinci and
Isaac Berger won gold in the bantamweight and featherweight lifting
competition. The next day's finals saw a United States sweep in the
400-meter hurdles, led by Ohio State University's Glen Davis. The slick
Bobby Morrow won the first of his three first-place medals with a
100-meter victory. At the same time, Harold Connolly, Greg Bell, and
Norman Read were winning the hammer, long jump, and 50-kilometer
walk. The Italians won team fencing, while Soviets Igor Ryback and
Fjador Bogdanovski lifted their way to victory. On Monday, 26 November

Al Oerter, USA, gold medalist in discus, 1956, 1960, 1964, and 1968 Olympic Games. Credit Track and Field News, Inc., California.

records tumbled as Tom Courtney (800 meters), Bob Richards (vault), Egil Danielsen (javelin), Betty Cuthbert (100 meters), and weight-lifters Tommy Kono, Arkady Vorobiev, and Paul Anderson asserted their superiority. On this fifth day, rowing honors were shared by athletes from the USSR, the United States, Italy, and Canada; France's D'Oriola won the individual foil, Morrow blasted another victory in the 200 meters, young Al Oerter won the first of his four consecutive discus gold-medals, the brilliant da Silva triple-jumped 53′7½″, and Elzbieta Krzesinska won the long jump by nearly a foot with 20′9¾″.

The Olympic flame continued to burn day and night. Several weeks earlier, at ancient Olympia, the sun's rays concentrated through a glass ignited the first torch, which was flown to Australia where 2,830 runners (the first was an aborigine) carried the symbol in one-mile stages from Cairns to Melbourne. Ron Clarke, world junior mile-record holder, carried the torch into the stadium on the opening day.

The sixth day of the games witnessed a Russian sweep in the 20-kilometer walk, impressive wins by Kuts in the 5,000 meters, Parry O'Brien, shot, Lee Calhoun over Jack Davis in the high hurdles, Shirley Strickland in the women's hurdles, Inese Yaunzeme in the javelin, and Lars Hall of Sweden in the modern pentathlon.

Two surprises occurred the next day as Chris Brasher won the steeplechase and Charlie Jenkins the 400-meter dash. Italy and Hungary were supreme in épée. Aussie John Henricks won the 100-meter swim sprint in 55.4 on the last of November. Haape won the women's 200-meter breaststroke, Tychkevith the ladies' shot, and Cuthbert scored again at the 200-meter spring. Canoeing victories were shared by Russians, Rumanians, Hungarians, and Swedes. Three magnificent decathlon specialists—Milton Campbell, Rafer Johnson, and Vasili Kouznetsov—divided honors in that classic event. Gillian Sheen, a London dentist, won a gold medal with her sensational foils skills against highly favored rivals from the Continent.

The ninth day, 1 December, witnessed more canoeing finals, a sensational last-place to first-place win by Ireland's 1,500-meter champion Ron Delaney, American victories in both men's relays, a gold medal at last for Alain Mimoun in the marathon, a host of freestyle wrestling and boxing finals, a 98–55 basketball score by the United States over the USSR, and swimming and shooting finals. The Australian men's 4 × 200-meter-relay team swam away from the Americans in the finals, winning by eight seconds in world record time on 3 December.

On the eleventh day, the Hungarians in sabre, the Soviets and Japanese in gymnastics, the Yugoslav-German tie in water polo, Australian-American swim domination, and Italian cycling skill wrote Olympic history. Yachting races ended on 5 December, with Sweden, Denmark,

New Zealand, and the United States the acknowledged class of the field. Gerald Ouellette of Canada pumped 600 shots out of 600, winning the small-bore rifle, prone, competition while Helsinki winner Anatoli Bogdanov won another gold medal in small-bore rifle, three positions.

A bloody semifinal water polo match between Hungary (4) and Russia (0) made international headlines, the animosity between the two nations venting itself, unfortunately, in the underwater "play." The Hungarians eventually won the final over Yugoslavia. The 1–0 field hockey win by India over Pakistan continued a great tradition by both teams. Greco-Roman wrestling champions from Turkey, Rumania, Finland, Bulgaria, Sweden, and the USSR were crowned. Italian, French, and Australian cyclists claimed victories in the 1000-meter time trial, the 1000-meter sprint, and the 2000-meter tandem. Rudolf Karpati kept the Hungarian tradition by winning the individual sabre competition. On 7 December, the French won the team road-cycling title, but Italy's Ercole Baldini won the 116.65-mile road race in 5:21:17. Murray Rose (1,500 meters) and Lorraine Crapp (400 meters) shared honors with diver Pat McCormick as the enormously appealing swim competition came to an end.

The fifteenth and closing day of these games of the sixteenth Olympiad was Saturday, 8 December 1956. The final soccer match saw the Russians run by Yugoslavia 1–0. The huge crowd enjoyed the farewell parade of athletes, no longer marching in national squads, but rather walking arm-in-arm with chosen friends from other countries. Brundage officially closed the games, calling for a youth reunion in Rome in 1960. The stadium scoreboard flashed: "The 1956 Olympic race is run. May all who have been present go forth to their homelands, and may the Olympic spirit go with them."

Mind-bending delays in Olympic venue construction had plagued the Melbourne Organizing Committee all through 1955 and 1956. Brundage flew to Australia and delighted world sport journalists with his colorful, direct chastisement of the games officials. No Olympic Games are even remotely near perfect. Small and large disorders were daily occurrences in Melbourne. An American hammer-thrower was sent home for insubordination on the eve of his competition. Cries of protest arose at the Olympic Village as Corporal Brian Agney blundered and raised the Communist Chinese flag rather than the Republic of China's banner. Soviet-Hungarian animosity spilled over, sometimes influencing the throngs of Melbourne spectators. Rhubarb and snafu were inevitable when 4,500 athletes from sixty-seven countries attempted to mingle with several hundred thousand Australians, visitors, and journalists. An English steeplechaser almost lost his precious gold medal following an accusation of interference. A Russian rower was beyond consolation as he bobbled his silver medal, losing it in the dark waters of Lake Wendouree.

No matter what Olympic fathers may say, the Olympic Games cannot place themselves above politics and war, but there is a certain sublimity in the sight of young men and women from scores of nations making an amazingly good effort to place them there. Even hardened journalists were impressed by Kuts's double victory and the surging acclamation of the crowd, which, for the moment, transcended every world barrier. The *Age* of Melbourne noted that "There can be no perfect games until there are perfect people, but we have watched a sincere attempt to achieve this human ideal."

These games have always stood as a grim but joyous, stubborn quest for peace and brotherhood. Neil Allen of the *London Times* agreed that, despite the games series barely escaping cancellation, the whole affair "has been great fun." The acknowledged common denominator—international athletic competition—while sometimes creating "incidents," is the reason why, as Coles Phinizy of *Sports Illustrated* pointed out, the common values and not the divergences need emphasis, and thus "there can be a moratorium at least in the minds of men." It was with this thought in mind that the International Olympic Committee was nominated for the 1957 Nobel Peace Prize eventually won by Canada's ceaseless ambassador of good will, Lester Pearson. Physical prowess interlocked with strength of character has always fascinated the human race and reminded men of their own integrated glory. Philosopher-physician-athlete Roger Bannister put it in a very homely way in describing the mental-physical strength of the Soviet champion: "Vladimir, Vladimir, Vladimir Kuts, Nature's attempt at an engine in boots." The sweetness and light uniformly displayed by the Australian people, mixed with the consistent intensity of the athletes themselves, combined and resulted in a cosmopolitan elixir that looked "forward from the Olympics to trials on a bigger scale than sport" and hinted at mankind's concealed divinity.

10 • Avery Brundage—High Priest of the Olympic Dream

During the 1950s and 1960s, the most important sports leader in the world was Mr. Avery Brundage of Chicago, Illinois. If this statement brings instant rise to argument from some, then certainly all voices will be silent when he is looked upon as the most controversial and least understood sportsman in the world during these same years. Brundage has been called a scurrilous capitalist, a fascist, a communist, a Nazi lover, a bigot, a racist, an unfeeling millionaire and a thoroughly unlikeable old curmudgeon. In a quieter voice, and usually not in North America, he has been called a great athlete, a magnificent sports leader, a connoisseur of art, an idealist, a loyal American and cosmopolitan, and the last link with the essence of sport and the concept of pure play.

Of Scotch-English ancestry, Avery Brundage was born in Detroit on 28 September 1887, attended Chicago's English High School, and received a degree in civil engineering from Illinois University in 1909. Outstanding academic honors and a gregarious interest in social and cultural areas marked these early years. He was a fine all-round athlete, good enough to make the 1912 Olympic team in the pentathlon and decathlon. The first "world's fastest human," Charlie Paddock, once said of Brundage: "I remember very distinctly that he was not so much a born athlete as he was a great fighter." Plunging into the business world, Brundage, a poor boy, made a million dollars by the time he was thirty. During these years, he was three-time American all-around champion. An amusing yet futurist article about him appeared in a World War I issue of *The World Magazine*. Marveling at the robust six-footer's ability to work all day and train "two hours every night exercising under the moon and stars," the article concluded that "it is not astonishing that Brundage is a bachelor." It was another ten years before he married Elizabeth Dunlap in 1926, a union that lasted till her death in June of 1971.

Brundage continued to make money in Chicago real estate, managed to beat nearly everyone in handball, served as president and manager of the

Avery Brundage, USA, President IOC, 1952 –1972. Credit United States Olympic Committee collection.

Western Conference Athletic body, and presided over the Big Ten Alumni Association. On 20 November 1928, he was elected president of the Amateur Athletic Union (AAU). He promised to oppose growing college athletic commercialism, and put his fiscal acumen to work by suggesting to the American Olympic Committee a continually renewed four-year search for monies instead of the frantic and frequently abortive efforts during the year of the games. Brundage set his jaw and announced that his unanimous election was unsolicited and had no strings attached.

The battle lines were drawn. Brundage—*die herausforderung,* the provocateur, the single-minded aggressor—issued a challenge to the world sporting community to look deeply into the delight of sport without profit as compared with the other kind, consummately skillful, commercial entertainment. During his innumerable world tours, Brundage collected several thousand Japanese *netsuke,* tiny, hand-carved wooden or ivory figures. Originally, these netsuke were carved with loving care for personal use by Japanese gentlemen to anchor perfume boxes hung from their kimona sashes. Some had imperfections, but these bore the stamp of the artist's personality. Later, as demand grew, professional carvers turned out thousands. Their work was more polished and displayed a superior technical skill, but, according to Brundage, was "cold, stiff, and without imagination." Here was the difference between amateurism and professionalism spelled out in a netsuke, at least according to one oriental art authority and sport philosopher. Author Robert Shaplen pointed out prophetically that it was, of course, an amateur carving of exquisite beauty that Brundage clutched firmly in his large hand that day.

It was at the forty-first annual convention of the AAU, held at St. Louis in November 1929, that President Brundage formally began his "Defense of the Amateur Code." He pronounced the obvious but not unimportant dogma that there is a high level of democracy found on the playing field that is attained in few other lines of endeavor. Unrelenting discipline coupled with the joy of effort reveal the vast possibilities of sport, he continued. "Buried way down deep in us is something brought out only under the stress of competition that enables one to excel himself," he extolled. The feeling is common to both the professional and the amateur, but, Brundage added, the former fails to understand "the spiritual side" of sport—the uplift and exhilaration of doing something for its own sake without thought of making money.

It was a good speech; Brundage had packed everything he believed into it. His personal flag of sport idealism was aloft and would neither change little nor be lowered throughout his life. For him, as for his moral mentor, Coubertin, no philosophy, no religion, preached loftier sentiments than the unvarnished amateur code of sport. The melding of physical fitness, flourishing intelligence, and a kind of omniscient fair play marked

Brundage's conception of the Olympic ideal and of amateur sport. Professionalized athletics, he said, and repeated a thousand times thereafter, are simply structurally incapable of such human ambition. The late Grantland Rice and Brundage shared, I believe, a similar view of the high place of noncommercial sport as, akin to religion, a kind of unitarian faith that looks upon good character as the fundamental virtue. Journalist Rice saw the spirit of fair play as indigenous to sport and religion. "Both," he once said, "stand against hate, greed, trickery, and muckerism of any sort; both give the race a higher, cleaner standard by which to live." Brundage, as well, believed in motives for sport involvement higher than career and profit. For him, sport was a meaningful supplement to and not a goal in life. His brand of sport, "like the religious feeling . . . comes from inside . . . providing instrinsic satisfaction; it is nothing more or less than an application of the Golden Rule—the essence of all religions."

Avery Brundage served as American AAU chief seven times from 1929 to 1936. On 19 November 1930, he was elected president of the American Olympic Committee, and, on the eve of the Berlin Olympics, replaced Ernest Lee Jahncke as a member of the International Olympic Committee. Thus, in late 1936, just before his resignation as head of the AAU, Brundage was deeply involved in all three national and world organizations. The depression wiped him out financially, but not otherwise. He redoubled his efforts—something he had learned to do long since—and his business spiral ascended eventually into the multimillion-dollar category.

After two years (1934–1936) of the bitterest internecine struggles among amateur sports leaders, the Brundage faction was successful in convincing the majority that the Berlin Olympics would be free of Nazism, racism, and militarism. The United States would participate. Mr. Brundage refused to accept the contiguousness of sport and politics. Even before his September 1934 visit to Germany, he said that the world would soon be presented with the greatest Olympic Games of modern times. "We should see in the youth at Berlin," he said, "the forebearers of a race of free, independent thinkers accustomed to the democracy of sport." In January of 1935, Brundage was presented the James Edward Sullivan award for his unrivaled contribution to amateur athletics. Reflecting on the Games of the Eleventh Olympiad, Brundage called them the largest and greatest; "young people imbued with the democratic spirit of competitive sport are not swayed by radical ideas," he said.

Brundage died in 1975, leaving sixty-five years of correspondence, among other bequests, to the University of Illinois, and, at the same time, revealing a darker, anti-Semitic side. Powerful segments of American liberalism, certain church groups, and "that New York City Jewish lobby" had joined forces to prevent the United States from participating in the

"Nazi-Hitler Olympics" of 1936. The bulldog, Brundage, was deeply angered at these efforts, and struck back with every weapon possible, including, unfortunately, personal invective against all Jews. The unauthored 1935 pamphlet *Fair Play for American Athletes* was a Brundage-approved document of the American Olympic Committee which said, in essence: "We, the sporting public, do not care about the 'Jew-Nazi altercation' in Germany, especially if it might prevent our great Olympic team from participation in the games." Logical arguments for American involvement in the Berlin games were neutralized by the use of glittering generalities, appeals to long-time fears of communism, and the omnipresent specter of bigotry.

Ten thousand copies of the pamphlet were published and distributed before the countering open letter to Dr. Theodore Lewald appeared. "Germany has violated the Olympic Code!" cried its author, Judge Jeremiah T. Mahoney, president of the AAU and implacable, long-time foe of Brundage. Mahoney reminded Dr. Lewald of the innumerable political intrusions of the Hitler regime into Olympic business, and, much worse, of monstrous incidents of racism, brutality, and genocide. American participation in the 1936 Olympic Games under the swastika must be totally abhorent, concluded Judge Mahoney, and, therefore, "I hope that all Americans will join with me in opposing American participation in the Olympic games and aid me in having the games transferred to another country."

Of course, the latter hope was impossible, with only ten months remaining till the scheduled Games of the Eleventh Olympiad. Brundage worked very hard to gain support in the other direction and was successful. German sport historian Arnd Kruger noted that Brundage's midwestern, middle-class, conservative background was fertile ground for his suspicion and mistrust of Jews, but that he was no different—except for his personal notoriety—from most of his kind. "Brundage," said Kruger, "reflected and verbalized the emotions and prejudices of his peers"; much of his writings were "merely a way of disguising American middle-class anti-Semitism." There is some truth to Kruger's self-righteous criticism of Brundage, but what may be even more accurate was the lifelong compulsion of Brundage (as of Coubertin) that the Olympic Games *must* be held every four years and that no earthly power be allowed to interrupt the celebration of the games. It was a successful ancient Greek idea, but one that was marked by the cancellation of the modern games in 1916, and, in 1935, the grim possibility of another postponement and of permanent nullification.

Rarely out of hot water and the national glare, Brundage allied himself with some of the nation's most strident isolationists in the years before Pearl Harbor. Conservative, dogmatic, and ideologically consistent,

Brundage saw sport as transcendent over all political or racial considerations. He headed the Citizens-Keep-America-Out-of-the-War Committee and shared a platform with Charles Lindbergh before 40,000 people in Chicago's Soldiers' Field on 3–4 August 1940. Brundage reminded all that he is not a pacifist, but was opposed to foreign entanglements. "We are wholeheartedly behind a strong defense program but against a program of aggression," he cried. Politics won out, of course, and Brundage impatiently waited out the passage of two Olympiads—each empty of a sporting festival. The world was preoccupied between 1940 and 1945. Smack in the middle of the war, Brundage enraged many by declaring that Japan and Germany should not be banished from future Olympic games. "Keep 'em both out . . . and Brundage, too," clicked many journalists' typewriters.

Only London, England, was brave and foolhardy enough to host the 1948 games. Brundage, now sixty-one years old, "remarkably flat-bellied, muscular and erect"—the bogeyman of sport—continued to withstand verbal brickbats. After reprimanding lovely skating champion Barbara Ann Scott for accepting a new car as a gift, Brundage was called "the country's No. 1 common scold," "choleric Donald Duck," "Slavery Avery," "champion of the sixteen-pound innuendo," and "a professional snoop." He countered with even greater pugnacity when asked "would anybody like to buy a tall, thin mind? See Brundage." Many agreed that his was "a mind that must have been caught in its infancy between two streetcars." Brundage, now the vice-president of the IOC as well as president of the USOC, punched back with "the true story" of the Olympic Movement. "It is," he said

the story of an idea of such universal appeal, and of such formidable strength that it has swept the world and captured the imagination of every civilized country.

During this period, Brundage wrote into the rule book his own definition of an amateur athlete as "one whose connection with sport is and has been solely for pleasure . . . and to whom sport is nothing more than recreation without financial gain of any kind, direct or indirect." Swedish authorities, already compensating their athletes for loss of salaries ("broken-time"), hurled vituperations at Brundage. Stockholm's *Dagens Nyheter* labeled him "apostle of hypocrisy"; *Idrottsbladet* got in a lick with: "It took Our Lord 800,000,000 years to create the world of today. How long a time will it take Mr. Brundage to learn to understand it?" The definition remained for a quarter century until the IOC, plagued with the very word "amateur," chose to avoid mentioning it completely in its rule 26, and carefully defined a professional athlete; all those remaining were eligible for the Olympic Games.

Brundage was fond of saying that professional athletics was not sport; it was, rather, he said, highly skillful and exciting entertainment. Amateur sports were free from the dollar sign and should be joyous activities, he repeated many times. None of us can remember if there ever was this sense of carefreeness in Brundage's own years of participation at the beginning of the century. Both Christianity and the Olympic Movement have made mistakes; no reason to abolish either of them, he said. One writer found the religious simile helpful in explaining Brundage's "inquisitorial attitude and his sense of mission." Sport—amateur sport, that is—"is not fun and games to Avery Brundage; it is a collection of solemn rites performed to dogmas he has spent a lifetime keeping pure." No question that the metaphysics and theology of Brundage revolved about the pure sport concept. On 17 December 1949, in Santa Barbara, California, while being honored by 200 civic, business, and cultural leaders, he deplored the world's sickness, alien doctrines and queer philosophies. "It may be that when the politicians adopt the principles of amateurism, fair play and good sportsmanship, it will find the antidote for its trouble."

Possibly the most significant day in Brundage's life occurred in July of 1952 when he was elected president of the International Olympic Committee, beating by a 30–17 margin Lord David Burghley, the Marquess of Exeter. King Haakon awarded the new president the Commander's Cross, Order of St. Olaf, with star clusters. Twenty nations would decorate him with highest honors. In addition to the Santa Barbara medal, he was given the first Medal of Merit from the city of Chicago; the first John Perry Bowditch Memorial for outstanding service to humanity; the University of Illinois achievement award; the state of Illinois Order of Lincoln; and honorary citizenship of some of the world's largest cities. Yet, as Red Smith once said, Brundage remains "the official target of abuse in every Olympic year since the invention of the discus." For most of his life, Brundage believed the Olympic Games to be imperishable. Only in his last years did he have some doubt. He felt that the games' organizers, as well as the Olympic philosophy, were sufficient to mute the effects of certain destructive ideologies.

In 1954, the 1 August *New York Times* noted that "athletics in Russia Impress Brundage"; his two-week inspection resulted in "a clean bill of health" for a Soviet sports program deemed amateur and free from direct political interference. He angered Australian leaders in the summer of 1955; Olympic Games plans were slow and inefficient, he said. Yet, on his way home, he stopped in West Germany where President Theodor Heuss conferred on Brundage the Great Service Cross with stars.

He always lived with these kinds of contradictions. Reluctant praise marks the brilliant biography of Brundage by senior *Sports Illustrated* editor Robert Creamer; the IOC president appeared more gregarious than usual, and, in an animated interview, shared some of his strongest feelings. Professional athletes are no less honorable than amateurs, he pointed out. But the former must win, Brundage continued, or it hurts their income.

> In triumph, Brundage lifted both hands high, like a man conducting a symphony. And there's the difference! Right there. As soon as you take money for playing a sport, it isn't sport, it's work.

There was always something of the evangelist in Brundage. "Amateur sport is a pure concept," he once said. "It is above profit, suppression, politics, intolerance, self-seeking . . . and I'll fight until I die to keep it from being polluted." He always felt that the professional takes from sport, while the amateur gives something to it.

In another sphere the esoteric world of oriental art, this complex person spent millions of dollars in a period of forty years. He gave the entire 6,000 pieces of his collection to the city of San Francisco—a forty-million-dollar gift which art critic Laurence Sickman called "the last comprehensive collection in this field that can be assembled in our time." All of it is housed in the Avery Brundage Wing of the M. H. de Young Memorial Museum. Oriental art was one of the greatest joys in Brundage's life. He smiled a lot when discussing art; few saw this side of the man. The tired definition of "amateur"—one possessing limited skill—found no applicability in either of Brundage's two worlds of art and sport. Noel F. Busch wrote that this Olympian of Asian art brought the deeper meaning of amateurism to art as well as sport. Busch, possibly influenced by the man he interviewed, concluded:

> Amateurism means the spirit of enthusiasm, creativeness and search for perfection that an artist or athlete brings to his task, a spirit which makes further incentive irrelevant.

Brundage found espousals of the joys of nonprofessional sport and art-collecting equally difficult to give up; both are like lotus-eating, he once said. One female art expert, who found him "enormously attractive, mild-voiced except when he roars at recalcitrant nations," recognized Brundage's two passions, pursued in tandem of amateur sport and art. "Hardly anyone knows more than he about the former; few know more about Oriental art." Another woman, Edith Weigle, seemed taken with his two great interests. She called Brundage "the man who has everything"; in an interview she noticed that "at 73 he has the powerful, wiry physique of an athlete of 30—one of the most amazing men in America. His two great interests are poles apart: Asian art and the Olympic Games." With apologies to Weigle, the two are not poles apart—at least not in the ambient air of idealism and excellence that always surrounded Brundage.

Never inconsistent in his view that professional athletes are honest entertainers but not sportsmen, Brundage always came under heavy fire from critics. One of them scored Brundage for failing to see that the great athletes—amateur or professional—give the last full measure of devotion to the task of extraordinary. Both have this same vision. "Brundage eats better, and has tenure," thus failing to understand the full tapestry, concluded the writer. Nonetheless, on his eightieth birthday in 1967, the city of Chicago hung out the Olympic flag for forty-eight hours and listened to the patriarch of amateurism call the Olympic movement "the most important social force in the world." Much closer to home, and on the same day, Brundage donated a tenth of a million dollars to promote sport among Chicago's poor children. This man Brundage, whose Grecian concept of the sportsman as the "seeker for perfection and lover of his efforts," faced the National Press Club members in Washington, D.C., on 17 September 1968. I was there that day and received a copy of his speech, distributed in advance of his presentation. He again called the Olympic movement the most important social force in the world. Citizens of every host city of the Olympic Games have benefited enormously, he continued. Staggering costs are unconscionable and must be reduced; yet, culturally and in real terms, a unique contribution is manifest in these international games. The complete man of the Golden Age of Greece is the Olympic goal and its philosophy, he continued in unashamed enthusiasm.

> The world, alas, is full of injustice, aggression, violence and warfare. . . . But this is no reason to destroy the nucleus of international cooperation and good will which we have created in the Olympic Movement. The Games are contests between individuals and not between nations, an oasis in an over-charged and over-heated world. We invite the youth of all countries, who are certainly not responsible for these evils, to accept our regulations and to participate.

Brundage's near-impossible posture of allowing no political interference in the Olympic Games, successful in the early days, has become more a wish than reality. Brundage's unequivocal opposition to political influence in the quadrennial festival leaves little room for criticism. The great fault lay in his monumental oversell regarding the benefits of Olympic involvement. Had Mr. Brundage (and all his predecessors) not professed so sharply and with such evangelic zeal these inexorable social, physical, and spiritual gains, they might have manifested themselves to an even greater degree. Cynics among the world's press, totally encapsulated in the athletics-for-profit atmosphere, might then give the Olympic sport-philosophy a more objective look. They might laugh less at Brundage's remonstrance that only when Olympic principles of fair play and good sportsmanship are followed in business and political fields can we expect a happier and more peaceful world. In the last years of his stewardship of the Olympic movement, Brundage became increasingly alarmed at the runaway growth of the games, their incredible cost, creeping commercialism, increases in the profit motive among many competitors, and virulent political intrusions. He fought these evils for over forty years. Secretly, as did Baron de Coubertin before him, Brundage feared that, as a viable social force for good, the Olympic Games might some day weaken and die. This "Don Quixote of the Twentieth Century," this defender of the faith, continued to look upon the Olympic movement as a revolt against modern materialism—a devotion to the cause and not to the reward. His reluctant admirer, William Johnson, admitted in a penetrating analysis that "Avery Brundage sleeps the sleep of the just."

Political pressures on the International Olympic Committee during 1968 and 1972 resulted in the banishment of Rhodesia and South Africa from the games. It was done over the strong objections of IOC President Brundage. It took a heavy toll, both physical and psychological, on the ageing and nearly blind American sports leader. His last years were torturous. His wife of forty-four years, Elizabeth, died in 1971. They had no children. The massacre of the Israeli athletes at the 1972 Olympics was a shattering experience worldwide and an especially traumatic one for Brundage. His beloved Olympics had been used for pillage, political blackmail, and murder—a travesty of all the Brundage utterances of a half-century. His puzzling ramblings at the Israeli funeral ceremony in the packed Munich stadium on 6 September 6 1972, were not altogether rational, an indication of the immediate trauma, and a sign of Brundage's rapidly failing powers. His last public appearance before his Olympic associates was especially painful. He never could speak a foreign language, and, on this particular occasion, his inept German was garbled and vacuous. One IOC staff member present at the meeting thought to himself: "What a horror; this lifelong strong man slipping." At eighty-five, he was a man from another era, as William O. Johnson pointed out in his 1972 book *All That Glitters Is Not Gold*—from "another time when the works of Horatio Alger were considered profound, when ethics could not be conditional. . . ." Right to the very end, Brundage reiterated the ancient litany that the Olympics are for those athletes for whom sport is merely recreational. The perceptive Red Smith called Brundage, at his 1972 retirement, "a rich and righteous anachronism," a man whose "wrath is the more terrible because it is so sincere and unenlightened." Brundage was a "true believer," and, as such, always ran the risk of myopic views on Olympic, nonprofessional sport. When Michael Morris, Lord Killanin succeeded Brundage in the fall of 1972, he pledged a modern, honest appraisal of the responsibilities and needs of Olympic aspirants and Olympic athletes. Brundage was rapidly left behind, his allegedly superannuated Olympic philosophy as old as the man himself.

In the spring of 1973, just short of his eighty-sixth birthday, Brundage married thirty-six-year-old Marianna Reuss, a handsome German woman of royal ancestry and a hostess at the Munich Olympic Games. The tall, extremely fashionable princess was fluent in six languages and an accomplished skier. They were together almost two years, during which her devotion and displays of tenderness to her husband were already a frequent conversational topic, when he suffered from a suspected heart attack and was hospitalized in Garmisch-Partenkirchen, Germany. Two weeks later, on 8 May 1975, he died in the small district hospital.

The major newspapers of the world took note of the extraordinary nature of the man, his single-mindedness, and his pugnaciousness. Very few of the obituaries carried much on his private life, his habits, friends, hobbies, or philanthropies. Brundage achieved the highest distinction in the masonic order, the thirty-third Degree in Freemasonry. At the same time, he allowed archivists and historians from Notre Dame University's International Sports and Games Research Collection to spend two months in his offices photographing a significant portion of his sixty-year collection of Olympic documents. A year before his death, Brundage contributed $333,000 to the University of Illinois, a fund earmarked to help gifted students who are at the same time exceptional athletes in so-called minor sports. The *Illinois Alumni News* noted that, for the academic year 1978–1979, twenty-five students, including wheelchair athletes, had been selected for Brundage scholarships. Thirteen men and twelve women, all top scholars, were active in archery, badminton, basketball, bicycling, bowling, figure skating, football, gymnastics, hockey, racquetball, rugby, sailing, soccer, softball, swimming, tennis, track, volleyball, water polo, and wrestling. And then, in 1977, this same university which had graduated Brundage in 1909 received the stunning gift of all his papers, books, tributes, gifts, and mementos from every continent in the world. This enormous and extraordinarily valuable collection, housed in the World Heritage Museum, Urbana-Champaign campus, in the university's special sport and physical education library, as well as 139 cubic feet of Brundage correspondence in the archives, is the subject of research by scholars from all over the world. In his own peculiar way, during his long life, Mr. Brundage prayed for peace. "Whatever happens in the world," he once said, "the dream does not wholly die. The sportsmanship of strength, of skill, of justice, and of gentleness survives."

As a college undergraduate in 1908, the young Brundage wrote an essay in the school paper called, "The Football Field As a Sifter of Man." Man's

ξin nature" is exposed and strengthened in honorable athletic combat,
ɔid. For the remaining sixty-five years of his life, he had no reason to
change his mind. He once told Robert Creamer of *Sports Illustrated:*

> What can't sport teach? What can't it achieve? But you can't say this, because
> people wouldn't understand that amateurism is a sort of religion.

Then he was off again, concluded Creamer, across the hotel lobby, "his
shoulders squared, his chin out, looking, as always, like a man carrying a
banner." Red Smith of the *New York Times* never had much love for
Brundage but he did "give the devil his due," calling him the world's
foremost guardian of the amateur ideal, "a position comparable to a
lookout in a prairie dog colony." Brundage subscribed wholly to the
principles of Coubertin, although he never knew the man personally.
Brundage was tough and intransigent, with an old-fashioned work ethic
that overcame poverty, weathered all the slings and arrows, refused to be
broken; he coveted and increased his personal fortune, while, at the same
time, he perceived these monies as means toward a holy purpose. Sitting
nearly unnoticed among the hundreds of boxes at the University of Illinois
Brundage Collection is a lengthy, disjointed, unpublished, typewritten
manuscript—a personal history of the Olympic movement and the
Olympic Games. Mixing fact and philosophy, as one must inevitably do in
writing such a history, Brundage said at one point:

> The world's sickness, social, economic and political, exists because of one and
> only one reason: lack of fair play and good sportsmanship in human
> relationships. . . . Peruvian and Bolivian Indians die when brought to sea
> level. The Olympic Movement must be kept on Olympic heights of idealism for
> it will surely die if it is permitted to descend to more base and mercenary levels.

It was as fitting an epitaph as any for a man who knew that the Olympic
Games, stripped of idealism, would be the poorest show on earth.

11 • Ascendancy of Olympic Games Glory and Crisis 1960 –1968

The inextricable hand of international politics once again created misunderstandings and waves of animosity within the Olympic community in 1959, the year before the Rome games. The question of the "Two Chinas" plagues the International Olympic Committee so much that a 28 May directive ordered the Olympic committee on the island of Taiwan not use "China" in its title, since only a fraction of the Chinese population was represented by that organization. Only the year before, mainland China's Olympic committee had withdrawn its membership, stating that it would return only on the day that "Avery Brundage, a tool of the imperialist State Department of the United States, will resign his presidency." Brundage repeated that the IOC never deals with governments, but only with Olympic sport administrators.

Brundage's garbled 28 May directive was misunderstood, and much of the world thought that the Chicago millionaire's committee had kicked Taiwan out of the Olympic movement. "If the politicians will only leave us alone," growled the IOC president. The island republic did compete as "Formosa"; the giant Communist state on the mainland has not competed in any Olympic Games to this date (1980) nor has it asked for readmission into the Olympic family.

Writing in the *New York Times* magazine section of 4 October 1959, the famous British Olympian Christopher Chataway stated that irrational spectator chauvinism is just about neutralized by the general air of friendship and respect between competing athletes at the Olympic Games. Thus, he concluded, these games are neither an evil nor a force for good. "They are worth while for what they are—the best sports meeting in the world," he said. Not all agreed. John V. Grombach, writing in *The American Mercury* of June 1960, reflected the feeling of many regarding the infiltration of politics into the Olympic Games. "Here can be seen," he warned, "the ultimate intent of the Soviet Union and the Communist block to bury us."

Squaw Valley in the United States was the unlikely site of the February 1960 winter Olympic Games. The brains and energy behind the selection of this unknown resort as an Olympic venue was a certain six feet six inch Alex Cushing, "a Boston Brahmin once removed," who had convinced the IOC to vote for the site and had extracted a financial pledge from the California legislature. Eventually, he returned eight more times to the California treasury. Walt Disney was hired and put in charge of entertainment, pageantry, ice statues, and daylight fireworks. Sport facilities were built with great difficulty, since the nearest city was Reno, Nevada. Even that western outpost couldn't escape the cold war, for, amidst the signs of welcome, Harold's nightclub displayed a banner proclaiming, "All American Society Dedicated to our Children's Future that they may not live a life worse than death under Communist slavery."

Multiple weather crises came and passed; the winter pageant began and ultimately was assessed an excellent competition. The usual stars and several superstars emerged from Squaw Valley, but the advent of the Soviet Union, with 37 athletes in the top six places, to the position of dominant winter-sports nation was shocking to Scandinavians and disturbing to many others not directly connected with sport. The three Scandinavian countries accumulated forty-four places, the United States had thirteen in the elite group, and Germany fourteen, followed by Austria and France with seven, Italy and Poland with six place-winners, Canada four, Switzerland four, Czechoslovakia, Holland, and Japan with two, and a single British fifth place performance in the men's 10,000-meter speed-skating. This American version of a winter Olympics was relaxed, almost casual, by comparison with the European model.

In 1960, Rome, the Eternal City, broiled in the hottest Spetember in half a century. The organizing committee's little book, *The Climate of Rome*, warned that midafternoon temperatures during the time of the games would hover around thirty-five degrees centigrade (ninety-five degrees Fahrenheit). They got much hotter than that, and tens of thousands of upper class Italians temporarily abandoned the city. Still, the magic of this very great city was such that a young Japanese student, unable to find modest-priced sleeping quarters, wrote home: "Rome and the Olympic Games. What an irresistible combination! When would I have such a chance again?"

Everything in Rome was on a grand scale, and the Italian government, working with the Olympic organizing committee (CONI), was determined to outdo even the colossal Berlin games of 1936. Italy's lack of a relatively orderly two-party system of government and pressure from Communists and the splinter groups created anxiety among the ruling Christian Democrats. Their desire for absolutely grandiose Olympic Games went far beyond sporting enthusiasm. Money was no object, and the $200 million

Olympic price-tag was paid, in part, from the lucrative *Totocalcio,* or soccer "betting pool."

The IOC always objects to Olympic Games expenditures which include the cost of major urban improvements—permanent benefits that might not have taken place without the catalyst of the great Olympic Games. Benito Mussolini had lived long enough to see completed several magnificent marble stadia in anticipation, if you will, of victorious 1944 Olympic Games in his city of Rome. They were still in good shape in 1960, mosaic pavements everywhere, with the word "Duce" embedded 264 times. Many of the new Roman arenas, built by Italy's top builder-designer Pier Luigi, were models of both beauty and functionalism. The sixty-nine-year-old Luigi, designer of the UNESCO building in Paris and the New York Port Authority building, felt that only structure was important and that "in any building, esthetic perfection derives from technical perfection." City fathers were positively thirsting for a great Games, having been denied the opportunity in 1904, 1908, and 1944. Twelve magnificent venues were ready for seventeen sports, not including the mammoth Palace of Science where a special thirteen-sectioned "Sport in History and Art" exhibition drew thousands of visitors and would have gladdened the heart of the late Baron de Coubertin.

The blowtorch Roman weather welcomed 5,348 athletes from eighty-four nations, with the politically-divided East and West Germany competing as a single national team. Crowds were small during the first week of competition. Track and field athletics, the jewel of the Olympics, were scheduled late in the program and thus the Italian holiday masses delayed their return to Rome. On 24 August, Pope John XXIII welcomed 3,500 athletes, including ten Russians; the next day were scheduled the always-impressive opening-day ceremonies, the competitive struggle beginning on the twenty-sixth. The Columbia Broadcasting Company paid $660,000 for Olympic television rights, thus, for the first time, including millions of vicarious Olympic spectators. A *New York Times* editorial on 25 August noted that, long before the efforts of the United Nations, "the quadrennial games were in many ways the strongest international fact that bound any number of nations together with ties both visible and attractive to most of the population here and abroad." This view was, of course, the optimistic side of the Olympic coin.

Swimming events opened these Games of the Seventeenth Olympiad and, astonishingly, athletes from Australia and the United States won every men's and women's individual and relay event, except for Britain's Anita Lonsbrough's upset in the 200-meter breaststroke. Gary Tobian and Robert Webster of the United States won the two men's diving events, while youthful Ingred Kramer of Germany won two gold medals in women's diving. Sixty competitors from twenty-three countries vied for honors in the modern pentathlon during this first week of the games. When the shooting, swimming, fencing, riding, and running cross-country was completed, Hungarians Ferenc Nemeth, Imre Nagy, and András Balczó had taken first, second, and fourth places, with Bob Black, third, and Soviets Igor Novikov and Nikolay Tatarinov rounding out the top places. Ten evenings of boxing at the Palazzo dello Sport proved, as always, that aggressive skill usually wins at these Olympic contests. Far too many questionable decisions marked the bouts. Blue-clad Italians delighted the home crowd with six of the ten finalists. Hungary, the USSR, Poland, and Czechoslovakia, each claimed a winner, while the three Americans were led by light-heavyweight Cassius Clay (Muhammed Ali). Tucked away just east of the Appian Way, a few miles south of Rome, is Lake Albano. The men and women from the Soviet Union won three gold, and one silver, and figured in every rowing/canoeing final. Denmark, Sweden, Hungary, and Germany also won championship medals. The antique Basilica de Massenzio was a perfect facility for Greco-Roman and freestyle wrestling; 339 athletes from forty-seven nations took ten days and 571 bouts to prove that Turkey was the top wrestling nation in the world, followed by the United States, Bulgaria, Germany, and Rumania.

Sixteen teams qualified for the basketball Olympics, including the top seven from Melbourne, the host nation, three non-European teams, and five qualifiers from a recent pre-Olympic tournament. No matter. The likes of Lester Lane, Oscar Robertson, and Jerry Lucas made it easy enough for the United States to win its fifth basketball gold medal over Russia, Brazil, and Italy. Cycling was another story, with the Italians winning the first gold medal of the games in the new event, the 100-kilometer team road-race. They added four more gold, sweeping every track event, their entire cycling team of twelve coming away with a medal. Field hockey was played at the Stadio dei Marmi and Velodrome Olimpico. Sixteen teams competed; Britain emerged in fourth place, Spain in third, and Pakistan dethroned India after thirty-two years in what the *British Olympic Report* called "a superb exhibition of scientific hockey, with masterful ball-control on both sides."

From 29 August to 10 September, the Palazzo dei Congressi was a veritable inferno as fencers from forty-three countries fought one another as well as overpowering heat. The Soviets won the foil championships, the Italians in épée, and, of course, the Hungarians in sabre. Fifty-year old Hungarian Aladar Gerevich, in his sixth Olympics, just failed to reach the sabre finals. Heidi Schmid of Germany won the individual women's foil, but the Soviets won the new team title.

Back at Lake Albana, the canoe races were over, and seven rowing competitions occupied 30 August through 3 September. Russia's Ivanov repeated in the single sculls, Germany and Russia dominated by winning nine medals, while twenty crews succeeding in getting into the finals. The idyllic Lake Albano, the interior of an extinct volcano, was fanned by cool breezes and provided a perfect 2,000-meter racing course. The athletes trained here, living in a Catholic institution run by nuns. The sensation of the competition was the upset victory of the German eight-oared crew. Radical reshaping of their rowing blades, the two middle oars swinging from the same side of the boat, a bewildering new slide technique, and superb physical conditioning all contributed to an unprecedented forty-seven-strokes-per-minute tempo and victory over Canadian, Czech, French, and American crews in 5:57.18, several boat lengths in the lead.

Another gorgeous Olympic venue was the Bay of Naples, where, in the shadow of Mt. Vesuvius and the Isle of Capri, yachtsmen (and one woman) enjoyed sunny days, crystal-clear water, and fine sailing breezes. Soviet, Norwegian, Greek, and American crews proved victorious, while Denmark's sailor, Paul Elvstrom, achieved an unparalleled fourth consecutive victory in the single-man dinghy class. R. N. Bavier, writing in *Yachting* magazine, said that the perfectly conditioned Elvstrom had a sixth sense for going the right way and an unbelievable touch. "He is unquestionably the finest single-hander the world has ever seen," he concluded. Amidst antique ruins of the Terme di Caracalla, Russian women and Japanese men won the lion's share of gymnastic honors. The Italians surprised and were the third best team present. Boris Shaklin, Larissa Latynina, Takashi Ono, Yuri Titov, Yukio Endo, Sofia Muratova, and the frail-looking Polina Aslakhova were several of the stars in the 1960 gymnastic firmament. The fabulous and popular Masao Takemoto, at forty-two years of age, was in two finals, winning a silver medal on the horizontal bar and fifth overall. Next to athletics, shooting was the most universal sport, with sixty nations represented. The Russians were again the most successful, claiming two gold, two silver, and three bronze medals in six events. Possibly the two most remarkable marksmen were William McMillan in the rapid-fire pistol and Aleksey Guschtschin in the free pistol, breaking Torsten Ullman's 1936 Berlin Olympic world record. Astonishingly, the old Swede, Ullman, took part in these Rome Games—as indeed he had in all games for the previous twenty-four years—and finished fourth.

Some of the weight-lifting competition lasted well past midnight, with the heavyweight final resolved at 4 A.M. Soviet and American athletes won twelve of the twenty-one medals, with Russia's phenomenal Yuri Vlasov wildly acclaimed the "world's strongest man." A kind of metaphysical atmosphere gripped the Soviet giant just before he totaled 537.5 kilograms (1184½ pounds); he recalled:

I was already losing contact with the world around me as my thoughts delved deeper and deeper into the sensations of my muscles, into the forthcoming exertion, into a precise chart of my movements. Time passed through me in waves. I rehearsed my muscle movements from start to finish.

The soccer final was played at Stadio Flaminio on 10 September. Denmark beat Hungary to gain the final, the semifinal tie between Yugoslavia and Italy being broken with a "decision by lot" favoring the Balkan country. Eyewitness expert Dr. Willy Meisl enjoyed the magnificent play of the Yugoslavs in the final as they outscored the Danes 3–1, "thus proving worthy winners of the Olympic title for which they had striven so long." They had lost to Sweden 1–3 in 1948, to the Hungarians 0–2 in 1952, and to the Russians 0–1 at Melbourne.

The traditional finale of the Olympic Games, just prior to the closing ceremonies, is the equestrian competition. Team jumping was won by the Germans, although Raimondo D'Inzeo aboard Posillipo won the individual title. Sergey Filatov rode Absent to victory in dressage, while the Australian team of Morgan, Neale Lavis, and William Roycroft emerged winners in the three-day event, their mounts, Salad Days, Mirrabrooka, and Our Solo, combining in an indistinguishable blend of skills from horse and rider.

In women's track-and-field, the USSR had six winners, with eighteen athletes in the top six places. German and British women placed twenty people in the finals, the American and Polish five each, and the Australian two. Wilma Rudolf ran spectacularly, winning three gold medals, and running fast enough to be acclaimed the fastest woman that ever lived. In the men's events, the Roman heat, absolutely first-class facilities, and inexorable physical improvement of the species, resulted in new Olympic records in every event except the 5-kilometer run, the 20-kilometer walk, the high hurdles, and the javelin. For the first time ever, the impressive combined East-and-West-German team secured gold medals in track events (100 meters and sprint relay). The Italian crowd went crazy when Livio Berruti won gold and a piece of the world record (20.5) in the 200 meters. Otis Davis outraced Carl Kaufmann at 400 meters, both timed in a world-record 44.9. The very young Peter Snell had to run hard four times, his 800-meters final at 1:46.3 good enough for an Olympic gold medal and the beginning of a brilliant athletic future. Herb Elliott had been called many things—lean and mean Aussie, a "raging tiger," and the "toughest s.o.b. in mile running"—all obtuse compliments to the Olympic 1,500-meter favorite who claimed that "no athlete in the Olympic Village has run more miles, except the marathon runners." The twenty-two-year-old Elliott proved his fitness in the final, running in the middle of the pack through 700 meters and then blasting the last 800-meters in 1:52.8 for an astonishing 3:35.6 world record. All six finalists ran the distance below

Ron Delany's Melbourne mark of 3:41.2. Murry Halberg of New Zealand outlasted the 5,000-meter field, winning by just one second in 13:43.4, while the unspectacular but Olympic-record-breaking Pyotr Bolotnikov won the 10,000 in 28:32.2. Germany's Hans Grodotzki was second in both races. The marathon was run in the early evening hours, and Abebe Bikila, a young, brilliant, bare-footed Ethiopian, destined for greatness, won in 2:15:16.2. The American hurdlers were awesome, winning all six medals in the high and intermediate barriers. The Polish steeplechase champion with the alphabet-nightmare name of Zdzislaw Krzyszkowiak broke the record with an 8:34.2 effort. The American 4 × 400-meter quartet had to run a world-record 3:02.2 to beat Germany by a few tenths. Golubnitschy of the Soviet Union and Britain's Donald Thompson won the two walking races. Soviet field-athletes won the high jump, the hammer throw, and the javelin, and were matched by American champions in the pole vault, long jump, shot, and discus. Jozef Schmidt won the triple jump, and Rafer Johnson won the most dramatic decathlon in the thirty-eight years that the event had been contested at the Olympic Games.

While the United States did very well, it did not dominate track-and-field as it once did, causing assistant coach George Eastment to mutter that things would get rougher at future Olympics. The State Department, he said, has done its work so well in spending millions of dollars helping foreign coaches and athletes "that they are catching up with us."

Life magazine called it the "Finest Olympic Show Ever." The *Economist* characterized the games as "La Dolce Vita—mostly good, clean fun." And yet it would be the last occasion in which South Africans competed. The 1–2 finish of African marathoners symbolized to *New Yorker* essayist A. J. Liebling "the escape of their continent from people like the . . . colonial powers, but [also] the Russians, whose intentions they suspected." Henry W. Morton, professor at C.C.N.Y., was convinced that Russian success in Rome was a devastating political victory. Sydney Skilton of *The Christian Science Monitor* sadly quoted from *Soviet Sport,* which praised all Soviet victors and the millions of youths ready to storm world records. "The party and government will help them all," ended the haughty Russian editorial. The truth about the Olympic Games probably lies somewhere between these two extreme views of sheer fun and the vindication of a political ideology through multiple Olympic victories.

Worldwide disquiet increased in the 1960s over the previous decade. Yuri Gagarin's feat in April of 1961 of walking in space brought joy to the Soviets, but uneasiness among many others—especially Americans. The infamous Berlin Wall went up in the summer of that year. The Cuban missile crisis and racial violence in Mississippi during October of 1962 were more than the president of the United States, John F. Kennedy, could handle. All through 1963, Kennedy tried to reduce the pressures of the European cold war. At the same time, he made the awful decision to actively support the government of South Vietnam. The nightmare of President Kennedy's murder on 22 November 1963 was followed by Lyndon Johnson's fatal decision to flood South Vietnam with American soldiers in 1964. It was, of course, also the Olympic year, and the scene was Tokyo, Japan, and the eighteenth games of the modern era.

From the moment the Japanese heard in 1959 that they would host an Olympic Games an amazing national solidarity, so typical of these people, swept the islands. They identified themselves without reservation with the idea of a world sporting festival, and most of them considered joyous good conduct and efficient management as national duties and "a sacred act."

Earlier that year, halfway around the world at Innsbruck, Austria, the ninth winter Olympics had seen Soviet Union athletes win eleven gold medals, Scandinavian champions capture eight first-place prizes, Austrians win four gold medals, France and Germany, three, and the United States, Canada, Holland, and Britain, one each. It was so often the same dozen countries. For these Japanese games, however, the torch relay, invented by Germany's Dr. Carl Diem in 1934, took on a truly global dimension as the "sacred flame" was flown from Olympia, Greece, around the world via the Silk Route, with stops in Istanbul, Beirut, Teheran, Lahore, New Delhi, Rangoon, Bangkok, Kuala Lumpur, Manila, Hong Kong, and northern Japan, through every one of that nation's provinces and was carried into the stadium by a nineteen-year-old national champion, born in Horoshima, in August 1945, on the day that city disappeared in an atomic blast.

Far more than any previous Olympic city, Tokyo urban renewal and civic improvements were accelerated by the pending games. Half a dozen sources agree that the equivalent of two billion American dollars was spent on this world's largest city in anticipation of the first Olympic Games on the Asian continent. *National Geographic* of October 1964, called the whole affair a "Peaceful Explosion" in this city of nearly eleven million. The highest economic growth of any nation in the world precipitated extraordinary prosperity, and, coupled with a kind of nationalistic "manifest destiny," resulted in possibly the biggest and "best" Olympic Games of them all.

Bet on it. The opening ceremonies were planned to the minutest detail, and the day was a memorable occasion. Puckish journalist Rex Bellamy saw the 10,000 pigeons rehearse day after day prior to their big event—carrying messages of peace. However, on the final day, two pigeons "with engine trouble" flew to a good vantage point, the press seats. The rest knew what to do, having been through it before. "They went home. But two pigeons stayed to watch." More than 5,000 athletes from ninety-four countries marched in the parade—an unprecedented gathering of the world's youth. A veteran of five Olympic Games, journalist Alan J. Gould, hoped that political antagonists might "test their skills on the athletic field rather than the battlefield." With every athletic stadia bursting with spectators, with 90 percent of the Japanese people glued to their television sets, and with the new era of global TV via Telstar involving hundreds of millions, the competitions began.

Now there are three levels of athletes at any Olympic Games: (1) less than great athletes, since each member nation may send one athlete in any individual event, regardless of ability; (2) national champions who are ranked among the best athletes in the world in their event; and (3) the "super" athlete or "model," whose extraordinary physical powers are, most interestingly, enhanced by a unique personality.

The easy cosmopolitanism of Rome in 1960 contrasted sharply with the omnipresent Japanese sense of national pride, and its total physical and psychic involvement in 1964. These may have been contributing factors to another harvest of world and Olympic records.

The "superstar" usually has something else going for him besides great inborn physical ability. Professor Hans-Wolfgang Heidland, a 1932 Olympic oarsman, does not use the phrase "superstar"; rather, he prefers "Olympic model," noting that a good athlete is often a simplistic creature who frequently captivates an audience, while "the model stimulates, develops other people's powers, looks for a group and lives in it." Betty Cuthbert was one of these model spellbinding "super-athletes." Triple-sprint gold-medal winner in Melbourne, the Australian flash came back eight years later, winning the Tokyo 400-meter dash in Olympic record time of 52.0. She was very special, on and off the track. A certain inner light plus an extraordinary runner's physique, set the defending Olympic champ, Peter Snell, apart from the hundreds of great athletes in Tokyo. The intelligent, charismatic, brilliantly-coached New Zealander was impressive in his eight Tokyo races, winning two gold at 800 and 1500 meters. He was easily the dominating personality in both races and, up to that time, the supreme middle distance runner in the hundred-year history of the sport. A third example of an Olympic model was Bob Hayes. No one ran like Hayes, nor had any one run so fast (10.0) for 100 meters. His every movement electrifying, the 190-pound powerhouse from Jacksonville, Florida, dominated the Tokyo short-sprint. The American Olympic track coach Bob Giegengack credited Hayes with only two speeds, "standing still and all-out drive." In Hayes's come-from-behind win in the sprint relay, he burst through the finishing yarn traveling forty feet per second!

Another Olympic model was Al Oerter, who, at twenty-eight, won his third consecutive Olympic gold medal in the discus throw. Never a favorite, the Kansas University graduate had the rare ability of "controlled psyche"—to perform literally at an Olympian level once every four years. Seriously injured in Tokyo, the 260-pound Oerter, "strapped like a mummy and hemorhaging with every violent twist," won his event from the rest of the world—the first man to break 200 feet at the Olympic Games. Incredibly, he won a fourth gold medal in 1968, and, as late as the 1980 American Olympic trials, the forty-four-year-old marvel was in contention for a spot on the team.

Australian Dawn Fraser was something beyond being a star. She was a role model for all athletes, possessor of "the creative personality" that would stamp her a great athlete in the midst of many good athletes. Dawn won the Olympic 100-meter freestyle in 1956 (62.0) and in 1960 (61.2). Shortly before the Tokyo games, she was badly injured in an auto crash that killed her mother. Despite this, and despite her half dozen Olympic medals, she showed up at the 100-meter starting blocks in the equisitely beautiful natatorium determined to win again. Sandor Barcs, in his *The Modern Olympic Story*, tells an amusing Fraser anecdote:

> The attractive young lady said she would not get married until she swam the [Olympic] 100 meters in less than one minute. Then she went to a fashionable dressmakers . . . and ordered a bridal gown, which could only have meant one thing!

Olympic history records that Dawn became the first woman to swim under one minute for 100 meters, winning two more medals in Tokyo. Worlds apart in many ways, and yet sharing a similar psychic and physical profile, was the Ethiopian foot-racer Abebe Bikila, the supreme marathon runner of the twentieth century's first seven decades. The quiet resolve, penetrating self-confidence, and the remorseless rhythm of the African soldier resulted in unprecedented back-to-back gold medals in Rome and Tokyo. Bikila—the "metronome on legs"—became a continental hero before his untimely death. Like all special champions, he had given that last full measure of devotion "from an instinct which is incomprehensible to the rest of us."

The queen of women's gymnastics, Larissa Latynina, great as she was in Melbourne and Rome, met an equally magnetic personality in Tokyo, the beautiful Vera Caslavska of Czechoslovakia. The two presented a rare double-view of grace, skill, and personal magic that had never been seen before, and, in the view of journalist Rex Bellamy, was "the embodiment of all that is young and lovely and happy."

The intense emotionalism of these Tokyo Olympics was embodied in the épée-fencing final between the composed, economical thirty-three-year-old British fruit farmer Henry Hoskyns and the much younger Grigory

Kriss of the Soviet Union, who, with fantastic acrobatics, managed the gold medal. And yet, neither was a loser, because, to quote Bellamy again, "The only failures were the indifferent losers." Neither Hoskyns nor Kriss was so guilty.

Other consecutive triple-gold-medal winners besides Oerter and Fraser were the peerless paddler Viacheslav Ivanov, and Hans Gunter Winkler of the German Grand Prix show-jumping team. Sport biographers consistently point out that all such people possess magnificent physical qualities in concert with less well understood inner drives. The three Pettersson brothers from Gothenburg—Gosta, Sture, and Erik—must have had both in abundance as they shocked the Tokyo Olympic cycling aficionados with their bronze-medal effort in the 109.89-Kilometer team race—pumping furiously for nearly two and one-half hours and averaging twenty-eight miles per hour.

There were, of course, other "super-athletes" at the 1964 Olympic Games, some of them partly hidden in the special athletic beauty of team sports. The rag tag American rowing eight, with only a few veteran performers, sponsored by four-time Olympian Jack Kelly, coached by the tiny firebrand Allen Rosenberg, and steered by the recent American immigrant Bob Zimonyi, beat the "unbeatable" German Ratzburg crew. Rhodes scholar Bill Bradley and his American college teammates still owned the game of basketball, besting the USSR 73–59. The unpronounceable Antal Szentmihalyl and his Hungarian compatriots won the soccer final over Czechoslavakia 2–1. Once again, the field hockey final was between India (1) and Pakistan (0), with far-flung Australia beating out Spain for third place.

The volleyball confrontation was at the highest level—especially the women's championships. This new Olympic sport had seen the Soviet men edge out the Czechs for first place. The real drama was in the electric atmosphere of the women's final—twelve Russian giants in scarlet uniforms, pony-tailed and grim, versus twelve little dark-haired Japanese factory-workers dressed in green and white, "who looked like a class of girls following their teachers, crocodile-like style, to school." These women had put in a thousand hours of the most unbelievably difficult training regimen, and they were ready for the Soviets, who, in turn, fought tenaciously and with considerable talent. The close victory of the Japanese was cause for a national celebration and opened the way for volleyball as an international sport.

Olympic water polo champions were from Hungary, with Yugoslavia, Russia, Italy, Rumania, and Germany rounding out the top teams. Special exhibitions of Japanese archery (Kyudo), wrestling (Sumo), and fencing (Kendo) were fascinating, but in no way as popular as the Olympic finals of judo, the ancient Japanese art of self-defense. Nakatani won the lightweight title, Isao Okano the middleweight gold medal, Takehide Inokuma the light heavyweight crown—all preliminaries to the heavyweight final between national hero, Akio Kaminaga, and the six-foot-four-inches, 240-pound giant from the Netherlands, Anton Geesink. Judokan Hall was packed, and all of Japan waited with trepidation, all aware that the great athlete from Europe had beaten their man previously. Kaminaga, the aggressor in the early going, was unable to throw the powerful Geesing, who, in turn, made several unsuccessful moves on his opponent. In the ninth minute, Geesing caught Kaminaga with the classic judo stranglehold. There was as much drama and agony among the massed audience as on the mat as the Dutchman relentlessly held his man, winning the world title, releasing a kind of collective sorrow among the Japanese, and solidifying judo as a permanent fixture in the Olympic Games. In an almost unique way, the Japanese had made a success of their games because they had cared for them, and cared desperately. Their very caring had assured the world of a very great sporting festival as well as perfected the communal phenomenon of a $2 billion expenditure.

The Mexican Connection was made for the Olympic Games. What an extraordinary festival were these summer games of the nineteenth Olympiad! Mexico City's thin air at its 7,500 feet above sea level caused serious problems to all distance runners, except a few extremely well-prepared Africans. Powerful and violent student revolts were squelched just before the opening ceremonies. The grim struggle between the Puma and Adidas shoe companies resulted in thousands of dollars illegally distributed to Olympic superstars. A Swedish pentathlete had his bronze medal revoked when he was declared legally drunk. The drug scandal became more widespread, a United States coach cried "foul" in freestyle wrestling, while five referees were withdrawn from the boxing ring because of incompetence. The new and stricter drug-testing often kept swimmers waiting for hours backstage, guarded by medical authorities waiting for the athletes to calm down sufficiently for them to get a reliable urine sample.

And there were more problems at these "hot-sauce" Olympics. Two black American sprint champions were summarily sent home after disrespectful conduct on the victory stand. Bitter denunciation of the high-altitude site came from some oxygen-hungry distance runners, from some coaches, and from a few medical doctors. When the famous Dr. Roger Bannister was asked how long it would take a sea-level runner to acclimate to Mexico City, he glumly replied, "Twenty-five years." Monumental traffic jams, an acute housing shortage for visitors, unusually heavy rain squalls, consistently inefficient communications problems, some dysentery crises among athletes, political sensitivity among some Czechs, Russians, Poles, Ghanaians, Kenyans, Cubans, a huffy attitude by the nonparticipants from North Korea, and the very serious internal IOC struggle resulting in the continued banishment of South Africa, all contributed to Olympic Games that were not the mirror-image of the Helsinki or even the Tokyo-staged games. And yet, from almost every side, despite "frictions, ineptitudes, displays of authoritarianism, and painful rumors," the bottom line was nearly unvarnished praise for a poor but proud Mexican people for hosting a colorful, essentially joy-filled Olympics.

The quarter-billion dollars in private and governmental monies was too much to spend on an essentially emerging nation, but there were many people in high places quick to dispute any such accusation, these same people pointing out enormous immediate and long-range benefits to the Mexican people. As Bob Phillips of *World Sports* said about this greatest Olympic Games congregation (5,931 athletes from 112 countries): "Baron Pierre de Coubertin could never in his wildest dreams have envisaged such a mammoth convocation of sport."

During the preparations for the tenth winter Olympics in Grenoble, France, scheduled for 6–18 February 1968, the very distinguished French biographer, novelist, and essayist André Maurois died at age eighty-two. An admirer of Pierre de Coubertin, he shared the baron's dream of universal respect and understanding through participation in a certain kind of high-minded, nonprofessional sporting festival. Maurois wrote of Coubertin that it was "his dream to unite the athletes of the whole world, and the poets and the artists in a new Olympiad. There, in the exuberance of noble struggle, men would set aside hate." Of course, objective proof is lacking that any such things ever happened. Conversely, no one can deny that something important, something good, may have emanated from an Olympic Games experiment that has served three generations of male and female athletes.

The youngest Olympic winter sport, the biathlon, or skiing-shooting trial of skill and endurance, is actually a 5,000-year-old form of hunting, and was won by an unknown thirty-one-year-old policeman from Trond-heim, Norway—Magnar Solberg. The Soviets won the team championship in this event. Super hero of these competitions, and winner of the downhill, slalom, and giant slalom, Jean-Claude Killy pointed out that his specialties "test character and courage," leaving little room for com-promise. Champion Karl Schranz said the same thing: "No coward will ever win the downhill." A forty-year-old veteran of many past Olympic honors, Eugenio Monti of Italy proved himself a genuine sport hero as he won two gold medals in guiding his two- and four-man bobsleds. A classic ice-hockey confrontation between the USSR and Czechoslovakia ended in a close, hard-fought win, 5–4 for the Russians, assuring them of the gold medal. Peggy Fleming skated superbly, gaining the women's figure skating title, the individual men's title going to the patient perfectionist, Wolfgang Schwarz of Austria. The veteran, synchronized skating-masters Ludmila and Oleg Protopopov ended their great careers with what Dennis Bird of the *Times* called "a program that was immaculate, artistic, perfect almost beyond the bounds of belief." Ludmila Titova won the 500-meter sprint, only two-tenths of a second ahead of three girls from the United States. Six skaters were bunched very closely in the men's 500, with Erhard Keller winning in 40.3. Anton Maier won gold and gained a world record in the 5,000-meter speed-skating finals; Cees Verkerk (Holland) and Johnny Hoeglin (Sweden) won the 1,500- and 10,000-meter races. The three longer women's races (1,000, 1,500, and 3,000 meters) were won by Carolina Geijssen, K. Mustonen, and Johanna Schut. Manfred Schmid of Austria won the men's luge singles, the East German men winning the double luge. Unfortunately, three East German women were disqualified for illegally heating their metal runners during the luge-singles final. Fragile-looking Erika Lechner of Italy turned in the fastest times for the event. Thirty-year-old physics teacher Toini Gustavsson of Sweden won both Nordic ski races, but could not prevent the Norwegian women from capturing the 15-kilometer relay race. Norway also won the men's relay, the fifteen-kilometer individual race (Groenningen), and the 50-kilometer cross-country struggle (Ole Ellefsaeter). Italy's Franco Nones broke the Scandinavian monopoly in the 30-kilometer race. In the Nordic combination (cross-country and jumping), the same monopoly was broken by the West German, Franz Keller. Canada's Nancy Greene surprised in the women's giant slalom; the powerfully-built world's champion, Marielle Goitschel, however edged out Miss Greene in the slalom final. In the downhill, Olga Pall won the first place in an event dominated by her Austrian teammates. And lastly, the spectacular 70- and 90-meter jumping events were won by a Czech, Jiri Raska, and in an upset victory, by the Soviet Vladimir Beloussov; Beloussov's startling leaps of 101.5 and 98.5 meters defeated Jiri Raska of Czechoslovakia. On the last day of competition, Japanese visitors and athletes distributed tiny national flags and artificial roses sheathed in perfumed lace—an exquisite welcome to a 1972 winter Olympics in Sapporo.

Jim Hines, Tommy Smith, and Lee Evans—all scintillatingly talented Americans—won gold medals and new world records in the 100-, 200-, and 400-meter dashes. Ralph Doubell of Australia also took advantage of the less-resistant air, racing 800 meters in 104.3 seconds—another world record. Kipchoge Keino started the East African domination with a record-breaking 1,500-meter win over Jim Ryun. Mohammed Gammoudi, Kip Keino, Naftali Temu, Mamo Wolde, Amos Biwoth, and Ben Kogo— all Africans—won nine of the twelve medals in the distance events. Davenport and Hemery blitzed the two hurdle events in record time, while the American relay teams posted nearly unreachable world records. Wladimir Golubnichy (USSR), Chris Hohne (E. Germany) won the walking events, while Gyula Zsivotsky, Janis Lusis, Randy Matson, Bob Seagren, and Viktor Saneyev won their hammer, javelin, shot, vault, and triple-jump specialties. Dick Fosbury startled the world with his high jump "flop" technique—torpedoing over the bar at 7'4¼". The venerable Oerter won his fourth consecutive gold medal, scaling the discus a record 212'6½".

No single woman dominated track-and-field competition. Maybe the level attained by women made it impossible. Wyomia Tyus (100), Irena Szewinska (200), Colette Besson (400), Madeline Manning (800), Maureen Caird (hurdles), Viorica Viscopoleanu (long jump), Miloslava Rezková (high jump), Margitta Gummel (shot), Lia Manoliu (discus), Angéla Nemeth (javelin), and the American relay team all added to the relatively new dimension of serious and near universal athletics for women. Bill Toomey and Ingrid Becker proved to be the greatest all-round track-and-field athletes, winning the decathlon and pentathlon classics.

For those with limited vision, it seemed inconceivable that such a wholesale onslaught on Olympic and world records might never again be duplicated. Only a dozen countries scored a first, second, or third place medal in men's and women's swimming-diving events, the lion's share going to athletes from North America. This was supposed to be the year that the United States finally lost an Olympic basketball game, but Spencer Haywood, Jo-Jo White, and company emerged unbeaten, with Yugoslavia and the Russians in runner-up spots. The eleven boxing gold-medals went to fighters from the United States, Venezuela, Mexico, USSR, Poland, East Germany, and Britain. The new concrete water canal, cut out of cornfields in a poverty corner of southeast Mexico City, was the site of socialist country domination in the canoeing and kayaking competition—part of their master plan to dominate the Olympic Games by paying particular attention to these "easy" events. It worked; fifteen of the twenty-one medals went to athletes from the Communist bloc.

Pierre Trentin, Daniel Rebillard, and Daniel Morelon symbolized the French domination of cycling at the Velodromo, while Dutch, Swedish, Danish, and Italian distance-men reigned in road racing. Bill Steinkraus of the United States, in his fourth Olympics, won a gold in individual Grand Prix jumping, the British, French, Soviet, Canadian, and West German riders winning the other equestrian events. Multimillionaire show rider from West Germany, Josef Neckermann, at fifty-six years of age, added a gold and a silver medal to his already impressive Olympic collection. Unremitting concentration, he said, is the key to business as well as sport success. He would add a bronze medal four years later in the Munich Games. A half-century domination of Olympic sabre honors by

Hungarian fencers was broken by Jerzy Pawlowski, a thirty-five-year-old major in the Polish army. This is not to say the Hungarians did poorly, for they were in every final of individual and team foil, épée, and sabre. The amazing growth in popularity of gymnastics spiraled upward. Among the most charismatic and skilled winners were Sawao Kato, Aklanori Nakayama, Yuklo Endo, Mikhail Voronin, Vera Casalavska, and Zinalda Voronina. The Mexican reverence for art and beauty led Rex Bellamy of the London *Times* to comment that the vast crowds "did not so much watch the gymnastic's competition as take part in it." After sixty-eight field hockey matches, two of the sixteen teams entered the finals, with Pakistan edging out the Australian "Roughnecks" 2–1. India and West Germany rounded out the top four teams. In the private world of the modern pentathlon, form held true as Bjorn Ferm of Sweden edged out Andras Balczo of Hungary and the USSR's Pavel Lednev for individual honors, the team title going to the Hungarians. The Soviet team was second, France third. The Swedes actually finished behind the Russians, but were disqualified when a member of the team failed the alcohol test.

Dutch, Soviet, Italian, East German, and New Zealand athletes' victories in rowing competitions seemed but preliminaries to the eight-oar final. Coaching genius Karl Adams of West Germany demanded and got a maximum effort from his crew—just enough to edge Australia over the 2,000-meter course, 6:07.00 to 6:07.98. The United States failed to win a single medal; the blow was especially heavy when the talented free-spirits from Harvard University, besieged by illness and injury, rowed poorly. Joseph M. Sheehan of the *New York Times* was there and suggested that the long-haired "shaggies" had become "over-involved emotionally in the efforts by some black athletes in other sports to use the Olympics as a vehicle for racial demonstrations." The always-large shooting competition, representing sixty-four countries, resulted in new world and Olympic records, the debut of a woman competitor, five medals for the Soviets, and three each for the United States and West Germany. Additional gold medals were won by shooters from Czechoslovakia, Poland, and Britain. When all the soccer hysteria had subsided, "the best team [Hungary] won", with Bulgaria, Japan, and Mexico runners-up. The same might be said of the Yugoslavs in water polo, who finally won gold after near success in five Olympics. They edged out the Soviets in a wild 13–11 final. The Yanks were even more impressive in swimming than they had been in Tokyo, winning more medals than all the countries put together. Don Schollander, Mike Burton, John Kinsella, Don McKenzie, Charles Hickox, Doug Russell, Carl Robie, Mark Spitz, Greg Buckingham, Gary Hall, Bernie Wrightson, Jan Henne, and Debbie Meyer wrote their names large in Olympic history, along with Mike Wenden of Australia, Roland Matthes of East Germany, Claudia Kolb of the United States, and the incomparable Klaus Dibiasi of Italy. The Soviet Union scored big, winning both men's and women's volleyball finals over Japan. Twelve world and fifty-nine Olympic records were broken in weight lifting as gold medals went to Russians Leonid Zhabotinsky, Boris Selitsky, and Viktor Kurentsov. Mohamed Nassari won the bantamweight class for himself and for his country, Iran. Yoshinobu Miyake of Japan won the featherweight title, his younger brother Yoshiyuki close behind in third place. Waldemar Baszanowski of Poland lifted 964¼ pounds in three lifts for a lightweight victory. Awesome middle-heavyweight Kaarlo Kangasniemi smashed the Olympic record with a lift total of 1140½ pounds, adding to an already glorious Finnish tradition. Freestyle and Greco-Roman wrestling medals were divided as follows: USSR, nine; Bulgaria, six; Japan, five; Mongolia and Hungary, four; Iran and Rumania, three; Czechoslovakia, Turkey, France, the United States, East Germany, and Yugoslavia, two. West German and Greek athletes took home single wrestling-medals. And finally, over in the bay at Acapulco, the yachting races, always incongruous to some Olympic critics, myself included, resulted in victories of Swedish, American (two), British, and Soviet crafts—all of them overcoming hot and very humid weather plus the most capricious winds and choppy seas seen in a good many years.

Black American sprint champions Tommy Smith and John Carlos had purposely insulted their own national flag during the 200-meter victory ceremony. The outrage that followed and the controversial expulsion of the two Americans created a front-page splash that somewhat dulled the edge of Bob Beamon's fantastic, even unbelievable long jump of 29'2½". His was the ultimate athletic performance. Every Olympic Games has had high drama both on and off the athletic field. These 1968 Mexico City games were no different. Transcending all athletic performances in all Olympic sports for its entire modern history was the leap of this skinny "slash of a man" from the depressing ghetto of South Jamaica, New York City. For two years prior to the games, the undisciplined Beamon had been recognized as an athletic talent of rare proportions, frequently jumping from the wrong foot, many inches back of the board, and yet approaching twenty-seven feet in distance. On Thursday, 17 October 1968, the unpredictable twenty-two-year-old Beamon fouled the first two of his three qualifying jumps; his last successful effort was from way behind the take-off strip. The next day, 18 October, in the long jump finals, Bob Beamon, Klaus Beer (East Germany), Igor Ter-Ovanesyan and Tonu Lepik from the Soviet Union, plus Australia's Allen Crawley, prepared themselves for what they thought would be fierce competition for the gold medal.

For forty years prior to these Mexico City Olympics, the supreme long jumpers of the world had thought in terms of surpassing twenty-six feet, the immortal Jesse Owens establishing a powerful record in 1935 of eight inches and a fraction beyond this mark. It took more than thirty years before an equally talented Ralph Boston became the first human to long-jump twenty-seven feet. This was the state of the art as the final competition began. The sky over the Olympic stadium at midafternoon this day was dark and threatening. I was ideally seated some fifty meters from the long-jump pit and the innovative gunsight measuring device paralleling the thirty-foot jumping area. Much was expected from Ralph Boston, who had established a new Olympic record of 8.27 meters (27′1½″) the day before.

On the fourth jump in the finals, Bob Beamon's first effort, athletics history was made. For perhaps thirty seconds, he jogged at the end of the runway, then abruptly began his long assault approach down the Tartan rubber runway. The long-legged, hugely talented Beamon, one of the fastest long-jumpers in history, possessor of enormous leg spring and elasticity, had decided to throw caution to the wind, and came down that rubber strip at top speed, probably faster than any jumper in history. By accident or design—no one knows—he hit the white painted mark absolutely perfectly and with his dominant leg. Specialists in the event, eyewitnesses to Beamon's takeoff, agree that there was no visible stamping of the take-off foot, so common in most jumpers. Beamon appeared to race off the runway, simply striding upward and outward through the thin stadium air, running on his body's center of gravity at the apex of his jump some seven feet above the surface of the sand pit. Every piece had fallen into place. As the young New Yorker finally began his descent into the pit, his legs spread wide and held high, his head and torso tucked between them, he appeared "like a huge, limby frog, his legs spread-eagled and his arms dangling between them." He hit the sand with such velocity, and so close to the end of the pit, that he bounded out on one hop, "like an airplane poorly landed." As Dick Schaap said in his insightful Beamon biography, *The Perfect Jump*, "It was, quite possibly, the greatest individual athletic achievement in the history of mankind." After many moments of almost comical confusion, the officials measured the jump at a new Olympic and world record—8.90 meters (29′2½″).

Young Beamon, the boy with the abysmally fractured personal background, knowing that he had done something extraordinary, leaped from the pit and ran around excitedly, waving his hands, in a state of highest agitation. What he had done was whirl past the twenty-six-, twenty-seven-, twenty-eight-, and twenty-nine-foot markers looking like, as Jerry Nason of the *Boston Globe* observed, "a typewriter ribbon unwinding in space. . . ." Beamon's unbelievable flight, beyond scientific logic, created a world record that has not been remotely approached a dozen years later, something unique in a record-breaking sport world.

His startling performance, called "terrifying" by Bob Paul of the United States Olympic Committee, was further complemented by ex-Olympic champion and athletics expert, Harold Abrahams, as "one world record which may never be beaten." The huge crowd, in a state of disbelief as the rotating electric scoreboard read 8.90 meters, was nothing compared to Beamon's ecstasy following the awkward moments of translating meters and centimeters into feet and inches. The young man danced in the infield, clapped his hands over his eyes at the impossible vision come real, was embraced and steadied by his friend, Boston. His uncontrolled joy so overcame Beamon that he slipped from Boston's arms, sank to the ground on his knees, bent over, and kissed the earth.

Medical doctor and sport scientist Ernst Jokl, in an attempt to bring some rationality to this whole existential scene, listed factors that contributed to what he called "the greatest single feat in the recorded history of athletics." In *The Physical Educator* of May 1970, Dr. Jokl noted that these unique factors and forces were acting in harmony that day, 3:46 P.M., October 1968, in Mexico City:

1. Negroes are more talented than non-blacks, and Bob Beamon was the most gifted of all.
2. Bob Beamon, super sprinter, ran with absolute recklessness.
3. The artificial Tartan surface, never used before in Olympic competition, was the fastest of its kind in the world.
4. The thin or rarified air in the stadium offered a significant advantage, lessening resistance to sprinters.
5. The maximally allowed following wind (2.0 miles per second) was blowing helpfully during those few moments that Beamon raced the 130-foot runway.
6. Beamon's completely uninhibited run, wiping out all long-jump inhibitions, somehow resulted in his hitting the take-off mark perfectly.

Dr. Jokl described Beamon's collapse in neurological terminology as a "powerless attack . . . a sudden loss of tone . . . a cataplectic collapse." No doubt it happened just this way to a person so ordinary in so many ways and from such a disadvantaged background. Schaap recognized this irony, making it the theme of his book. Bob Beamon, he said, was "the ultimate 'ordinary' human being, [performing] the ultimate extraordinary feat, setting a world record so startling that he became, for a flickering moment, an international figure. . . ."

Michael Morris, Lord Killanin, President IOC, 1972 –1980. Credit IOC Archives.

12 • Lord Killanin—Reluctant Descendant of Coubertin and Brundage

Prior to the 1972 Olympic Games in Munich, West Germany, the International Olympic Committee had invited Rhodesia and 120 other countries to compete in the great quadrennial festival. The Rhodesians seemed to have met the letter of the IOC regulation, but, upon their arrival in the Olympic city, displayed an arrogance that irritated many and deeply angered many blacks. Powerful pressures were put on President Brundage and the IOC resulting in an emergency vote (36–31) to rescind their own invitation and to expel Rhodesia from the games. Brundage was enraged, deeply hurt at this first major countermand of one of his wishes. Amidst this electric atmosphere, the IOC presidential elections took place on 23 August. France's multimillionaire Count Jean de Beaumont, a sixty-eight-year-old Brundage-like industrialist, was narrowly defeated by a jovial fifty-eight-year-old British peer, Sir Michael Morris, Lord Killanin. Although he did not take charge of the Olympic Movement till 10 September, Killanin was under enormous pressure, noting that he had "one hell of a job" following Avery Brundage; "He's such a big man." Indeed, Killanin was also a "big man," but in an entirely different mold. He was, as Clive Gammon said, "the new Pope John, sent to heal the scars of twenty years of autocratic Brundage rule."

Thirty-three days after Michael Morris was born, on 30 July 1914, in London, his father, Lieutenant-Colonel George Henry Morris, became one of the first World War I casualties when he was killed in action near Villers-Cotteres, France, leading the first attack of the Irish Guards on the western front. Michael's mother, Dora Maryan Wesley Hall, born in Melbourne, Australia, was remarried in 1918, to Lieutenant-Colonel Gerard Tharp. The Morris family, always supportive of English kings, was Roman-Catholic Irish from Galway, Ireland, and traced its lineage back to the fifteenth century. The future Olympic-committee president inherited the title of Baron Killanin when his unmarried uncle died in 1927, during

193

the youngster's schooling at Eton College. (His grandfather was named a baron by Queen Victoria in 1885, when Ireland was still part of Britain and was pressing for its independence.) After graduation in 1931, Michael spent a year at the Sorbonne in Paris, returned to England, and enrolled in Magdalene College, Cambridge University, receiving his bachelor of arts degree in 1935 and a master's degree the following year. In addition to majoring in English and history, this future Renaissance-man boxed, rowed, was president of the dramatics club and editor of the *Varsity Weekly*, and, while still studying, joined the staff of the London *Daily Express* as a crime reporter in 1935. Within a year, the third Baron Killanin moved to both the London *Daily Mail* and *Sunday Dispatch* where he served till 1939 as a gossip and political columnist.

In 1936, Killanin spent a three-week vigil at Fort Belvedere, the private home of King Edward VIII, waiting for confirmation of the king's abdication. The next year, the *Daily Mail* assigned him to cover the Sino-Japanese War. He joined the British Army (Sixtieth Rifles) in 1938, when he heard the news of Neville Chamberlain's Munich agreement with Hitler. In that same year, the young second lieutenant wrote about the Munich treachery in a volume called *Four Days: 25–29 September, 1938*. By 1943, he had risen to brigate major, going ashore on D day with the thirtieth Armored and finishing his army stint in 1945 with several decorations.

Although devoid of the aristocratic "landlord mentality," Killanin returned to Ireland in 1945, rebuilt the family house at Spiddal, County Galway, met and married Sheila Dunlop, and plunged into a variety of enterprises in journalism, business, the cinema, and public service. First, though, he discovered that he was no country squire, he sold his estate and moved to Dublin, on Lansdowne Road, close to the Irish national rugby stadium. In 1948, he completed the biography *Sir Godfrey Kneller and His Times, 1646–1723*, followed by a twenty year involvement in the production of motion picture films, several of them directed by his close family friend John Ford. Killanin's association with Shell Oil Company of Ireland in 1947 resulted in a blizzard of business responsibilities as well as the writing of the *Shell Guide to Ireland* (1962), a skillful, authoritative book, coauthored with Professor of Archaeology Michael V. Duignan.

During these energetic years of the 1950s, the six-foot tall, somewhat overweight Killanin pursued so many interests that it was "difficult to distinguish between those that are merely titular and those that are the foundations of his fortune." He served some of the largest corporations in Ireland, and somehow managed to retain his association with many of them when a new, nearly all-consuming involvement presented itself in

1952. Killanin's brilliant response in 1950 to the internecine Olympic struggle in his own country (he was president of the Irish committee) led to his promotion to the International Olympic Committee in 1952. An eventful, twenty-year apprenticeship with the IOC more than adequately prepared him to step in as the seventh president of this most powerful world sport organization.

Lord Killanin, Michael Morris's business, his Irish Olympic interests, and his wife, Sheila, and their four children (Redmond, Deborah, Michael, and John) frequently had to wait as he moved up the international Olympic ladder from I.O.C. member, to executive board member, and, in 1968, to vice-president. All this while he watched closely the decision-making process of Avery Brundage. It helped him relate every bit as much as Brundage to the cause of Olympism, but, because he was not cut from the same cloth as the American, a peculiar iron-fist-in-velvet-glove approach marked Killanin's style. For example, he was traditional enough to be appalled by the 1964 hard-sell approach of ninety-seven Detroit business and civic leaders who attempted to win the 1968 Olympic Games for their city. "Show-business vulgarity," was Killanin's comment, and the IOC agreed with him. A Killanin letter to President Brundage, dated 6 June 1968, cautioned against any IOC endorsement of a proposed film based on the distorted Olympic image portrayed in the book *The Games*. More importantly, he predicted correctly that "we will no doubt have a good deal of trouble from Africa during the next eight to twelve years." One of the great errors in IOC history, he ventured, has been to select members who did not meet the approval of their own national Olympic committee. "This is like sending an ambassador to a foreign country who starts off by being persona non grata," concluded this consummately practical-minded man, a polished committee person, strong-minded but not militant, and a persuasive reformer who made waves but roused little disagreeableness in anyone. In a three-part conversation with Paddy Downey of Dublin's *Irish Times* (December 1968), Vice-President Killanin's topic, "The Olympics: Ideal and Reality," was a perfect definition of the man's dual but not necessarily contradictory points of view regarding international Olympic amateur athletics. "Melbourne was the last of the old-fashioned Olympics," he lamented.

In the early 1970s, just before his own election to the IOC presidency, Killanin was hard at work preparing the way for a radical departure from bye-law 26 of the *Olympic Charter*. Brundage's untrammeled, simon-pure amateur stance was unacceptable to Killanin, who felt strongly that deserving athletes training twenty-five hours a week should be significantly subsidized. In a letter dated 19 February 1971, and addressed to Killanin, Jean Beaumont, and Herman van Karnebeek,

Brundage disapproved of such unprecedented generosity, snorting that an athlete receiving such state aid "may be better off than when he is working."

Brundage was a great sports leader, but he may have been around a few years too long. Count Beaumont lost the 1972 election for IOC presidency to Killanin because the Frenchman seemed too much like the outgoing president. "We felt," one member confessed, "that twenty years of Brundage had been ample." Brundage ran a one-man show, but this would not be Killanin's way. John Hopkins, in the London *Sunday Times* of 11 July 1976, noted that Killanin is a committee man, with "a noticeable homely, paternal touch. . . ." Working with Brundage "was like pulling teeth," recalled Charles Palmer of the International Judo Federation. "Killanin is sweetness and light by comparison." Brundage frequently worked with trip-hammer forcefulness, while Lord Killanin moved with ease, wit, cleverness, marginal guile, and a thirty-five year belief that almost anything can be achieved through arbitration.

In a word, Killanin was a pragmatist. "Maybe it's because I was a political journalist for so many years," he confessed to A. F. Gonzales in a December 1974 *Illustrated London News* interview. Lord Killanin's remark, "I try to deal with things as they are, not as we'd like them to be in a more perfect world," stamps him as pure realist, while his predecessors, Coubertin and Brundage, constantly espoused sport idealism. And yet this Irish "Lord of the Olympics" had the profoundest respect for Coubertin, Brundage, and all those who work toward the proliferation of sport for all, the uninterrupted but controlled spread of the Olympic movement, and its ultimate manifestation, the games, all encapsulated in a kind of international fair play that all three men called Olympism. In this special regard, Killanin was as much the philosophical disciple of Brundage as Brundage was directly beholden to the man he greatly admired, Baron Pierre de Coubertin. Only with regard to the granting of subsidizations or real help to the aspiring nonprofessional athlete did Killanin radically differ from his predecessors.

Beginning in 1972, the year he took office, Killanin engineered major efforts to reduce the severity of the amateur code, which not only sensibly prohibited financial gain from sport involvement, but unnecessarily prevented the modern world-class athlete from his or her twenty-five hours a week of hard training. Killanin and the liberal wing of the IOC changed this in 1974 and 1975 with the implementation of *Olympic Charter* bye-law 26, which allows for substantial help to the gifted, serious athlete with Olympic Games aspirations. (Chapter 8 of this text deals with this special problem and its modern-day resolution.) The unflappable IOC president, who had promised "changes, but no sweeping reforms," was wrong in this prediction because this new Killanin-inspired rule-change is revolutionary and of great importance to athletes from the western and capitalist nations. Had Brundage been president in 1973, the Varna, Bulgaria, Olympic Congress would probably have been a failure. But, with the new perceptive and affable sports diplomat at the IOC helm, that organization worked closely for a week with all the world's national Olympic committees and all the Olympic sport federations—a first such meeting in forty-three years.

Killanin insisted that the IOC was the last word, but guaranteed the sometimes suspicious NOCs and IFs that "under my presidency the IOC will not be the club which it may have been many years ago." These were soothing words to many. Killanin added, with a figurative backward look to bygone IOC presidents, that he personally believed it "better for the Olympic movement not to put itself on too high a pedestal . . ." He spoke with candor and discussed such possibilities as multiple Olympic Games sites, aid to athletes, nationless athletes competing under the Olympic flag, simplifying the pomp and ceremony at an Olympics, the reduction of team sports at the games, and the need for highly qualified females as members of the IOC. One thing he did not consider for even a moment was the persistent communist-socialist proposition of a one-country, one-membership on the IOC.

Clive Gammon's perceptive Killanin biography in the 9 February 1976 *Sports Illustrated* called the unpretentious aristocrat a man of "genial, commanding presence and an instant likability," a person without false dignity, devoid of delusions of grandeur. And yet, Lord Killanin was every bit as adamant as was Brundage regarding the need to continue the nondemocratic, self-selecting characteristics of the IOC, and to strengthen rather than diminish the power of its presidency. He simply operated differently from his predecessor, refusing to storm and shout at even the most crucial meeting. As an IOC member told Gammon, Killanin's "mellifluous English voice flows on," exercising his power discreetly, with that

> . . . nice, fey Celtic way of pleasing people, flattering them a little, appearing to be impressed by them, saying, "That's an awfully good point. I really think we should take that up."

In a London *Times* profile on 12 July 1976 Brian Connell found Michael Morris a totally engaging person, a man sometimes poking fun at himself. "One of the odd things," revealed Killanin, "is that when I was diplomatic journalist, I could never meet any high powered politicians. Now I don't seem to be able to avoid them." He met some important people in the United States during a February 1974 visit, warning that any direct governmental control over its own monies allocated to a 1980 Lake Placid winter games "would risk putting the U.S.A. out of the Olympics." The liberal reformer wanted it made clear that, as Gammon said, "it would be a grave mistake to believe that the Olympic ideal of amateurism died with Avery Brundage." A close twenty-year friendship between Brundage and Lord Killanin cooled noticeably during those cruel last years of the American's tenure as IOC president. But Killanin, in his own way, was equally devoted to the cause of Olympism, frequently pointing out that something large, something good can come out of international sport if we work hard at fostering realizable goals of the Olympic movement. If we fail, he said in a 1974 speech, "we shall retreat into barbarism." Abandoning his realist training as a historian-journalist, in that same *Sports Illustrated* article, President Killanin looked to the future:

> I'de love to see the anthem-playing and the flag-raising go. . . . I can see the time coming—but well after my own time—when the Games might be spread over a wide area, say Benelux (Belgium, The Netherlands, and Luxumbourg) or the geographic British Isles.

In every conceivable way, the sixty-two year-old Lord Killanin was under pressure and on trial during the long Montreal fortnight of the Games of the twenty-first Olympiad, 17 July to 1 August 1976. In addition to a parade of record-breaking feats, endless anecdotes of friendships made, a thousand gestures of largess amidst a unique splendor, there were also "political wrangling, propaganda ploys, security fears," and the stupendous billion-dollar cost. Killanin was on the hot seat but refused to be outwardly flustered. The *Toronto Star* of 11 January 1975 reported that, despite a massive strike by 1,200 iron workers forcing complete shutdown on the incomplete four-hundred-million-dollar stadium, Killanin would not fly to Montreal with a Brundage-like "take-charge" attitude and get the men back to work. The next eighteen months were a nightmare of delays and escalating costs, and were described with bitterness and bias in Nick Auf der Maur's *The Billion-Dollar Game—Jean Drapeau and the 1976 Olympics*. It suffices to say that Killanin arrived in Montreal prior to opening ceremony having already faced mountainous problems.

Trouble for Killanin and his committee grew rapidly as the Canadian government announced its inability to allow athletes from the Republic of China admittance to the country since Canada did not recognize that nation's existence, even though China was a member of the IOC. Killanin's group, after days of nasty wrangling, offered the China member the opportunity to compete, but only if they would do so as the delegation from Taiwan, not the Republic of China. Killanin's typical compromise suggestion was flatly refused, and one less country impacted these Montreal games. Brickbats were tossed around by the consummately political host government, by the grimly intransigent Chinese, and by Killanin—who failed to grapple and solve the two China problems (at least as far as Olympic competition was concerned) several days before the Montreal games began.

Even before the opening ceremonies on 17 July 1976, Tanzania, and then Uganda and Zaire, pulled out and went home in protest over a recent New Zealand rugby tour of South Africa. Killanin refused to expel New Zealand, and twenty-two more African countries sent their athletes home. "Now everybody is using the Olympics as a political tool," was IOC Director Monique Berlioux's bitter comment. It was a view probably shared by President Killanin. But he kept a typically low profile and allowed the defection to happen without any intervention from the IOC. The Taiwan issue was still hot, the African withdrawal lacked credibility even in the most liberal press, and Killanin sat smoking his pipe, at least in the figurative sense, waiting for the Olympic pageant to begin. Probably it was the wisest move—or lack of action—on his part.

The Montreal Olympic Games sorely missed the African athletes and the Olympic movement was shaken, but neither suffered irreparable damage. Lord Killanin had learned, as a young journalist in a Hitler-infested Europe, to act swiftly, but only after all the facts were in hand, which, in effect, allowed a "cooling-off" period. He acted accordingly when a furious Soviet administrative delegation threatened to go home when their seventeen-year-old diver, Sergei Nemtsanov, fled the Russian team and could not be found by the boy's comrades, and when no one stepped forward to return him. A reminder from Killanin that a Soviet withdrawal would jeopardize its chances for a 1980 Moscow Olympic Games did the trick, and that minor incident, easily capable of exaggeration, was defused. Killanin's laissez-faire attitude, so unlike Brundage's, may have prevented any single Olympic unhappiness from getting out of hand. And there were many minor troubles. A champion Soviet fencer was caught double-wiring his blade, a coach was accused of trying to fix the diving competition, and a sixty-five-year-old shooter was disqualified for taking amphetamines, as was a Canadian yachtman. Gross misconduct by several American weight men, by an East German female javelin world-record holder, and more, prompted a veteran Associated Press special correspondent to wonder if Killanin and his committee were aware that

The erosion of principles—permitted if not promulgated by the sacrosanct IOC—is being followed by a deterioration of spirit. . . . Where is there a soul as strong as that of Coubertin or the late Avery Brundage?

Killanin survived the Montreal games, but was not remembered for any forceful decision making that reduced political interference. It was not his style to step in the fray, to accelerate polemics, to meet fire with fire. His day would come, he felt, at post-Olympic meetings of the IOC. As these 1976 Olympics ended, highly successful in many ways, Lord Killanin's conciliatory balm would become, he hoped, the healing process. He held out a figurative olive branch to Africa and the two Chinas, urging them all to be in Moscow in 1980. We must not throw in the towel, said Killanin, sadly admitting that a gold medal for politics should be awarded these Games of the Twenty-First Olympiad. Everyone was "desperately sad" at some of the political shenanigans. Unlike Brundage in many ways, Killanin agreed with his predecessor that every eligible athlete from every nation in the world should be encouraged to participate. "We want to see the People's Republic of China back to the Olympics," he said in an interview on 2 August 1976. He felt very strongly on this point, and would dedicate himself to this nearly insurmountable and, as he called it, "delicate situation." Killanin was good at interviews, reducing the waves of heavy dialogue with some humor—in between puffs on his pipe. Steve Cady of the *New York Times* found the topic of the nude "streaker" that disrupted the closing ceremonies worthy of comment. With dead-pan countenance, Lord Killanin replied, "I don't see how he got through all those security forces. He obviously wasn't wearing an identity card." But make no mistake, Killanin was already planning reprimands and warnings to uncooperative NOCs and certain federations; he was consumed no less than any previous IOC president with the perpetuation of the Olympic movement and its most spectacular manifestation—the games.

Sir Michael Morris, Lord Killanin, heavy-set or "fair of flesh," collapsed in April 1977, from a heart attack after seeing his son win the major race of the day at Dublin's Fairyhouse track. Killanin was taken to St. Vincent's Hospital; he progressed sufficiently well to be released in time to address the seventy-ninth session of the IOC on 15 June 1977 in Prague, Czechoslovakia. Looking wan and thin, he pounded away at political intervention with the committee, and, just as importantly, aggressive political bias by some IOC members themselves. No political persuasion, right, left, or center must ever influence the individual member, he warned. Sport can act as the common denominator, and governments are encouraged to give assistance—but with no strings attached. Under no circumstances, he repeated, must the national Olympic committees and their athletes become "the instruments of government direction." It was a good and forceful speech and he looked directly at IOC violators of this Coubertin code.

Five years to the day after his election to IOC presidency, Killanin was back in Dublin, "five years older and twenty kilos lighter, but I can say that every moment has been interesting." His shirts fit less well, but, in everything else, the fit was good. He seemed perfectly capable of fulfilling the arduous role, although, at that moment, he was again preoccupied with the growing politicalization from within his IOC. "We have intentionally increased our numbers," he said to Alex Frere in an 17 August 1977 interview. "Once you get more members," Killanin continued, "you are apt possibly to get bigger political groupings within the IOC." Political and diplomatic journalist that he was, Killanin ran on about the Taiwan and mainland China problem, "the seesaw between Washington, Moscow and Peking," and the unacceptable socialist-Third World attempts to gain domination of the IOC through a one-nation, one-vote plan. He spoke disapprovingly of the new apparition of possible political intrigue from within the United Nations Educational, Scientific and Cultural Organization (UNESCO) to take away from the IOC certain international sporting jurisdictions. Allocation of Olympic television monies—that two-edged sword—concerned him greatly as did the Moscow and Lake Placid games sites and the tremulous decision about Los Angeles as a possible 1984 Olympic Games location. Killanin had few definitive answers, but this aplomb and directness were a reporter's delight. And, to make things perfectly clear, the momentarily not-so-jolly Irishman closed the press conference with the warning that, in the future, any nation boycotting the Olympic Games would be subject to severe sanctions by the International Olympic Committee.

Lord Killanin, seventh IOC president, like his predecessors in several important ways, was, on the bottom line, a maverick. Pierre de Coubertin, Henri de Baillet-Latour, J. Sigfrid Edstrom, and Avery Brundage—all conservative men—were followed by this man whose natural inclination was optimism couched in realism, a Renaissance man, as Gammon said, possessing "all the talents needed to drag the Olympic Games into the last quarter of the twentieth century. Indeed, to save them." No less a believer in Olympism than Brundage was, Killanin's approach was to take the risky route of constantly anticipating inevitable change with alternatives and modifications that do not, at the same time, violate the most sacred tenets of the Olympic movement. It is a riskier road than the inexorably straight and narrow one taken by Coubertin and Brundage. Killanin's innately affable personality, his unceasing hard work as a business man for thirty-five years, a joyously happy home life with lots of children about, so unlike the life-styles of Coubertin and Brundage, all stamped him an optimist and a more accessible human being than his two famous predecessors. Coubertin spent his entire fortune on the games and movement that he re-created. In a half century of Olympic involvement, Brundage spent several million dollars of his own money. Killanin worked very hard at his many business, professional, social, and philanthropic interests, and yet, quite amazingly, punctuated these with several dozen air flights a year on Olympic duties. Unlike the Coubertin-Brundage duo, however, Lord Killanin was compensated financially for his Olympic travel expenses. Small wonder that he seemed to have a special sensitivity for the unwealthy, nonprofessional athlete—something that was not said about the Baron or Brundage.

Killanin loved the Olympic movement no less than the aforementioned giants. It just seemed that Killanin comprehended more deeply than they did the awful fragility of the Olympic Games and the impossible fruition of the excessively lofty goals built into their structure. Killanin could live with an imperfect Olympics; Coubertin and Brundage could not, even though they had to, time and time again, "I'm philosophical," said Killanin after the Montreal Olympic successes and failures. "If something goes wrong, there is nothing one can do except try and help it. I don't stay awake worrying." This attitude, far short of resignation, was a Killanin trademark, an attitude that helped him serve the Olympic cause for thirty years. There's a new word in the Olympic vocabulary: "Killaninism." Lord Killanin always had the habit of getting things done. Even the man he defeated for IOC president, Count Beaumont, had praise for Killanin, completing the bottom line with the comment: "Michael is doing a fine job. Nobody could do it better."

13 • A Billion Spectators—Munich through Montreal 1969–1976

"A Summitry of Sport" was one journalist's definition of the 1972 Olympic Games. The winter version began in exotic Sappora, Japan, and ended in one of Europe's most interesting cities, Munich, West Germany. But, to appreciate both these settings, at least from an American's point of view, the immediately preceeding years, 1969 through 1971, should be reviewed. The United States was in a special turmoil during these years. Concentration on the Olympic Games was difficult for most youthful Americans, emotionally and physically involved in a hateful, impossible-to-win Vietnam War. In an extraordinary mass display of petulance, affluent and sometimes spoiled youth protested every aspect of the war, seeing more clearly than their elders that the whole thing was beyond rationality, that the idyllic Age of Aquarius was over, and, as Arthur Schlesinger, Jr. said, the era "was turning sour." College campuses in the States were in a turmoil. The New Left, the contradictory and appealing rhetoric of Herbert Marcuse, the Students for a Democratic Society (SDS), the Weathermen, "the hippie scene," drugs, "pigs," "Black Panthers," Charles Manson and the counterculture—all contributed to a national instability. Dr. Benjamin Spock, the world's most famous baby doctor, had been an Olympic gold-medal winner in eight-oared crew in 1924, but, in 1968, neither reputation meant much as he was brought to trial for conspiring to encourage draft resisters to violate the Selective Service Act. A controversial President Nixon visited China in February of 1972 just as a Sapporo, Japan, winter Olympics began, and, at the same time, the Vietnam War statistics revealed nearly four million tons of bombs dropped, a cost of $400 billion, and countless lives lost. Nevertheless the eleventh winter Olympics opened on schedule with 1,100 athletes from thirty-five countries ready to thrill over 50,000 spectators and an ever-growing world television audience. The darling of the slopes, Austria's Karl Schranz, was singled out by Avery Brundage for especially blatant violations of the amateur code and was banished forever from Olympic competition. The "Frostbite Follies," as the *New York Times*'s Arthur Daley called the Sapporo games, took place anyway, and Emperor Hirohito, his family, and a great audience were treated to scintillating displays of speed, power, grace and daring. Nineteen countries placed at least one athlete among the top six places, but five nations—Russia, East and West Germany, Norway and Finland—dominated as usual, with 110 places out of a total of 208. Standing literally and figuratively above all the others was Ard Schenk, "The Flying Dutchman," the 6'2", 194-pound winner at all three long-distance races. Without the help of announcers, television cameras, and electronic scoreboards, too many of these winter athletes seemed endlessly alike, a real effort being required to pick out superstars Anne Henning, Marie-Therese Nadig, Annemarie Proell, Erhard Keller, Gustavo Thoeni, Yukio Kasaya, and several others. The Soviet hockey players skated beautifully, defeating the United States. Bobsledding and luge racing were dominated by German, Swiss, and Italian teams. The Japanese hosts had again outdone themselves in efficiency, thoughtfulness, and money spent in bringing to successful fruition the winter festival at their Hokkaido hideaway.

The 1972 Munich games were an extraordinary pageant at an extraordinary price. British social scientist Sir Geoffrey Vickers was of the opinion that the world was changing at an alarmingly accelerated rate, faster than responses could be made; thus, he said, "this brings us nearer the threshold beyond which control is lost." Something like this happened during the fifteen-day celebration of the summer games of the Twentieth Olympiad in Munich, West Germany, 26 August–11 September 1972. When it was all over, there was no consensus, even among veteran Olympic watchers. Vernon Morgan said that Munich was a disaster—"a hoodoo over a fated city." Jerry Nason refused to join the cry of "Doomsday," insisting that the underlying Olympic philosophy of good would prove stronger than "the misguided nationalism that currently tints them [the games]."

The West Germans, especially Bavarians and citizens of Munich, had put together, with amazing skill and huge amounts of love, the grandest and most visually handsome Olympic Games of the century. Somewhere between 1,972 million German marks ($780,000,000) and four hundred million English pounds ($850,000,000) lay the cost of hosting the Munich games. Whatever the cost, the defenders of such expenditures said that, without the incentive of having the Olympic Games, the host city would have delayed indefinitely much needed construction of highways, subways, airports, housing facilities, recreation areas, and athletic venues.

In affluent West Germany, the cost to the individual tax payer was diffused by the clever machinations of Munich's Chief Mayor Hans-Jochen Vogel. Revenues from lotteries, the sale of commemorative coins, and television income accounted for half of the huge Munich costs. The other half came from the combined resources in the city of Kiel, the Olympic sailing site, the states of Bavaria and Schleswig-Holstein, the coffers of the central government in Bonn, and, lastly, Munich's contribution from public funds. While many IOC members saw the expenditure of nearly a billion dollars as a real threat to the continued existence of the Olympic Games, the dynamic Willi Daume, IOC member and president of the 1972 organizing committee, saw it differently:

> The world would be a poorer place without the Olympic Games. . . . And since the experience gained in Munich, insofar as economic matters are concerned, can be used by other countries on a suitable scale and according to their particular circumstances, I wanted this report to show that the future of the Olympic Games need not be jeopardized by material [money] problems.

What the Germans and Munich visitors got for these six years of construction was a spectacular, futuristic city of sport, concentrated outside the main city, with no site more than one kilometer's walking distance. The steel-and-Plexiglas "tent-roof"—larger than fourteen football fields—was an architectural marvel, costing $45 million. The number and quality of the athletic stadia were unrivaled anywhere in the world. Improvements in the Bavarian capital vaulted the already wealthy city into a universal showpiece. Of course, six unrelenting years of construction prefaced the "slow strangulation" of old ways, and prompted automobilists of a conservative bent to display bumper stickers crying, "Come Back, Mad King Ludwig II, and to Hell with the Olympics." The German technocracy was up to the challenge, sending thousands of specialists to Munich—a kind of construction summit meeting. Four hundred companies were involved, the German electronics giant, Siemens, getting a whopping $20 million worth of orders. Rome, Tokyo, and Mexico City had been big, but this Munich extravaganza was one of mankind's largest engineering and building sprees. President Avery Brundage had seen almost all the Olympic Games since 1912, and he knew that it was too much of a good thing and said so repeatedly. Although powerless to do much about it, IOC President-elect Lord Killanin felt the same way. Eighty thousand spectators packed the main stadium on opening day, 7,131 athletes from 122 countries assembled at midfield; 5,000 doves were released; 7,000 press, radio and television personnel were on hand. The "magic eye" beamed pictures to one billion people—"three times as many as those who watched the first landing of a man on the moon in 1969."

The Olympic dream is to visualize thousands of talented young men and women from almost every country in the world together in a radiant gathering of fraternal, high-level, athletic competition. The dream is not altogether false, for the idealistic dimension of the Olympic Games absolutely does exist. However, the main preoccupation of the best athletes gathered in Munich that opening day was to win. Some were very tiny, very young, like seventeen-year-old Olga Korbut, multiple winner from the Soviet Union. And then, contrastingly, there was the grizzled West German warrior-wrestler Wilfried Dietrich, who had begun his Greco-Roman and freestyle Olympic-medal collection back in Melbourne when Olga was a year old. In five consecutive games, this modern "pot-hunter" fought for and won a gold medal, two silver medals, the bronze medal twice, and a fourth-and-fifth-place finish in his own German Olympics of 1972. Let the record show that these Munich games mirrored more perfectly the two sides of man—his transcending glory as well as his inept, error-filled, and even, during one eighteen-hour stretch, his bestial side—than any previous Olympic festival. To repeat the litany of all Olympic Games, world and Olympic records were broken in wholesale lots. In Munich, against "the supreme sports landscape" that was once a giant trash heap for World War II rubble, athletic excellence spiraled upward.

The running track inside the main Olympic stadium was impeccable, and, for the first time in history, a full capacity crowd of 80,000 saw both the morning and afternoon sessions. It was worth it, this showing up at 8 A.M. in order to get a seat in a packed stadium for preliminary running, jumping, and throwing events. No record was safe, except Bob Beamon's unearthly mark set at the previous Olympic Games. Valery Borzov, Vince Matthews, Monica Zehrt, and Renate Stecher dominated the sprints; Rod Milburn, John Akii-Bua, and Amelia Ehrhardt owned the hurdles, while Lasse Viren, Pekka Vasala, Dave Wottle, Hildegard Falck, Kip Keino, Ljudmila Bragina, and Frank Shorter were crowned Olympic distance-running champions. The run-from-behind style of 800-meter star Wottle was a wonder to behold; "I was just trying to catch up," he said to a BBC interviewer. Kenya, the United States, and East and West Germany won the four relay races, while Peter Frenkel, Bernd Kannenberg, and Nikolai Avilov won the short walk, the long walk, and the decathlon, respectively. A thirty-four-year-old secretary and mother from Belfast, Mary Peters, broke the world's record in the pentathlon, her first gold medal, after placing fourth at Tokyo and ninth in Mexico City. Ruth Fuchs, Faina Melnik, Nadezhda Chizhova, Heidi Rosendahl and Ulrike Meyfarth won field events were won by Juri Tarmak, Randy Williams, Viktor Saneyev, Wolfgang Nordwig, Wladyslaw Komar, Ludvik Danek, Anatoli Bondarchuk, and Klaus Wolfermann. Instantaneous photographic and timing devices kept the finish line free of officials, while hammer, discus, and javelin throws were measured by an invisible beam "shot" from high in the viewing stands and instantly reflected onto huge electronic scoreboards.

For a week and a half, Mark Spitz, the California dolphin, owned the Olympics. His seven gold medals and seven world records were unprecedented, as was the near domination, once again, in men's swimming by athletes from the United States. Australian women won eight medals while their counterparts from the States took home eighteen swimming and diving Olympic symbols of excellence. Japanese, Soviet, and East German athletes dominated men's gymnastics, while Olga Korbut, the great Turishcheva, and the Russian female team won highest honors in women's gymnastics, the East Germans, Hungarians, and Americans following in that order. The "old guard" prevailed in fencing, especially among the Soviet and Hungarian stars, who amassed four gold, six silver, and five bronze medals. In rowing competitions, the USSR, East Germany, and West Germany did well, but it was the stunning New Zealand "eights" victory over the United States and East Germany that led former gold-medal winner Hans Lenk to proclaim it "the end of an era." His brilliant Karl Adams-directed Ratzburg crew finished fifth, unable to stand up to "the powerful, fanatically motivated giants from the Antipodes." It was not surprising for the yachting competition held in the harbor at Kiel-Schilksee to be called "the most thoroughly organized . . . ever held." It is the German way, and the Germans did a super job in hosting over 300 sailors from forty-two countries.

Poland met Hungary in an exhausting soccer final, both teams having already played six hard matches in twelve days. Thirty thousand spectators saw Poland endure 2–1, with the East Germans and Soviets tied for third place. *Philadelphia Inquirer* sports writer Frank Dolson called the bizarre finish and victory of the Soviet basketball team over the United States a sordid and surrealistic affair, "decided in a room, behind closed doors, not on a basketball court." Putting emotion aside, and after careful analysis of all available evidence, it must be concluded that, despite lackluster American play, the United States should have won the game 50–49. The spirit of Olympism took it on the chin that night. Unfortunately, the Olympic ideal was bruised again when Germany won out 1–0 in the field-hockey final, the Pakistani supporters and losing Pakistan hockey team showing uncommonly poor manners. Goals came thick and fast as 105 points were scored by the top six handball finalists. Yugoslavia prevailed over Czechoslovakia, with runners up from Rumania, East Germany, USSR, and West Germany. Teofilo Stevenson of Cuba, 6'5", 214 pounds, his boxing as impressive as his looks in the Olympic heavyweight division, won the gold and joined, with two fellow Cubans, champions from Yugoslavia, Russia, West Germany, the United States,

Poland, Bulgaria, Hungary. There were twenty weight-classes in Greco-Roman and freestyle wrestling. The USSR team won fourteen medals, the Bulgarians won seven, the United States six, and the Japanese, four. In addition, gold medals were won by grapplers from Rumania (two), Hungary, and Czechoslovakia.

Two of the world's best weight lifters, Belgium's Serge Reding and American Ken Patera, failed to make a valid lift in the opening press and were disqualified from further competition. Eyewitness Steffen Haffner concluded that "both men lived beyond their means, metaphorically speaking." Bulgarian and Soviet lifters won the lion's share, with gold-medal winners also from Poland, Hungary, and Norway. Alexeev raised the Olympic record for three lifts to 1,411 pounds (640 kilograms). John Williams, an 18-year-old from Pennsylvania, captured the archery gold-medal with a stupendous 2,528 points out of a possible 2,880. A thirty-year veteran of archery competition, Doreen Wilber of Iowa, won the woman's title in a very close match with shooters from Poland and the USSR. Canoeing and kayaking honors were dominated by athletes from the Eastern European socialist countries—part of their long-time master plan to emphasize those Olympic sports usually neglected by the traditional big winners at the games. Peerless Daniel Morelon once again became an Olympic cycling champion, and was joined by Hennie Kuiper of the Netherlands, Knut Knudsen of Norway, Niels Fredborg from Denmark, the winning tandem team from the Soviet Union, the victorious West German pursuit team, and the 100-kilometer team-winners from Russia. All the fencing medals were won by men and women from Poland, Hungary, France, USSR, Switzerland, Italy, and Rumania—for several generations the dominant nations in this sport so consistently on every Olympic Games program since 1896.

Japanese judo stars won three gold medals in the lighter-body weight classes, Shota Chochosvili winning the light-heavyweight class, while the Dutchman, Wim Ruska, was supreme at the heavyweight and open classes. Fifty-nine participants from twenty countries vied for modern pentathlon recognition. In this event, swimming, riding, shooting, and fencing culminated in a 4,000-meter cross-country finale, ending in the main stadium, with an amazingly large crowd of 80,000 watching Andras Balczo of Hungary beating back three Soviets, a Britisher, and Bjorn Ferm of Sweden. Some amazing firing took place in pistol, rifle, and clay-pigeon shooting as world and Olympic records fell before marksmen from North Korea, the United States, Poland, Sweden, Italy, West Germany, and the USSR. Maybe the editor of the *1972 United States Olympic Book* was somewhat biased when he said that "there was never a better Olympic water-polo tournament competition-wise" than the Munich finals. After all, the United States won its first water polo medal, a bronze, in forty years, the silver going to Hungary, and the gold to the USSR. The best twelve men's volleyball teams ended the preliminary competitions with five wins and zero losses for both Japanese and Soviet teams. Intermediate rounds, however, saw East Germany advance to the finals versus Japan, and the USSR versus Bulgaria for places three and four. The Japanese were crowned champions of the world in this rapidly growing sport. Eventually, the top six women's volleyball teams turned out to be the USSR, Japan, North and South Korea, Hungary, and Cuba. The traditional finale of the summer Olympic Games are the equestrian events, and the West German hosts were, once again, very strong, winning first and third places in grand prix dressage, second in team result, first in grand prix team-jumping, and third in the three-day team scoring. Individual champions were Richard Meade, Great Britain, riding Laurieston, West Germany's Liselott Linsenhoff on Piaff, and Graziano Mancinelli on Ambassador.

The Munich games were thus concluded, or rather, "limped to an end" one day later than scheduled. A tragedy of incalculable proportions had spoiled an athletic festival of the highest athletic standards and one near-perfect in organization. But the murder of eleven Israeli athletes on 5 September 1972 cast an "invisible shadow" over everything—a cloud that would, for as long as the modern Olympic Games last, haunt the German people, all those who love untrammelled sport and the whole of humanity.

The urbane world traveler from *The Saturday Review,* Horace Sutton, on the eve of the Munich Olympic Games, called that city an emerging international community

fairly singing with youthful ebullience, steaming with new industry, energized with new citizens, gleaming with new chrome, athrob with old culture and new learning, and not unwilling to become, as it is often already called, the unofficial capital of a democratized Germany.

West Germany had come full circle from the Hitler days of the 1936 Olympic Games. Willie Daume, president of the German Olympic committee, was eager for a new, democratic Munich to help erase a demonic past and bestow on that Bavarian capital "the world's gift of renewed trust in Germany. . . .

And yet, halfway through the Olympic Games festival, on 5 September 1972, with finality, the dream was shattered. Eight Palestinian guerrilla fighters somehow gained admittance over the heavily-guarded cyclone fence around the Olympic Village and, in twenty-one horror-laden hours, murdered eleven Jewish athletes; in the process, they were themselves blasted to kingdom come by German police. This was the ultimate unthinkable—terrorism as a spectator sport. The terrorist's massacre of innocent athletes, an act of the purest blind, patriotic fanaticism, is chronicled in angry, pitiless, minute-by-minute detail by the French journalist Serge Groussard in his 464-page savage account, *The Blood of Israel*. The book spares no one except the slain athletes. IOC President Avery Brundage, with only a week left in office, refused to cancel the games, and ordered a day of mourning to be followed by a memorial ceremony. His singular decision, made hastily, in a blind, old man's rage, and without prescribed consultation with every member of the executive board, ended two days later with his memorial eulogy in which he condemned equally, and in the same breath, African sport politics and Palestinian murderers. It was not a dignified, rational way for the patriot of Olympism to end a sixty-year career in international sport.

World shock and outrage eventuated in a reluctant acceptance of the brief halt to the Games. There was no satisfactory alternative, with the possible exception of a longer, more contemplative three-or four-day period of mourning. The games ran their course, the world press as preoccupied with the horror as with the women's kayak finals or Kannenberg's Olympic victory and record in the 50,000-meter walk. The games had "lost their soul," a catastrophe had occurred that left a veteran *Time* magazine correspondent limp in the full glare of "yet another notch on an ever-rising scale of grotesquerie." An age of violence invaded what some had perceived as a sanctuary, and in the eyes of some, like *The New Yorker* roving correspondent E. J. Kahn, the potentially glorious Olympic Games would always possess "an invisible defect." A few saw the barbarian outrage inside Munich's Olympic Village as the beginning of the end for these revived games. The "insane intrusion" proved the inseparability of politics and sport; from now on, the IOC, the NOCs, and the sport federations could only hope to keep a lid on political machinations as they moved in the direction of "the once gentle backwater sport." The venerable journalist of the *New York Times*, Red Smith, was joined by others in calling for the discontinuation of the Olympic Games since, in their opinion, the games had come to have "an irresistible attraction as forums for ideological, social, or racial expression." Still others suggested that future games be held in totalitarian countries where terrorist outrages could not possibly happen. Through it all, Canadian observers were planning a massive, hopefully foolproof security system for their own 1976 version of the Olympic Games.

There was no end to the editorial aftermath of the Munich successes and the Munich carnage. But the next games in Montreal were on, and no degree of unsureness about the value of so huge an athletic festival could alter those preparations. Of course, the world could get along without the Olympic Games, but it has always been a mountain-peak individual experience for thousands of young people, fulfilling human yearnings for competition and the need for human contact. And yet, the memory of Munich's mad violence was fresh in the minds of many, such as the television broadcaster, Jim McKay, who said that the Olympic lesson was that nothing, not even "unspeakable atrocities can stop the spirit of man to keep living; to try to make something out of the world as it is." Interestingly, opinion about the Olympic Games future caromed in three directions, the first of which predicted their imminent downfall, another that hoped for salvation through immediate and total disassociation from international politics, a sports Valhalla for the innocent. The third view, eloquently pronounced by Professor Hans Lenk of Karlsruhe University in West Germany, urged careful, effective political involvement by the IOC in order to free itself from intolerable political pressures. For the Olympic movement to try to stand loftily above the materialism of world politics is only to hasten its own end, said the 1960 Olympic gold-medalist. The Olympic Games have to be politically as well as philosophically defended, and this can only occur, he said, when

> the I.O.C. itself has unavoidably to take political steps to assure the relative political independence of the Games. On a metalevel, so to speak, the I.O.C. must act politically to be relatively free from special political forces.

In October of 1974, the International Olympic Committee, once unfairly called a "multinational gerontocracy," met and awarded Lake Placid, New York, and Moscow the Olympic Games of 1980. Brundage died the following May, and, in February of 1976, unprecedented police protection looked over the shoulders of a thousand Olympic athletes at the winter games in the Tyrolean Alps at Innsbruck. The event was beamed worldwide, and, in an instant, great athletes became superstars and celebrities. Listen to the names: Franz Klammer, Karl Schnabl, Gustavo Thoeni, Piero Gros, Heini Hemmi, Rosi Mittermaier, Galina Bulakova of the Soviet Union, Bill Koch of the United States, Tatiana Averina, Peter Mueller, Sheila Young and Dorothy Hamill. Ice dancing and pairs figure-skating were won by wonderfully skilled Soviet skaters. East Germans won both men's and women's luge racing, as well as two- and four-man bobsled; the Soviets prevailed over the Czechs in ice hockey. There were more "greats," each one every bit equal, if not superior, to those that had come before them. The upward escalation of special athletic skills seemed endless. But a specter hung over the whole thing, a disconcerting phenomenon of escalating cost, "gigantism," commercialism, and political interference—all the result of near universal acceptance of Pierre de Coubertin's Olympic Games as the most important and exciting of all sporting events. David Miller of London's *Sunday Telegraph* called the games "a monster that has become greater than the sum of the people who constitute it." Final proof of that brand of pessimism has not yet been gathered.

When the dust settled and the cost could be calculated, the games of the twenty-first Olympiad in Montreal, Canada, cost one and one-quarter billion dollars. Lord Killanin was stunned by the final figure, and said it must never happen again. The staggeringly expensive main stadium cost $350 million. Its architect, the prima donna Parisian Roger Taillibert, justified the cost (and his estimated several-million-dollar fee) by pointing out that the structure would stand as a permanent monument to Canadian civilization. A year after the games, Canadian outrage at the runaway cost had not lessened. Taillibert's reply was typically pompous, or, possibly, insensitive:

> The West will one day have to acknowledge that sports installations, however costly they may be to build and maintain, must be included in the State's budget in the same way as the manufacture of arms.

Taillibert, like many key people in the Canadian Olympic Organizing Committee (COJO), never talked about economy. Taillibert and Mayor Jean Drapeau stated over and over again that these Olympic Games must transcend the concept of money and, rather, "respond to and express the higher levels of the human spirit." Fraud, corruption, fumbling ineptness, cost-boosting, and carte-blanche abdication of construction responsibilities are all themes in Nick Auf der Maur's *The Billion-Dollar Game*. Although unfairly one-sided, there is massive corroborative evidence to substantiate most of his revelations. Twelve men died in stadium construction, the cycling arena alone cost $70 million, $60 million for two garages, $14 million for a viaduct walkway, and $8 million for a cascading fountain. At one point, during the last year of construction, Auf der Maur pointed a finger at the

> forest of almost 200 cranes on the site, some brought in from as far away as Calgary and rented for anywhere from $105 to $300 an hour, twenty-four hours a day.

"For two weeks of fun," said playwright Michel Tremblay, "we are in debt for twenty-five years." Costs skyrocketed in every direction, including a grimly necessary $100 million bill from the federal government for massive police security. For sure, the bottom line was a discouraging price to pay for what turned out to be, in a great many ways, an extremely successful Olympic Games. Talk of a permanent Olympic Games site, a serious alternative to a few historians, journalists, and sportsmen, gained several new adherents after Montreal.

It has been said that the modern Olympic Games, ever since massive global television coverage in the mid-1960s, provide a potentially greater political forum for sovereign states than the United Nations or any other human institution. The London *Sunday Times* of 18 July 1976, repeated a trite phrase not without truth when it said that international sport is the grandest, least harmful form of politics available to world nations—"a continuation of war by other means." The implication, surely in contradistinction with Coubertin's cosmopolitan Olympism, was inescapable as examples of Olympian politicization grew with every quadrennial festival. It was discouraging for sport purists to fully comprehend that sport cannot be isolated from politics, and is, in fact, being used today "as a legitimate and important political weapon by individuals and nations alike." Athletes and nation-states successful in playing politics with sport are threatening to kill the Olympic Games.

Two blatantly political events, occurring almost simultaneously, and, by some curious human chemistry thus reducing their impact, singly or collectively, cornered front-page and sport headlines for days prior to the opening ceremonies. The *Spectator* of London called them the Canadian government's ridiculous "exclusion of Taiwan and the foolish African boycott." As early as April of 1975, the Canadian government indicated to President Killanin and his IOC that there existed problems with respect to the participation of Taiwan as the "Republic of China." Neither the Canadians nor Killanin addressed the matter until early July 1976, a week before the games began. It was a classic dilemma. The IOC had, for many years, recognized as a member in good standing the island nation, The Republic of China (R.O.C.). Mainland China, the People's Republic, was not a member of the Olympic family, nor had it any inclination to join as long as R.O.C. was a member. The Canadian government did not recognize Taiwan as a sovereign nation; rather, for diplomatic and important commercial reasons, Canada did recognize the People's Republic of China. All this was known long in advance, but nothing was resolved on the eve of the games. The Chinese were not allowed admittance into Canada, and adamantly refused the government's conciliatory offer to compete as athletes from Taiwan rather than from the Republic of China. Vituperative editorials were leveled in four directions: at the stubborn R.O.C. delegation for not accepting "half-a-loaf" and participating in the games as Taiwanese; at the intransigent Troudeau government's love affair with mainland China and Canada's violation of the *Olympic Charter*; at the indecisive, never-act-hastily Lord Killanin; and, finally, at the Peking government, a nonmember Olympic nation, that had so strongly objected to any compromise that would have allowed the Taiwan team to use the flag and anthem of the Republic of China, but not that name, during the fifteen-day Olympic Games period.

Hard on the heels of this China fiasco was the even more unreal boycott by thirty nations, most of them African, in protest over the presence of New Zealand because a rugby team from that nation had gone on a tour of racially troubled South Africa. Officials of the Supreme Council for Sport in Africa, swollen with power at the relative effectiveness of their demands at the previous two Olympic Games, demanded that an allegedly racist New Zealand be kicked out of Montreal because it had sent a football team to South Africa. Slowly, painfully, tearfully, the African athletes, some of them world champions, packed their bags and returned home. Surprisingly, and unlike the Mexico City and Munich games, the world press this time did not sympathize with the African boycott. Somehow, the Taiwan crisis and an improbable and weak case against New Zealand by the Africans had turned things around. As sports editor, Larry Eldridge of the *Christian Science Monitor* said, on the very day of the walkout, 19 July 1976: "At least 20 countries, including Great Britain, France, and the U.S., had sporting contacts with South Africa, and it was hard to see why New Zealand should be singled out any more than the U.S., for instance." The competitive excellence of these Montreal games was measurably diminished by the loss of the African athletes, but, of course, other champions stepped into the vacuum left by their absence. It is the way of athletics. The influential publication, *Track and Field News,* in a rare sympathetic tone regarding I.O.C. leadership, allowed Gary Hill to say:

> Roll over Monsieur de Coubertin! Rattle your chains, Mr. Brundage! You Pierre. You had lofty goals when you reestablished the Games. Many have scoffed at your thoughts. Too idealistic we said. You Avery, you Curmudgeon. We didn't like your crusty, dictatorial ways. Your harsh, unbending attitude towards maintaining the amateur ethic. Not practical, we said. Maybe you were both right.

The Olympic movement has been consistently in error in claiming or even hinting that, through its efforts, world peace has been brought a little closer. As Hans Lenk put it, such exaggerated claims "overload the Olympic Idea and, by that, detract from its actual social effectiveness." He is right, of course, for the real uniqueness of the once-every-four years Olympic Games is the fantastic gathering of 10,000 young men and women in some kind of social chemistry difficult to define. One observer called it "shared struggle, shared enjoyment, and shared pride in human abilities." The athletes speak, in the most eloquent way open to them, with world record after world record. Hal Willard of the *Washington Post* called it "the only truly worldwide festival"—an opportunity for the triumph of man's spirit. Without indulging in sophomoric sweetness, it is enough to say that mankind, outclassed by machines and computers, can find some

Main Stadium, 1976, Montreal, television screen and Olympic flag. Credit Ronald Smith collection.

humanistic recompense by direct involvement in or vicariously watching the Olympic Games drama.

Darrell Pace and Luann Ryon, both from the Unites States, set world and Olympic records, outshooting sixty-four archers from twenty-five countries. The king of Olympic sports, track-and-field athletics, was dominated by the United States, the Soviets, the two Germanys, the West Indies, and Scandinavia, although fifteen different countries had at least one gold-medal winner. Rising above even their fellow gold-medalists were Donald Quarrie, Alberto Juantorena, Lasse Viren, Edwin Moses, Waldemar Cierpinski, Viktor Saneyev, Mac Wilkins, Bruce Jenner, Irena Szewinska, and Tatiana Kazankina. For eight days that decided thirty-seven championships, an astonishing total of 880,000 spectators watched the morning trials and afternoon finals from inside the concrete stadium. Athletes from seventy-four nations contributed to track-and-field world and Olympic records in wholesale lots. Dean Smith did a masterful job in coaching the United States' men's basketball team (considered ripe for upset) to a 95–74 finals victory over Yugoslavia. The young American women were too good for everyone but the Soviet basketball team, losing to them 112–77. The twenty-two finalists in the eleven boxing weight-divisions were dominated by six Americans and six Cubans. Better fighters and better officiating made the 1976 Olympic Games version one of the very best.

One Canadian silver-medalist prevented an extraordinary sweep by the Communist-socialist countries of all thirty-three places in the canoe-kayak competitions. The enlarged rowing program now included seven women's and eight men's events. Athletes from the following countries won medals: East and West Germany, the Soviet Union, the United States, Bulgaria, Rumania, New Zealand, Britain, Norway, Czechoslovakia, and Finland. Scratch sprinting, 1,000- and 4,000-meter time trials and pursuits, plus 100- and 180-kilometer team time-trial and individual road race gave Montreal's Velodrome, the Trans-Canada Highway, and the grueling, inner-city Mount Royal course full opportunity to see the world's greatest cyclists. The United States equestrian team was the best that country had ever produced, based on the four medals earned in Montreal. West Germany, Switzerland, Australia, France, and Canada did admirably well in this "sport of kings." The best men's teams in foil, épée, and sabre fencing were from West Germany, Sweden, and Russia. The Russian women had the best foil team in Montreal, although not the individual champion.

The eye of the television camera could never get enough of gymnastics, especially of Nadia Comaneci, for her Montreal performances were the most brilliant female gymnastic routine in the history of the games. Nelli Kim, Olga Korbut, Ludmila Tourisheva, Nikolai Andrianov, Alexandr Ditiatin, and Vladimir Marchenko—all from the Soviet Union—outshone even the brilliance of Japan's Sawao Kato, Eizo Kemmotsu, Mitsuo Tsukahara, and Hiroshi Kajiyama. Peter Kormann began the American gymnastic resurgence with a bronze medal in the floor exercise. Men's and women's team-handball finals were won by Soviet athletes, with central and eastern European countries, where the game is very popular, dominating the remaining honors. The African defection seriously affected the soccer program, although the two best teams in the world, Poland and East Germany, made the finals before 71,619 spectators, the German Democratic Republic team earning a hard 3–1 victory. The best field-hockey teams, in order of their finish, were New Zealand, Australia, Holland, Pakistan, West Germany, and Spain. India went unplaced. The "down under" teams played a rough, unnerving brand of hockey. The *1976 United States Olympic Book* commented that "the Australians drank gallons of beer in celebration while Indian journalists spent hundreds of dollars telephoning New Delhi and Bombay to explain what happened." Eight champions from the Soviet Union and Japan, two from Britain, and one each from Cuba and Korea battled in six-division judo finals, all of them inching closer to the once unbeatable Japanese. The always unpredictable Olympic team from Great Britain surprised the sporting world by winning the team championship in the modern pentathlon, Poland's Janusz Pyciak-Peciak taking the individual title. The world's best athlete in this event, Red Army Major Boris Onishenko, disgraced himself by cheating in the Olympic tournament, and was sent home. Olympic honors in rifle, pistol, trap, and skeet shooting were divided among eagle-eyed champions from the United States, West Germany, Russia, East Germany, Czechoslovakia, Italy, Portugal, Holland, Poland, and Austria.

Almost every single men's and women's swim final resulted in an Olympic or world record. The two Germanys, Russia, and the United States produced the majority of medal winners. Swim records fall so rapidly that it is difficult to predict if the next generation of swimmers will remember Montreal champions Jim Montgomery, Bruce Furniss, Brian Goodell, John Naber, John Hencken, David Wilke, Matt Vogel, Mike Bruner, Rod Strachen, Kornelia Ender, Patra Thumer, Shirley Babashoff, Ulrike Richter, and a whole additional firmament of stars. Italy's super nova, Klaus Dibiasi, won his third consecutive gold medal, beating the precocious California teenager Greg Louganis in the men's high-board diving. Phil Boggs, Jenny Chandler, and Elena Vaytsekhovskaia also won highest honors in diving. Hungarian water-polo specialists won their fourth gold medal in the last eight Olympic Games, finishing ahead of Italy, Holland, Rumania, Yugoslavia, and West Germany.

The remarkable growth of volleyball culminated in a men's final that was electric with excitement, the Polish team finally emerging as winners over the Soviet Union. Cuba, Japan, Czechoslovakia, and Korea also played superb volleyball. The very determined Japanese women regained their Olympic title by besting their long-time rivals, the Russian volleyball team. The next four teams were from Korea, Hungary, Cuba, and East Germany.

In retrospect, it still seems difficult to believe that Olympic weight-lifting records were broken in every one of the nine weight classifications, and, still more remarkably, all by strong men from Russia, Bulgaria, and Poland. Something similar happened in the awarding of sixty gold, silver, and bronze medals to freestyle and Greco-Roman wrestlers. Twenty-five medallions went to the Soviets and the Bulgarians; Japan, the United States, and Rumania won six medals each, the rest distributed among eleven nations. And finally (to repeat myself), that most incongruous Olympic sport, yachting, was contested at Kingston, Ontario, on the eastern tip of the lake. Even here, police protection was very tight—a grim reminder to all of the Munich nightmare of four years earlier. Sailing honors in the six classes were shared by East and West Germany, Sweden, Russia, the United States, Australia, Denmark, Spain, Britain, and Brazil.

American historian Arthur Schlesinger, Jr., in a bicentennial speech titled "America: Experiment or Destiny?", reminded his listeners that "The Founding Fathers had an intense conviction of the improbability of their undertaking." In a quite similar way, Pierre de Coubertin, founder of the modern Olympic Games in 1896, was never sure all during his long life that the Olympian experiment would work. He worried about the loyalty and commitment of his IOC, and he was profoundly cynical of the bureaucrats and politicians that everlastingly buzzed about his Olympic Games honey pot. He often chose to overlook some official's decisions and frequent gauche spectator behavior. But never once in fifty years did his faith in the essential integrity of the majority of athletes wane. His was a consistent hymn of praise for that essential Olympic commodity, the participants in the games. The year before his passing in 1937, he wrote a brief farewell essay, "Aux Coureurs d'Olympie-Berlin," in which he addressed the athletes, reminding them that no greater preparation for the future exists than their present, intense transitory preoccupation with athletics. He never stopped believing that preparation for and participation in the Olympic Games could be an ennobling experience, that excellence in life is still possible. It was always to youth that he looked for this elusive, transcendent dream. And so must we.

Index